BRITAIN'S DEVELOPING CONSTITUTION

BRITAIN'S DEVELOPING CONSTITUTION

Peter Bromhead

Professor of Politics, University of Bristol

ST. MARTIN'S PRESS
New York

AFFILIATED PUBLISHERS: Macmillan Limited, London
also at Bombay, Calcutta, Madras and Melbourne

PREFACE

A constitution is the framework of norms and practices which define and regularise the management of political relationships. Some of the norms and practices are normally embodied in laws, and in nearly all modern societies (though not in Britain), the most important of these are embodied in a special law entitled 'the Constitution'. The absence of a 'constitution' need not be very significant; in any case the whole body of norms and practices is only one aspect of the political system, which is a much wider concept.

There is no limit to the types of information needed for an effective study of a political system: information, for example, about the countless different relationships of people with the process of production, about countless varieties of perceptions of those relationships, and about the influences which produce those perceptions. But the people's relations with the production process, actual and perceived, are only a small part of the whole mass of factors which influence the political system's orientation. The totality of these factors is so great and so uncertain that any selection of elements for examination must involve a large subjective element.

This book will try to set out the main lines of the British constitutional system as it operates in the mid-1970s, concentrating on those aspects which concern the structure of power: the choice of persons for elite positions; the means of expression of public demands and aspirations through the system of representation; the means by which office-holders are made to account for their actions and policies. A study of a constitution must be mainly descriptive, though it may legitimately attempt to ask why the constitution is what it is, or why elements of it are what they are. Having suggested purposes or objections underlying particular forms or phenomena, it may evaluate the forms in relation to these purposes.

Evaluation is relatively easy with a constitution which has been produced at a given moment by the deliberate act of people then possessed of sufficient power to be able to prescribe a whole new set of rules and definitions of objectives. Their constitution has been made with a definite purpose, whether that purpose be to preserve rights to life, liberty and the pursuit of happiness, or to promote the nation's success in attaining domination over others, or to keep the people firmly in subjection. Institutions so produced may be evaluated at a given time with reference to their success in achieving the proclaimed objectives.

When a constitution is not the product of any single act, evaluation is less easy because there is no prescribed set of standards by which to evaluate its working. The last English revolution was nearly 300 years ago, and even it did not claim to innovate; it merely claimed to declare the validity of some principles that had been violated: that power must be exercised to maintain order, but only subject to the will of Parliament, whose purpose was to discuss what had been done and what was to be done.

All government is concerned with choice: identifying and evaluating options, and choosing between them. This book deals with the framework of institutions, defining the manner in which the choosers, at different levels, are chosen, the limits which they must observe, and the checks to which they are subject. It deals with the nature and quality of discussion, and of the representative process on which that discussion is based. It is concerned with the machinery of government in its main political aspects, and for this reason it deals with the laws, conventions, practices and assumptions which comprise the political elements of the Constitution as it is in the mid-1970s. It pays particular attention to changes of the past few years, identifying changes and seeking reasons for them; it looks for reasons both for change and for lack of change; and where a purpose can be discerned behind a constitutional practice it assesses the consistency between the practice and its apparent purpose.

The British system is so lacking in precision that there is room for subjective elements in the choice of the materials for study. Written constitutions do not normally include provisions for the internal working of parliamentary assemblies, but in Britain some such rules (notably those dating from the seventeenth century) by which the House of Commons successfully established its special claim to authorise taxation and public expenditure, are commonly included in constitutional textbooks. But other internal parliamentary rules and usages, including some introduced very recently, are today even more important for any real discussion of the working system.

The internal rules of political parties may have an even less obvious place in a book about a constitution, but so long as the British political system works in such a way that either the Labour or the Conservative Party provides the government, the processes by which those parties provide for the choice of their leaders are essential to the process by which the effective chief executive is appointed to his office; omission of all discussion of these party practices leaves us with a mere skeleton.

Some other aspects which are often treated at length in constitutional treatises are omitted here, because in a book of restricted length some topics must be sacrificed. Questions of the freedom of speech, of the Press and of public meeting will not be discussed, partly because they are only in a rather special way part of the organisation of political power, partly because they are expressions of a single principle – that anyone may do what he likes provided that he does not harm anyone else or the public at large.[1]

This survey pays particular attention to those aspects of the subject which are most evidently in a state of change or uncertainty, or in which recent innovation needs to be identified. Ministerial responsibility to Parliament is uncertain, and attempts have been made to adapt Parliament's means of operation, in relation to ministers and their policies, in response to this uncertainty. Britain's entry to the EEC has brought other changes; the relationship with Northern Ireland has been redefined and that with other geographical sections of the kingdom is being examined with a view to change. Topics of this kind are discussed, changes described and evaluated, because the changes show the constitutional system adapting itself to the changing world in which it has to work.

This book then is about the constitutional system as found in the 1970s. It is neither a legal textbook nor a history; it is a political assessment. Hence it includes no table of statutes; it deals with the past only in so far as it affects the present; and it does not seek to define public rights and duties.

There are many ways in which the study of a political system may be divided. Looked at from the point of view of its institutions the conventional divisions are probably the most useful. Hence the study is divided into four sections. The first deals with the entity commonly known as 'the Government', the Queen and the ministers who take decisions on her behalf; the second looks at the role of Parliament as the body without whose approval the ministers cannot act; the third examines the Parliament's source of power in the people, through the electoral process; and the fourth considers an aspect which has become prominent lately, the relationship between the central authority and the subordinate authorities that derive their existence, powers and duties from it; these include the constituent 'nations' of the United Kingdom and the local authorities within them.

---

[1] A number of laws forbid some types of private behaviour on the ground that they are repellent, or damaging to the whole fabric of society. These derogations for the general libertarian principle and the terms in which they need to be discussed, illustrate the special moral and legal, rather than constitutional, character of the principle itself.

CONTENTS

I

Introduction

For a definition of 'constitution' we may well use that given by Professor Hood Phillips: 'the laws, customs and conventions which define the composition and powers of organs of the State and regulate the relations of the various state organs to one another and to the private citizen'.[1]

Almost every contemporary State has a written constitution, but in Britain there is only a collection of customs and practices, together with some laws which provide for some parts of the system of government – and these laws, though they are laws about the constitution, have no special status, and can be changed by the same process as any other laws.

The written constitutions established elsewhere in the past 200 years were all made in response to great upheavals, and Britain has until now not experienced any such upheaval since 1688. The events of that time, the departure of King James II and his replacement by William and Mary, were in the nature of a revolution, and they did produce something like a constitution in the form of the Bill of Rights, which still remains in force. Constitutions, in the modern sense, had not yet been written in any of the States of Europe. The Bill of Rights was a pioneer, showing the way towards the formulation of comprehensive instruments defining political powers. It was supplemented by further enactments soon after, such as the Act of Settlement, each one to serve the needs of the time. These enactments were not complete innovations, but rather responses to new needs for clear definition of some elements of the system of government. Since that time further new definitions have been made by statute, some of them against fierce opposition. Meanwhile other innovations have crept in, without intention or plan, and become accepted as regular practices or conventions – a term often used but without specific meaning. Even after full-scale

[1] O. Hood Phillips, *Constitutional and Administrative Law* (Sweet & Maxwell, 4th ed., 1967), p. 6.

constitutions became the standard form in other states, the few
advocates of a similar device for Britain had had no success by 1973.

Hood Phillips suggests that a constitution defines the powers of
state organs; in Britain we may find definition in statutes and (less
certainly) in conventions, of the powers of particular agencies, but no
definition of the concept of 'the State'. Instead there is the more
concrete fact of the existence of the Crown, which is in practice the
same thing. There is no prescribed limit to what the Crown may do;
safeguards against arbitrary or oppressive actions are provided instead
by expectations of restraint. The Queen can do no wrong, but there
have been, from the Norman Conquest onwards, expectations that the
occupant of the throne should consult particular persons or groups,
and respect the advice given;[1] and when the Sovereign has acted in
defiance of the expectations the result has been upheaval, leading to
closer though fragmentary definitions of the processes by which the
Sovereign is to act, of the relations between the Crown and its servants
and those who claimed to speak for the community.

The Bill of Rights of 1688 was the most important in this series of
definitions. It began with a declaration that some of James II's actions
had been subversive of 'the laws and liberties of this kingdom'; and
'utterly and directly contrary to the known laws and statutes and
freedom of this realm'. The list of his offences assumed that he had
broken binding custom, and demanded that such breaches should not
be repeated. It condemned

'. . . the pretended power of suspending of laws or the execution of
laws by regal authority without consent of Parliament; . . . levying
money for or to the use of the Crown by pretence of Prerogative without grant of Parliament for longer time or in other manner than the
same is or shall be granted; . . . the raising or keeping a standing army
within the kingdom in time of peace unless it be with consent of
Parliament.'

The enactment did not limit the power of Parliament, or of the King
in Parliament. It simply assumed that so long as Parliament was freely
elected, left with free speech, and involved in taxation, legislation and
the keeping of a standing army, there was no need for further safeguards. Unlike the French and American revolutions, the English
revolution of 1688 could claim to be essentially conservative, a return
to old processes from which there had been an improper deviation. It
was a response to a particular situation, and it left some big questions
unanswered. On the one hand it was clear that the new occupants of

[1] Cf. Ronald Butt, *The Power of Parliament* (Constable, 1967).

the throne held their position only by virtue of their acceptance of specific limitations on their personal powers; to this extent the solution contained elements to satisfy those who believed that power was held by virtue of a contract, though it came nearer to Locke's less defined notion of a trust. On the other hand it did not attempt to destroy sovereign power; provided that there was agreement between the Crown and Parliament (as representative of the people) it set no limits to what these two agencies together could do.

The English Bill of Rights provided the inspiration for the constitution of the thirteen original American states, followed by that of the United States and by those of the other states added to the Union in later years. Other constitutions, first in Europe, then outside it, in the nineteenth century and after, owed some debt to the English Bill of Rights, though as time went on the debt was so indirect that it could plausibly be ignored.

In one respect the English solution was soon outmoded; full written constitutions set clear limits to the powers of any legislative or executive bodies that might be set up under their terms. The American notion, widely adopted elsewhere, was inspired by the idea that no persons, no individuals, no groups, should have untrammelled power: that all should have only delimited functions prescribed for them in the constitutional document. But the Americans recognised that there must be a need to provide means of changing the constitutional documents themselves, and the need to provide the exercise of the sovereign power of constitutional amendment has been a source of difficulty for all constitution-makers.

Written constitutions differ from one another in the provisions made for amendment. Any constitution, being made at a particular point of time, is devised for the environment of that time. But that environment will inevitably change, and even the dominant values are not permanent. In recognition of all this, some formula has to be found to define an amending process, and no formula can be devised which is entirely satisfactory.

Two extreme solutions are possible: at one extreme no provision for amendment at all, at the other a provision that amendment can be made by the same process as ordinary legislation. The most rigid extreme is scarcely practicable, the least rigid has the effect of giving the constitution no special standing. It is not quite the same thing as having no constitution, because the authority which changes it has to produce reasons in support of a change in the fundamental law. All the same, if that authority is the legislature, and it can amend the constitution in exactly the same way as it passes ordinary laws, the constitution is hardly a check on its current power.

If a constitution is to have the special authority which is expected of it, there is a case for making it include some restriction on its amendment. It can be provided that a change in the constitution requires a majority of more than half of the members of the elected assembly. Or if there are two houses of the legislature there must be a majority in each, or in a joint session of the two. But machinery arrangements of this kind are unsatisfactory for many reasons. Why should a majority of an elected assembly be prevented from taking action which it thinks necessary, just because a previously existing agency, perhaps a body similar to itself, has made prescriptions in ignorance of the future? And in any case the ability to pass a constitutional amendment by a large majority depends at any given time on adventitious factors. A party or group of parties may at some time have a majority large enough to enable it to amend the constitution as easily as it can change an ordinary law. If in Britain there were a constitution capable of amendment by a two-thirds or three-fifths parliamentary majority, too much would depend on the size of the last general election majority.

A popular referendum as a means of constitutional amendment has obvious attractions; at least it returns decision-making power to the people. But experience with this device shows how it can be abused, even made to serve authoritarian purposes.

Objections of this kind could be adduced to defend the British failure to write a constitution, but they are not the explanation for it. The British have until now managed with the collection of statutory and other definitions and half-definitions which have filled out the Bill of Rights, partly because every government has been occupied with current problems, partly because there has been no pressing need to define the rules of the system more rigidly.

In the last 280 years many new statutes affecting the constitution have been added, but the more important developments have come through the adoption of new practices, some of which are commonly said to have acquired the status of 'conventions'. A constitutional convention may be said to exist when a process has been repeated on a number of occasions, and when there is wide agreement that it ought to be repeated, and on the reason why it should be repeated. Conventions define both important and unimportant processes, and in many cases it is uncertain whether or not a convention exists.

The most important conventions are those which have developed with respect to the position of ministers. The Queen still appoints the chief political office-holders, as before the Bill of Rights. By 1800 it could be said that there was a convention that she should act on the advice of ministers, and that she should appoint to ministerial offices only persons who were acceptable to Parliament. This was a reasonable consequence of the fact that, by law, they could not obtain or spend public money without parliamentary approval. Similarly, once appointed they became answerable to Parliament for their policies, and an expression of parliamentary disapproval demanded resignation. The office of Prime Minister developed as a response to a need for a chief among the ministers (particularly after the Hanoverian kings had withdrawn from most decision making). Then came the convention that the Prime Minister advised the Monarch on the appointment of other political office-holders, and that all together as a team were collectively responsible for the whole of their policies and actions. This collective and individual responsibility is the central feature of the whole system, and it has a major function as a safeguard against the abuse of governmental power; but its real effectiveness is doubtful in the light of the modern party system, along with the convention that the Prime Minister may ask for the House of Commons to be dissolved, to suit his purposes, and expect his request for a dissolution to be granted.

The House of Commons derives its authority from the people who elect it, and the franchise and other matters concerning elections have been defined in great detail in a series of statutes. Here the most important feature is that the electoral process normally produces a House of Commons in which one party has an overall majority which is very unlikely to reject its own leaders as ministers. Parliamentary standing orders and practices are indispensable to the Constitution's working, but they are meaningless except in relation to the balance of seats among the parties.

A vast mass of minor definitions, by statutes or established practices, understandings and assumptions, fills in this skeleton.

The Labour Government appointed a Constitutional Commission in 1968. There had never been any such body before, and the creation of this one could have seemed to indicate an intention to produce definitions which might provide the basis for a new and complete formulation. The appointment at that time was curious, in that many changes of constitutional significance had been made during the previous few years, and other possible changes were already under consideration, involving the relations between Government and Parliament, the structure of Parliament itself, and the system of local government.

The terms of reference of the new commission suggested a rather restricted purpose. Its concern was apparently with the Constitution only in the sense of the composition of the United Kingdom.

'To examine the present function of the central legislature and govern-

B

ment in relation to the several countries, nations and regions of the United Kingdom:

to consider, having regard to developments in local government organisation and in the administrative and other relationships between the various parts of the United Kingdom, and to the interests of the prosperity and good government of our people under the Crown, whether any changes are desirable in those functions, or otherwise, in present constitutional and economic relationships:

to consider, also, whether any changes are desirable in the constitutional and economic relationship between the United Kingdom, Channel Isles and the Isle of Man.'[1]

The chairman was Lord Crowther, former editor of *The Economist*. He died in 1972 and was succeeded by Lord Kilbrandon, a judge. The members included three professional academics (a lawyer, an economist and a political scientist), a woman who was a former civil servant but currently principal of an Oxford college, a legal peer, two senior members of the House of Commons (both ex-ministers), a trade unionist, two representatives each of Scottish and Welsh interests, and one of Northern Irish, and the President of the northern group of the Royal Institute of Public Administration. Both the terms of reference, and the fact that two-fifths of the members represented national or regional concerns, indicated that the part of the Constitution involved was the relation between the central United Kingdom government and the constituent parts of the kingdom: something which went beyond the local government reforms already expected, and which might reasonably have preceded or coincided with those reforms, rather than coming after them. The appointment of the commission was apparently a response to two distinct demands of which much had been heard: first, a demand in Scotland and Wales for a greater degree of national independence, and in England for increased local independence from the central government; and second a demand, currently articulated as an extension of democracy, for increased public participation in political decision making. The two demands were inter-connected, as decentralisation could be expected to promote increased participation.

The terms of reference explicitly prevented the commission from raising the question of the monarchy, because it could only inquire into the system 'under the Crown'. These words, which did not occur in the preliminary indication of the terms of reference which was given in the Queen's speech of October 1968, or the Prime Minister's first explanation of the project in the House of Commons, were inserted to

---

[1] H. C. Debs, 11 February 1969, cf. H. C. Debs, 31 October 1968.

make it clear that the continued inclusion of Northern Ireland within the United Kingdom, under the Crown, was not in question.

The commission, now known as the Kilbrandon Commission, made its report in November 1973. The report, which was not agreed by all the members, concentrated its proposals on the development of new bodies to express regional interests. The majority favoured the establishment of an elected assembly for Scotland; a smaller majority favoured a similar assembly for Wales; a majority recommended the creation of co-ordinating and advisory councils for five regions of England. But, apart from these proposals on devolution, the commission did not make any proposals regarding the fundamental principles or working of the Constitution as a whole. If any action is taken on the basis of the report, it will almost certainly not take effect before 1977 at the earliest, and the general principles, including the broad relations between statutes, conventions and practices, will not be affected.

The Central Executive Power

It is at the centre of the political structure that changes have been least clearly defined. Since the greatest single change, the transfer, during the eighteenth century, of the Monarch's effective power to a Prime Minister, the main developments have concerned the checks and limits, through responsibility to Parliament, on the powers of the Prime Minister and his close colleagues, and (establishing the nature of that responsibility) the manner of their appointment and removal.

In form the Monarch still appoints the Prime Minister from a small group of leading politicians, but the amount of discretion available to her has been reduced, until now she automatically appoints the person who has been chosen as leader of the party which has a majority of House of Commons seats. If the machinery of election and the internal party rules should fail to produce an automatic nomination she might still have to make a real choice, but in that case, within the system now established, the solution would probably be in the nature of a stop-gap pending the return of a normal party situation. Although she still appoints the other ministers, she does so entirely on the Prime Minister's advice. Effectively he decides not only who is to be appointed to which office but, subject to some technical constraints, what offices there shall be.

Although the Prime Minister determines the shape of his Government, his office cannot be described except by reference to its evolution within the group of royal advisers. Some such group has existed continuously since Norman times, when there was no thought of any clear distinction between legislative, executive and judicial functions.

The record of the conflicts of the Middle Ages suggests that there was a general expectation that the King should follow two principles: he should give high offices only to people of the right sort according to the established values of the time, and having appointed them he should consult them and respect their advice, acting always in agreement with prevailing norms.

A group of royal advisers and officers known as the 'Privy Council' became important under the Tudors, and although Henry VII and Henry VIII made the monarchy something close to an arbitrary dictatorship, not much restrained by traditional norms, they also developed the standing of the council as an institution, as well as that of Parliament. Their Privy Councillors were chosen for their loyalty and competence and it suited the Tudor monarchs to act through them, so that the council attained a new degree of stability and institutionalised authority, to which Parliament in general gave its consent.

Although the Privy Council still survives as the body through which many prerogative powers of the Crown are exercised, it has never again had the real powers of Tudor times. The Stuarts made use of smaller groups of advisers, and 'Cabinet' was just one of the terms used to describe such bodies, often with unfavourable implications. Later the term 'Cabinet' came into general use as the description of a meeting of the chief officers of state coming together to make real decisions about policy, and the wider Privy Council tended more and more to confirm cabinet decisions. For a long time now the Privy Council has had only formal functions, but the modern Cabinet still exists, as an institution, as that group of members of the Privy Council which determines state policy.

By convention, custom or prescription every person on appointment as a cabinet minister is made a member of the Privy Council by letters patent for life. Membership is also conferred (also for life) on the holders of some other posts (such as ambassadors) or as an honour. There are some 300 members now. There have been two removals from the council in this century, and an Order in Council was used in each case. In 1962, when Mr John Profumo asked to be removed, the lack of precedent for such a request was found to be no obstacle.

For a long time meetings of the Privy Council have been held only for the purpose of exercising prerogative or statutory powers of the Crown, without discussion, to give effect to decisions taken by the Cabinet. The quorum is three, meeting with the Queen at Buckingham Palace (or elsewhere if urgent necessity requires it, as for the sudden proclamation of a state of emergency.[1] The judicial functions of the

---

[1] On 3 August 1972, the Cabinet decided that it was necessary for the Privy Council to meet in order to make an order proclaiming a state of emergency,

Privy Council still survive, but in modern form, based on legislation of the past 150 years; they are exercised by the Judicial Committee, whose membership is determined by statutes of this period, and the committee is now part of the system of Courts of Law, being the final Court of Appeal in a small class of cases.

The Privy Council as such was finally replaced, as an effective instrument of government, in the eighteenth century, by a smaller body, which became stabilised around 1740. By this time the term 'Cabinet' was in general use to describe it. More important in the eighteenth century was the gradual but unsteady process by which the chief executive power passed from the Monarch in person to the most prominent among his ministers. The Bill of Rights had unwittingly provided conditions favourable to this development, but the change was not foreseen or intended by the men of 1688.

What the revolution of 1688 did produce was a new definition of the relation between Monarch and Parliament, so that the Executive certainly could not make laws or impose taxes except with Parliament's consent, given by a majority vote.

The Crown kept (and still keeps) a residue of prerogative powers, or common law powers, not derived from statute. The only significant one not exercised by ministers is that of appointing ministers, and the Crown's actions here are by now inescapably determined by conventions which will be discussed below. All other such powers are exercised by ministers who must answer to Parliament for the manner in which they exercise them. The most important are those involved in 'acts of state'; the Crown may declare war or make a treaty without Parliament's authority, but if it did such a thing contrary to the wishes of the majority of the House of Commons the House's displeasure, expressed by vote, would call into play the Government's responsibility to Parliament. In practice the most nearly-independent exercise of the

---

giving special power to take measures to reduce the damage likely to be caused by a dockers' strike. The Queen was on the royal yacht in Hebridean waters. The Lord President and three other ministers flew to the island of Islay; they were taken by car to the quay at Port Ellen and by small boat out to the royal yacht, where the Privy Council meeting was held. The ministers then returned, carrying the proclamation signed by the Queen, and were in the House of Commons by the end of question-time.

When the Monarch is incapacitated, or absent abroad, her functions are performed on her behalf by a Council of State, temporarily appointed, according to precedent, for the purpose (e.g. in 1972 the Queen's son, mother, sister and uncle – though the presence of all four was not necessary for a meeting to be valid). The Queen was touring in the Pacific when the general election of February 1974 took place. She returned to London so as to be available to appoint a new prime minister if necessary.

prerogative now is with respect to the appointment of persons to public offices, military and civil, in so far as they are not governed by legislation. There is still legally a power to dismiss civil servants at will, but it is not exercised.

The chance that the first two Georges, after 1715, could not speak English well and were not absorbed in English political affairs, left a vacuum. When Walpole became the recognised leader of the group which met regularly as a 'Cabinet', King George II did not formally appoint him as Prime Minister; it was just that he came to have a pre-eminent position among his fellows, and his *de facto*, unplanned pre-eminence set a pattern that was to be followed afterwards.

Meanwhile the notion of ministerial responsibility to Parliament developed, and determined the conditions of ministerial appointment. It is easy enough, looking back, to suggest reasons why. If the King's powers were subject to Parliament's approval, and exercised by ministers under the King, Parliament could refuse to grant money to ministers of whom it disapproved. From this it was a fairly short step to the principle that it could require the ministers to give an account of their actions, in order that Parliament could have knowledge on which to base approval or disapproval. Hence the notion of responsibility. The House of Commons could effectively force the resignation of any minister, or of all the ministers together, by refusing to grant money so long as he or they held office. The Bill of Rights did not create this new parliamentary sanction against ministers, but it created conditions favourable to the development of such a sanction if it should occur to Parliament to use it. That development took place slowly, and it brought with it an informal parliamentary influence over appointments.

For a long time after 1688 the appointment of ministers was still regarded as the Crown's prerogative, and William III did not appoint his ministers wholly from the majority party. Parliament at that time concerned itself with the various items of policy rather than with ensuring the appointment of ministers all acceptable to its majority. In the early eighteenth century the Executive obtained parliamentary support for its policies by using its influence, directly and indirectly, to get well-disposed persons elected to the House of Commons. Now and then ministers resigned, but the causes of their resignation could not be attributed to the operation of the principle of responsibility to Parliament as it was to develop later.

The general election of 1741 produced a House of Commons which Walpole could not effectively command. His resignation soon after that election has often been regarded, in retrospect, as pointing the way towards ministerial responsibility, but it did not seem at the time to have any such significance. For forty years after this, ministers succeeded in obtaining parliamentary support so long as the King had confidence in them. But in 1780 the House of Commons voted 233–215 in favour of Dunning's resolution 'that the influence of the Crown has increased, is increasing, and ought to be diminished', and in 1782, after the British disasters in the American war, the House passed unanimously a motion against its continuation. Lord North resigned, and his resignation was an important stage in constitutional development. It set a precedent and may be regarded as having installed the principle of responsibility to Parliament. Almost a hundred years had passed since the Bill of Rights had created conditions favourable to the principle, and another fifty years were to elapse before the 1832 Reform Bill, which set seriously in motion the process of reducing the effects of influence on the process of election.

The device of impeachment has never been abolished by statute, but has not been used since 1806, and must now be regarded as obsolete. There can now be no suitable machinery for imposing penalties on public men for political acts; the House of Lords, an assembly where members support parties, could not now properly undertake such a function.

The responsibility of ministers to Parliament has for a long time been the key principle of the constitutional system. But it has never been defined by law, and by now, in view of the facts of the party structure, the principle is of doubtful value.

The gradual development of the notion that each minister was responsible to the House of Commons, and that all the ministers collectively were responsible together, was soon followed by the growth of a rigid two-party pattern in the House of Commons, which suffered considerable setbacks but has seemed, since 1935, to be so firmly entrenched that the definition of its meaning needs some difficult logical gymnastics.

3

Appointment of the Prime Minister

THE MANNER OF APPOINTMENT

When the Queen appoints a Prime Minister her choice is governed by a number of conventions and facts of political life, which have been so developed that the choice is normally very simple. If one party has an overall majority, she appoints the person whom the members of the House of Commons belonging to that party have chosen as Leader by a process defined by party rules. If an election should produce no single-party majority the choice would be more complicated, and the conventions must provide for this eventuality.

The essential rule is that the Queen must consult persons who are in a position to give her sound advice as to which of the possible candidates is most likely to be acceptable to a majority in the House of Commons. Normally this means persons in the party with most seats in the House of Commons, who are not themselves candidates for the office, and who have substantial authority in the party. Common sense suggests this, and both past and recent practice confirm the convention.

What is not so clear is exactly whom the Queen should consult: in particular whether she should consult the outgoing Prime Minister or rely on other members of the party. The most recent cases give no answer to this question. In 1957 Eden resigned through ill-health. The Queen may have asked him for his views on the succession, or she may not; we have not been told. We do know that she consulted two prominent Conservatives who were not candidates, Lord Salisbury and Churchill. In 1963 however, when Macmillan resigned, the Queen consulted him only. This difference in practice between the two cases must be taken [as an indication that flexibility is recognised. Both Eden and Macmillan resigned through ill-health, and indeed

Macmillan was in hospital recovering from an operation at the time when the Queen went to see him. The conditions for consulting him were more unfavourable than the conditions for consulting Eden.

One might look for evidence of differences between the two resignations on the basis of the conditions which led to them, but such an inquiry is not particularly helpful. Both men were to some extent under a cloud politically when they resigned. Eden had just perpetrated the Suez invasion and the whole enterprise had collapsed in disaster, but the party as a whole was still supporting his policy and pretending that it had been a success. Macmillan on the other hand had suffered some political misfortunes which were embarrassments rather than disasters, but he was becoming rather stale, and his party were rather impatient with him.

When the Queen accepted Mr Heath's resignation in March, 1974, an invitation to Mr Wilson was the obvious next step.

The next question is how those who are consulted should proceed in advising the Queen. Their task is not to give their personal preferences; the Queen needs to be told who will be supported by the House of Commons. To fulfil their task they must inform themselves. In this matter there have been big changes. In the nineteenth century they were mainly concerned with the party's leadership group: which man of high standing would be prepared to be a minister in who's Cabinet? For a Prime Minister and his Cabinet, once appointed, to be able to survive in office with parliamentary support, the balance of relationships within the leading party group was inseparable from the ultimate questions about prospective parliamentary support. The process which produced the name to be put to the Sovereign was subtle and not always exactly the same; the Conservatives, until quite recently, claimed that a Leader of their party 'emerged'.

All this is now past history. The Labour Party came into Parliament with a different conception, reflecting the Party's egalitarian values. If all Labour Members of Parliament are equal, the only proper way for them to produce their Leader is by electing him. The Conservatives, while not themselves embracing those values, have arrived at the conclusion that the method of choosing a Leader predicated by them is more effective than the old process of emergence. The advice given to the Queen has thus been changed in character so that it is now, in most normal circumstances, a report to her that a person has been duly elected as party Leader by the majority party's members in the House of Commons, together with advice to appoint that person as Prime Minister.

The Parliamentary Labour Party has always elected its Leader when not in power. In 1957 the party's National Executive passed a resolution to the effect that no person was to accept the office of Prime Minister with Labour support unless he had first been formally elected Leader of the Parliamentary Labour Party by a defined process. Thus if the Labour Party has a majority it does not matter whom the Queen consults, because she can only be advised to follow the decision made within the party by the machinery which it has itself established. The process of electing the party Leader, by exhaustive ballot among the Labour members of the House of Commons, must be taken as an important part of the working Constitution, although in this case the formal basis is merely a resolution of the party's National Executive. If the Executive should make a new rule, then that rule in turn would affect the working Constitution.

There is still room for some slight uncertainty about the working of the system. The Labour members of the House of Commons, when in opposition, elect their Leader at the beginning of a parliamentary session and for the duration of that session. At the moment when the result of a general election is known to have given the Labour Party a House of Commons majority the existing Leader derives his position from the fact that he was elected at the beginning of a previous session by the Labour members of the old House, and he is subject to re-election. It might reasonably be argued that the spirit of the party's rules required that he should not accept office as Prime Minister until a new party election had been held. If the new House includes say 150 Labour members of the old House and 200 new members who had no part in approving the leadership before the election, why should the leadership, and the office of Prime Minister, be determined by such a stale majority, with the new membership left out of the process of choice? Such an argument would be rather pedantic. The facts of political life make it unlikely that the Party would go into a general election without a recognised Leader. In 1964 the outgoing Conservative Prime Minister resigned as soon as it became clear that Labour would have an overall majority in the new House, and Mr Wilson accepted office immediately afterwards. If he had been opposed and defeated in an election for the leadership of the PLP after the assembly of the new Parliament, he would no doubt have resigned. The machinery is there, but it has never been effectively used.

A new Labour Party rule, adopted late in 1970, made provision to insure against a potential future difficulty. As there is no Parliament between the dissolution of an old Parliament and the assembly of a new, there can be no Parliamentary Labour Party during that period. If the Leader died or became incapacitated during the election campaign, no machinery existed for electing a new Leader until after the assembly of the new Parliament. The lack of an established Leader at that time could be disturbing to the electorate (and could lose votes for the Party's candidates). In the event of the party's winning the election the Queen would presumably have to be advised to defer the appointment of a Prime Minister until after the assembly of Parliament and election of a Leader.

The new Labour Party rules of 1970 have done something which is unusual in British constitutional practice; they have made provision for an eventuality which has never actually arisen, so as to be fore-armed if it should actually arise. They provide that if the Leader dies or becomes incapacited during the dissolution of Parliament, the old PLP shall meet and proceed to elect a new Leader.

It is unlikely that this new rule will ever be needed, but it is of some constitutional interest in that it ascribes a very important function to a group of people at a time when the existence of that group as such has only a residual legitimacy.

In 1965 the Conservatives adopted a procedure similar to that of the Labour Party for electing its Leader and potential Prime Minister, but they still have no procedure for annual election, and certainly nothing so detailed as a procedure to provide for the death or incapacity of a Leader during a period when Parliament is dissolved.

The change of 1965 may be regarded as a consequence of the party's experiences of the past generation, though there may be a hint of a response to new values. The last two Leaders to emerge smoothly, Neville Chamberlain and Eden, were peculiarly disastrous Prime Ministers, and Churchill, who is generally considered to have been successful in his first term of office, was appointed in 1940 as a result of discussions involving notables of major parties, because it was agreed that a coalition government was needed. When Eden resigned in 1957, after less than two years in office, no successor had emerged, but Butler and Macmillan were almost equally prominent. Of the two, Butler seemed to have the greater claim, but Macmillan was appointed, on the advice of Churchill and Lord Salisbury, an elder statesman and a peer who was a member of the Cabinet.

Lord Kilmuir has disclosed that Lord Salisbury advised the appoint-ment of Macmillan, after he and Kilmuir (then Lord Chancellor) had asked each member of the Cabinet, one by one and privately, for his opinion.

'To each Bobbety (Salisbury) said "Well, which is it, Wab or Hawold?" As well as seeing the remainder of the ex-Cabinet, we interviewed the Chief Whip and Lord Poole, the chairman of the party. John Morrison, then chairman of the 1922 Committee, rang me up from Islay the next morning. An overwhelming majority of Cabinet ministers was in favour of Macmillan as Eden's successor, and back-bench opinion, as reported to us, strongly endorsed this view.'[1]

Churchill's advice appears to have been merely an expression of his personal preference. Exactly how the Chief Whip (Heath) ascertained back-bench opinion has not been disclosed, but it has been said that back-benchers were listened to when they gave their views. Kilmuir has said that Butler had 'damaged his position both in the Conservative hierarchy and in the parliamentary party', by 'publicly hedging his bets', and that he has no doubt that a straight vote in the party would have left him in a small minority.[2] All this may well be true, but the truth has never been demonstrated fully enough to dispel suspicions that there was a high-level determination to keep Butler out.

Professor Alexander is perhaps being legalistic when he suggests that, as the Cabinet resigns with the Prime Minister, it is absurd that the outgoing Cabinet should have a decisive voice in the choice of a new Prime Minister; but he is surely right when he says that, /

'. . . there was no suggestion [as there had been in 1931] that the Monarch had acted unconstitutionally, but there was some feeling, especially in the Labour Party, that the exercise of the Monarch's prerogative in such circumstances as those existing after Eden's resignation involved the Monarch, willy-nilly, in intra-party politics and, as such, her position became, to quote the Deputy-Leader of the Labour Party, "embarrassing".'[3]

In 1963, when Lord Home was appointed, Macmillan's advice to appoint him was based on a very complete inquiry by the whips among all Conservative members of the House of Commons. This inquiry was an *ad hoc* arrangement, devised at very short notice after Macmillan had announced that he was resigning. The procedure followed was publicly disclosed some time later. The Chief Whip explained in a television interview that every Conservative member of the House of Commons had been asked to state his first and second preference and also to indicate whether there was any particular person whom he would not wish to see appointed. The replies had been put down on paper and tabulated, and the result of the tabulation showed that there was more support for Lord Home than for any other candidate and less opposition. The precise mode of calculation was not disclosed; it is in any case not now of much significance, except as a sign that the party was moving towards a new and regular procedure.

[1] Lord Kilmuir, *Political Adventure* (Weidenfeld, 1964), p. 285.
[2] *Ibid.*, p. 286.
[3] Alan Alexander, 'British Politics and the Royal Prerogative of Appointments since 1945', *Parliamentary Affairs*, (1970), pp. 251 f.

The processes used in 1963 were unsatisfactory, both because the nature of the publicity that surrounded them was bad for the party and because some of the leading ministers in the Cabinet objected both to the processes and to the result which they produced. A small group of the top party leaders made a last-minute attempt to prevent Home's appointment but they failed. The suggestion that the opinion of prominent ministers should override that of the majority of MPs looked like a return to the nineteenth-century ideas, and it ran counter to the contemporary trend.

The new Conservative Party rules were not inspired by any new egalitarian philosophy; rather they were a response to the unsatisfactory working of the old arrangement. Sir Alec Douglas-Home's position as Prime Minister was weakened from the beginning by the circumstances of his appointment, and after all the party did lose the ensuing general election (albeit by a smaller majority than had seemed likely during Macmillan's last months). It was also said that the new process of formal election was good in that it protected the Queen against the possibility of being accused of intervening in intra-party politics – though it also reduced to almost nothing her one surviving power – except when there is no party with a clear House of Commons majority.

When the general election of February 1974 produced a House of Commons in which no party had an overall majority the Prime Minister then in office at first sought to ascertain from those holding to the balance whether he would find enough support among them to avoid defeat. When his enquiries produced a negative result he decided not to wait for the meeting of the new Parliament, but at once offered the resignation of his government to the Queen. She accepted it, and took the only course then open; she appointed the Leader of the Labour Party, who then hoped to enjoy majority support. If he had failed in his turn, he would presumably have advised a new dissolution. The situation was complicated by the presence in the new House of three groups each big enough to affect the outcome of an eventual vote, but the government survived several months without defeat – helped no doubt by the common opinion that in any new election it would be likely to get an overall majority.

If, in a situation in which no party had an overall majority, a party holding the balance between the biggest parties should offer support to one of them, but under a Prime Minister other than its leader, the Queen would be somewhat involved. She would be likely to need to try to persuade the parties involved to agree, and in the event of failure she would have no option but to appoint the Leader of the biggest party, and dissolve Parliament if he should then advise a dissolution.

The first months of the minority Labour Government of 1974 were remarkable for the fact that the government was not defeated; the Conservatives in opposition feared that a new general election would be disastrous for them.

The Queen's theoretical power to dismiss a Prime Minister, at the head of a Government backed by a solid majority, is probably obsolete because its exercise would involve intervention in politics beyond any accepted norms. If she used this power she would, within the Constitution, need to find a successor who would be supported by a House of Commons majority. She could succeed in this only if the dismissed Prime Minister was so far out of favour with his party that it was ready to accept her action. But such a situation could arise only if the party's dissatisfaction with its Leader were so strong that he could not practicably have continued as its Leader; the party itself would force his resignation without any royal initiative.

During the life of a Parliament a Prime Minister's resignation is normally the outcome of his own voluntary decision, and really severe and open pressure for his resignation is unlikely to come from his own party. To be effective, such pressure would need to be open and loud enough to constitute serious disunity in the Government and in the party supporting it. Every political calculation suggests that such disunity must be damaging to the party, and to its prospects at the next election. A Prime Minister thus enjoys a rather high degree of security in his position, so long as his party maintains its majority.

QUALIFICATIONS FOR THE OFFICE OF PRIME MINISTER

There seems to be little doubt that a person appointed as party leader, and thus as either Prime Minister or Leader of the Opposition, is bound to be a member of the House with many years of experience there. He must have been for some considerable time one of the party's recognised leading group, though he may well have had a period out of office because of disagreement. When a successor has to be found for a Prime Minister who has resigned or died, with no change of party majority, the successor is almost certain to be one of a group of no more than five or six of sufficient standing to be capable of being elected to the leadership by the party's MPs. He is therefore likely to have had considerable ministerial experience, and the appointment as Prime Minister must come as the culminating point in a series of promotions in a long parliamentary and ministerial career. He must owe his availability for the highest office in part to his predecessor, because the Prime Minister in power has absolute effective control over the process of appointing his own colleagues.

In establishing the list of persons from whom the next leader of a party will be selected there are now two immediate influences: the existing party leader and the whole group of party members of the House of Commons. The relative powers of these still differ as between the Conservative and Labour Parties. At this point the private rules of the parties perform functions so closely linked with the Constitution that it is tempting to regard them as part of it.

A Conservative Leader, once elected, has absolute discretion, either as Prime Minister in allocating ministerial posts when the party is in power, or as Leader of the Opposition in choosing the members of the Shadow Cabinet and allocating posts among them. But in making his appointments the Conservative Leader is likely to be somewhat influenced by what he knows about the general opinion in the party concerning its members. He can also remove people from office, though by doing so he does not necessarily remove them from the list of those with a chance of being elected to the leadership. (Mr Heath dismissed Enoch Powell from the Shadow Cabinet in 1968, but Powell's position in the party was not thereby diminished.)

With the Labour Party the Leader's freedom to choose his closest associates is limited, in opposition, by the annual election of the officers and twelve members of the Parliamentary Committee. If he becomes Prime Minister he can choose his ministers without any formal need to refer to the parliamentary party as a whole. At first he needs to include most of his old Parliamentary Committee, but after a few years in office his discretion is no less than that of a Conservative. To this extent a Prime Minister in office is a major contributor to the choice of his successor.

Since the 1920s it has commonly been assumed that it is a convention of the Constitution that the Prime Minister must be a member of the House of Commons, and not a peer. This rule is a good example of a constitutional convention. It appears to be binding though it is not quite certainly so; it cannot be said with certainty when it was established, though a particular choice at a particular time (1923) can be cited as a precedent; it is fairly new, representing as it were an unwritten amendment to the unwritten constitution; and there are good and clearly definable reasons for it, arising out of political developments which correspond with the rise of a new set of values – in this case egalitarian values.

Except for the appointment of Lord Home in 1963, which is discussed below, the last occasion on which a peer was appointed Prime Minister was in 1895, when the Conservative Lord Salisbury, a hereditary aristocrat, followed the Liberal Lord Rosebery. Already the balance between the Conservative and Liberal peers in the House of Lords had been altered by the desertion of the Liberal Unionists from the Liberal Party in 1886. By 1900 the Conservatives had such a solid majority in the House of Lords that it could have been breached only by a massive creation of peers opposed to the Conservative Party. The crisis of 1909–11 emphasised the role of the House of Lords as a Conservative stronghold, and the Parliament Act of 1911 responded to this situation by circumscribing its powers. That response was a constitutional innovation brought in with loud and furious controversy. The growth of a convention to the effect that the Prime Minister should always be in the Commons was another innovating response, brought in without any deliberate calculation or specific plan, but an inevitable complement to other constitutional and social developments.

In 1923, when the Conservative Prime Minister Bonar Law resigned through ill-health, the King had to appoint a successor from the same party. In many ways the Conservative with the strongest claim to the office was Lord Curzon, but Baldwin was appointed instead, after leading Conservatives had advised against Curzon on the ground that any member of the House of Lords was ill-placed for the office of Prime Minister. Curzon's peerage may have been an excuse, but it was certainly convenient that his peerage should be regarded as the cause of his not being appointed.[1] The fact that Curzon was passed over can be cited as the major precedent for the supposed convention that a Prime Minister should not be in the House of Lords, though one of the factors of 1923, the virtual non-representation of the main Opposition party in the House of Lords, no longer applies now.

The events of 1940 confuse the issue a little. When Chamberlain resigned after a vote of the House of Commons in which many of his own party abstained (although there was still a majority) one of the available successors was Lord Halifax, whom King George VI favoured. The Government Chief Whip, Margesson, seems not to have doubted that the majority of the Conservative Party (who had a majority in the House of Commons) would support Halifax if he were appointed to the post. However, it was agreed on all sides that it was desirable to have a new Government which would be a grand coalition of all three parties. They all supported the war, and a clash between Government and Opposition was unlikely to promote successful war-making. The Labour Party would not support Lord Halifax, not so much because he was a peer but because he was identified in its mind with the policies of Chamberlain, whom they had just rejected. In a discussion with Chamberlain and Churchill Lord Halifax expressed his reluctance to take on the premiership because having 'no access to the House of

[1] Cf. The memorandum of King George V's private secretary, Lord Stamfordham, quoted by Harold Nicolson, *George V* (Constable, 1952), p. 377.

C

Commons', he 'should speedily become a more or less honorary Prime Minister, living in a kind of twilight just outside the things that really mattered'.[1] In the event Churchill was appointed with Labour support, and he formed a coalition Government. The fact that Lord Halifax, though a possible candidate, was not appointed can be cited as a further precedent to add to that of the non-appointment of Curzon in 1922; but it could also be argued that the convention was weakened by the mere fact that Lord Halifax was seriously considered, in spite of his peerage.

The convention was criticised for one potential danger: it might exclude the possibility of appointing the best man for the job. If Churchill had happened to succeed to the dukedom to which he was very close, there would have been difficulties about his becoming Prime Minister.

A clear acceptance of a convention that no peer could be Prime Minister had one serious inconvenience: if the best man for the job should happen to be a peer, his exclusion for such a fortuitous cause would be unjust to him and against the public interest. The Peerage Act of 1963 dealt with the problem by allowing a peer to renounce his peerage, and so to become eligible for election to the House of Commons. More particularly, it made it possible for Lord Home and Lord Hailsham to be serious candidates for the Prime Ministership when Macmillan resigned. The appointment of Lord Home as Prime Minster, while he was still a peer, was acceptable only because it was known that he would at once renounce his peerage. A confident expectation that he would be elected to the House of Commons was fulfilled within two weeks.

[1] Lord Halifax, *Fullness of Days* (Collins, 1957), p. 219. Cf. W. S. Churchill, *The Gathering Storm* (Cassell, 1948), p. 523, and J. Wheeler-Bennett, *King George VI* (Macmillan, 1958), p. 443, in which he quotes from the King's diary for 10 May 1940.

4

Ministerial and Minor Offices

Every Executive needs to be organised in departments, and no constitution can alter this fact. The work of government is a response to needs, and the needs are by their nature compartmentalised – though the definition of the needs, and of the function of dealing with them, depends on economic and social factors, on currently accepted values, and on the interpretation which those currently in power place on their functions and objectives. If it is commonly agreed that the education of children is a private matter for their parents, there is no need for a Department of Education. External relations, military forces, internal order and the management of state finances are divisions of executive work that have not been dispensable to known organised states (though it is easy to imagine the scrapping of military forces). But many of the other sections of contemporary executive work have grown up in response to changing needs or expectations of industrial societies.

British Prime Ministers enjoy wide freedom to create new offices, to merge or abolish existing ones, and to change the functions of the holders of ancient offices whose original functions have become archaic.

Most British offices are fairly new, and those which have ancient names have mostly changed their real functions. The office of First Lord of the Treasury is wholly subsumed in that of Prime Minister. The offices of Lord President of the Council, Lord Privy Seal, Chancellor of the Duchy of Lancaster and Paymaster-General have all become virtual sinecures, and in this century have been used to provide places in the Government for people to do all manner of jobs, some of them temporary. Two of these formal posts, those of the

Lord President and Lord Privy Seal, have lately been used for the Leaders of the House of Commons and of the Lords respectively, and it looks as though we may have reached a settled practice. Since 1915 there has sometimes been a Minister without Portfolio too, when the sinecures have not been able to accommodate the Prime Minister's needs.

Nobody has bothered to rename the Chancellor of the Exchequer prosaically as Minister of Finance. The Lord Chancellor still does the work that a Minister of Justice would do. Under this curious title he is not only a minister but also a judge and the person who normally presides over the sittings of the House of Lords – an anomaly which has survived because there has been no immediately pressing cause to remove it.

Departments may be established or abolished or reorganised with little constitutional hindrance, though changes of this kind sometimes require legislation, which can always be passed with only slight inconvenience. There is a constant process of creating new departments to correspond with new governmental functions, or dividing or amalgamating existing departments.

Butler and Freeman's *British Political Facts*[1] lists over sixty separate departments with ministerial heads which existed for short or long periods between 1900 and 1960, and ninety designations of their chiefs. The rate of change accelerated between 1960 and 1970. Of the departmental headships which existed in 1960, only four survive with unchanged designations today (those of the Chancellor of the Exchequer, Home Secretary, Secretary of State for Scotland, and Minister of Agriculture), and there have been some boundary changes even here – notably the separation, in 1968, of the new Civil Service Department from the Treasury, which had formerly performed the new department's functions.

Recent changes in the control of the national finances give us an example of the flexibility of offices. In the 1930s the Treasury was thought by many people to be so deeply identified with its old function of balancing the budget that it could not adapt itself thoroughly to a new role in managing the economy in a broad enough way. When Labour came into power in 1945 an additional department, concerned more broadly with economic affairs, was set up. Sir Stafford Cripps, who was appointed as its head, was a man of higher standing in the Government, and in public estimation, than Hugh Dalton, who was made Chancellor of the Exchequer. But the separate department did not survive long, and after two years Cripps became Chancellor of the

[1] David Butler and Jennie Freeman, *British Political Facts, 1900–1967* (Macmillan, 1968), pp. 48 ff.

Exchequer himself and his former department lost much of its importance. Again in 1964, when a Labour Government returned to power, Wilson set up an Economic Affairs Department, and Mr George Brown, who had been elected by the PLP as Deputy-Leader, was placed in charge of it. Within two years Mr Brown had left it for the Foreign Office, and the department appeared to have a reduced importance. Later the Prime Minister took charge of it himself, with a newcomer to cabinet rank in charge of its day-to-day operations, until in 1969 the department was abolished and its functions were redistributed.

It would be tidy and reasonable to say that new departments are set up to satisfy new needs, but that is not the whole story. Sometimes a new department is really just a new focal point in the Government's shop-window, and it may be ephemeral, a sign that the Government is reacting vigorously to some crisis or to some party or sectional or popular demand. Such innovations are not always hollow. A new minister in a new office may have an impact which could not have been obtained without him.

Secretaries of State

One of the older titles is that of Secretary of State. For a long time there were two Secretaries of State, one for foreign and one for home affairs; these two offices have existed continuously since the eighteenth century. Other Secretaryships were added from time to time, with named functions: War, India, the Colonies, Air and Commonwealth Relations. Three of these have now been merged into the renamed Foreign and Commonwealth Office, the War and Air Departments have gone into the Ministry of Defence.[1]

---

[1] The background may be explained by a quotation from E. C. S. Wade and G. Godfrey Phillips, *Constitutional Law* (Longmans, 3rd edn., 1945), p. 143:

'The office of Secretary of State springs from a [humble origin, and it is not easy to say at what precise moment in history the King's Secretary became a definite office. In the Tudor period the Secretary became a channel of communication for home and foreign affairs, and the office seems to have grown in importance, largely perhaps on account of the personal rule of the Tudors. From about 1540 two Secretaries of State were appointed, but not at first as an invariable practice. It was when the Privy Council sought to combine deliberative and executive functions that the office assumed its present importance. The Secretaries of State ceased in fact, though not in law, to be servants of the King and his Council and became one of the motive forces in the Cabinet. On two occasions before 1782 a third Secretaryship was added for the time being. It was in that year that the Home Office and the Foreign Office came into existence as separate departments. . . . On 27 March 1782, the Foreign Office came into existence as a result of a circular letter addressed by Fox to the representatives of Foreign Powers in London, to the effect that he had been entrusted with the sole

In the first half of this century most new departments were headed by office-holders entitled 'Minister', and though there were certain formal duties attached to a 'Secretary of State' (and the Commons journals still refer to Mr Secretary X), the title of Secretary of State implied neither superiority nor inferiority to that of 'Minister'.

In very recent times there has been a wholly new tendency to use the term Secretary of State to indicate that the holder of the office is superior to most of the persons designated merely as 'Minister'. In some cases the term has been used when two or more departments have been joined under a single ministerial chief.

The slow changes in the reorganisation of defence showed the way. For a long time each of the Armed Services was under a minister with a seat in the Cabinet. The Secretary of State for War, the First Lord of the Admiralty, and (later) the Secretary of State for Air, were equal in status. The three Services directed much of their aggressive talent against one another in competing for money, and their political chiefs became instruments of their rivalry. In 1936, in an attempt to remedy the dysfunctions, a Minister for the Co-ordination of Defence was appointed. The office was mainly futile because it lacked authority. When war began in 1939 its holder, Admiral of the Fleet Lord Chatfield, was appointed to the War Cabinet, but so were the three Service ministers. Churchill, who was then First Lord of the Admiralty, comments that their inclusion 'profoundly affected Lord Chatfield's authority as Minister for Co-ordination of Defence'. Churchill's hundred-page narrative of the seven month period when, as one of the Service chiefs, he was being co-ordinated, does not mention his co-ordinator at all, except to say that in September 1939 Chatfield accepted the presence of the Service chiefs in the War Cabinet 'with his customary good nature',[1] that a few weeks later he supported one of Churchill's minor plans,[2] and that on 3 April 1940, when his job had become redundant, he proffered his resignation 'freely'.[3] The experiment with a co-ordinating minister in 1936–40 was not very productive.

When Churchill became Prime Minister he 'assumed the office of Minister of Defence, without however attempting to define its scope and power'.[4] Attlee followed suit in 1945 and kept the title until he

direction of foreign affairs, while his colleague, the Earl of Shelburne, had been appointed Principal Secretary of State for Domestic Affairs and the Colonies. The Home Secretary from that date took precedence over all other Secretaries. At that time he had very few of the statutory powers and duties which subsequent legislation has conferred upon him. The other Secretaryships of State may be said to have been created out of this Secretaryship.'

[1] W. S. Churchill, *The Gathering Storm* (Cassell, 1948), p. 328.
[2] *ibid.*, p. 422.   [3] *ibid.*, p. 463.   [4] *ibid.*, p. 526.

appointed a separate Minister of Defence in December 1946, as the undoubted superior of the Service chiefs, although two of them were still entitled 'Secretaries of State'. Attlee kept the service chiefs in his Cabinet, but Churchill for the first time (in peace) left them out in 1951; the Minister of Defence's superiority was now more clearly marked. Then new weapons and new strategic needs made it expedient to reduce the autonomy of the three Service departments. In 1963 the title of the supreme minister was changed to Secretary of State for Defence, and the three Service ministers were brought within his ministry and called Ministers of Defence (Army), etc. These reforms required legislation, but the Defence (Transfer of Functions) Act was passed with little trouble except for some nostalgia about the demise of that traditional figure, the First Lord of the Admiralty. Changes made in 1967 reduced the separate ministerial representation of the Services to the level of Parliamentary Under-Secretary, with two Ministers of Defence, one for Equipment and one for Administration, under the Secretary of State. In 1970 these two were replaced by a single Minister of State.

In 1964–70 Mr Wilson was energetic in creating new offices of Secretary of State. Some merged two or more old departments into one; Commonwealth Relations absorbed the Colonial Office, then both were absorbed by the new Foreign and Commonwealth Relations Office. By stages Health, Pensions and National Insurance were merged under a new Secretary of State for the Social Services. The new creation of Secretaries of State had some glorification effect, highlighting the Government's special concern with first one field of governmental activity, then another, though the fate of Economic Affairs showed that the glamour could be short-lived. At the same time, these innovations made it possible to restrict the number of departments while governmental activities were expanding.

In October 1970 Mr Heath soon continued the trend, with two new Secretaries of State, one for the Environment, covering local government, housing, public building, and transport, the other for Trade and Industry, covering technology and trade. By then there were ten Secretaries of State, all presiding over expanded or spot-lighted departments, except for the Home Secretary and two whose offices expressed devolutionary objectives.

It may seem that the Secretaries of State for Scotland and Wales are hardly holders of offices of enormous importance in the Government. A Scottish department, headed by a Secretary, was set up in 1885, and since 1925 the head of the Scottish office has been entitled Secretary of State for Scotland. The use of the title was partly a window-dressing device to satisfy Scottish demands for recognition of

Scotland's existence as a nation within the UK, but there were good objective reasons for it too. Internal administration in Scotland has always had to reflect the distinctions of Scottish education and law, and the Scottish Secretary has presided over the whole of Scottish internal administration. His three under-secretaries have specific functions, which have been altered in the past few years.

The creation of a Secretary of State for Wales in 1964 must be attributed almost entirely to the Government's wish to placate Welsh demands, and to its fear of the vote-winning potential of the Welsh National Party. It corresponded with new measures of administrative devolution, but ran counter to the main trend towards concentration of ministerial responsibilities, which by 1970 had reduced the number of departments to sixteen, only one of which had its chief outside the Cabinet, as compared with nine outside in 1957.

Mr Wilson created his new offices of Secretary of State one by one. Mr Heath made all his changes soon after taking office, then left the system stable for three years, except for the creation of a Secretary of State for Northern Ireland when the devolutionary system for the province was suspended in 1972.

MINOR OFFICES

Almost every department now has at least one political assistant to its chief, with the title of Parliamentary Under-Secretary of State or Parliamentary Secretary. Junior ministers are politicians who assist the heads of their departments in general departmental operations and in speaking for the departments in the House of Parliament to which they belong. The precise relationship between a junior minister and his chief has never been defined; in some cases a specific sub-section or division of the department is entrusted to a junior minister. The most obvious case of this is the Scottish Department, in which the three Parliamentary Secretaries can be regarded almost as though each were a minister for the particular section of Scottish administration with which he is concerned. Alternatively, the junior minister may simply assist the minister over the whole field of the department's activities. The designation of special functions for junior Ministers has become more usual since 1964, though it does not transfer responsibility from the departmental chief.

There has recently been a great proliferation of a new type of under-minister, more grand than a Parliamentary Secretary. In May 1941 Churchill brought Lord Beaverbrook into his Government with the novel title of Minister of State (a kind of non-portfolio office). Two months later Beaverbrook was given a departmental office, but the title of Minister of State was given to Oliver Lyttleton when he was sent to be a minister resident in the Middle East; he remained for a little over six months. These uses of the title Minister of State seemed to be little more than Churchillian inventions for particular purposes. A little later, in September 1943, the title was given to Mr R. K. Law when he was appointed to assist the Foreign Secretary, and it was felt that his office should be at a higher level than that of Parliamentary Under-Secretary of State. The Labour Government of 1945 included two Ministers of State, one at the Foreign Office, one at the Colonial Office. After 1951 the Ministers of State began to multiply, until by 1960 there were eight. By 1968 there were eighteen, and the two ministers under the Secretary of State for Defence were Ministers of State in all but name. Mr Heath's reorganisation of October 1970 left only nine Ministers of State, but there were in addition six 'Ministers' who were subordinate to Secretaries of State.

Whips
The Machinery of Government Act, 1964 made a further innovation which was of considerable constitutional interest, though it attracted little attention at the time. Political life in contemporary Britain involves a set of relationships within Parliament between ministers and the general body of their supporters – and a parallel relationship exists in the shadows on the Opposition side. The relationship requires channels of communication; such channels have developed most effectively outside the constitutional framework. Members were appointed as party whips as long ago as the eighteenth century, and the whips' function has become steadily more sophisticated in the modern world in which communication becomes ever more important. In so far as they tell the leader what the rank and file are wanting or thinking, and try to get the rank and file to do what the leaders wish, they are performing a strictly party function. Their role in relation to the organisation of parliamentary business is less obviously a party function, and is in a sense a service to the House as such.

Until 1964 there was always some hesitation about recognising the position of whips as members of the Government, and a typical compromise was employed, with some whips appointed to archaic offices (with pay) such as Comptroller of the Household. The Chief Whip was Parliamentary Secretary to the Treasury. Meanwhile, half of the Government whips held office without pay, being described simply as 'government whips (unpaid)'. The Act of 1964 allowed the payment of salaries to these as well as to the other whips, thus clearly including them in the ministerial team.

Ministerial Salaries

Politicians desire and love office for its own sake, not for the remuneration. It can reasonably be argued that a Member of Parliament who is a minister should continue to be paid as a Member of Parliament, but receive nothing for being a minister. However, until 1908 Members were not paid at all, and ministers had always been paid as servants of the Crown. Also, an MP who is not a minister may receive remuneration for other work in commerce or in a profession, while a minister, holding a full-term appointment, is not allowed to receive any other salary. When payment for MPs was introduced, ministers continued to be paid as such, and did not receive the parliamentary salary so long as they held office.

The rate of ministers' pay was until recently fixed quite arbitrarily. In the nineteenth century it was appropriate to a man of substance in a highly inegalitarian society. By the 1960s the rate was still fairly high, but it had been overtaken by the pay of senior civil servants (itself somewhat influenced by the market rates for high ability). A committee was set up to examine the question, and it recommended large increases, partly because it was not asked to discard a set of values linking pay with prestige, partly because some were finding that the sacrifice of income from other sources on accepting office was very great. The Labour Government introduced legislation providing for an increase of ministers' pay, but less than the increase which the Lawrence Committee had proposed. In 1971 there was a further big increase, giving the Prime Minister £20,000 a year, and other ministers between £5,000 and £14,000.[1] All ministers in the Commons receive the parliamentary allowance[2] in addition to their ministerial salaries.

It seems likely that, particularly when the Conservatives are in office, the minister's pay is not an important factor in making him maintain solidarity. It is the fact of holding office that he finds attractive.

---

[1] This time the question had been referred to the Top Salaries Review Committee, whose chairman, Lord Boyle, had been in an earlier Cabinet. The committee found twenty-six cases of MPs who said they had refused office because they did not relish the drop in income that it would cause.

[2] See below, p. 112.

5

The Office of
Deputy-Prime Minister

If the Prime Minister is ill or absent someone must act in his place, but there are difficulties in the way of formally designating him as Deputy-Prime Minister. To do so might seem to imply a derogation from the Sovereign's rights in appointing his successor. Churchill wrote that by November 1941 Clement Attlee was 'now generally recognised as Deputy-Prime Minister'.[1] This was specially appropriate for the exceptional conditions of the time, with Attlee as the Leader of the second party in the grand coalition, though not regarded as Churchill's potential successor. From 1945 Herbert Morrison was regarded as Deputy-Prime Minister under Attlee, and his definition may be regarded as authoritative:

'Including and since Churchill's War Government, the position of Deputy-Prime Minister has been publicly announced, though not constitutionally recognised. . . . The Deputy-Prime Minister might be specially considered by the Sovereign, though there would be no obligation to do so, especially as I gather that *the Sovereign does not recognise such an office.*' (My italics)[2]

The title of First Secretary of State was an ingenious device, invented in 1962 by Macmillan, for giving a constitutionally-correct formal recognition to Butler's *de facto* position as Deputy-Prime Minister. *The Times Book of the House of Commons* for 1964, in its entry for Butler, says: 'He had been Deputy-Prime Minister and First Secretary of State since July 1962'; here the first title seems to depend on the second.

Until 1970 the Parliamentary Labour Party's internal rules compli-

[1] Herbert Morrison, *Government and Parliament*, (Oxford University Press, 1953), pp. 76–7.
[2] *ibid., loc. cit.*

cated the position in that they provided for a post of Deputy-Leader of the PLP, whether the Party was in power or in opposition. The common (but constitutionally irregular) acceptance of Morrison's position as Deputy-Prime Minister in 1945–51 depended in part on his party position – though a constitutional purist would be offended by such an assumption. In 1964 George Brown held the party elective post of Deputy-Leader, and had also been runner-up when Wilson was elected Leader in 1963. The title of First Secretary of State was conferred on him. The arrangement was convenient as an indication of his personal eminence, but it also indicated the special importance of his office as Secretary of State for Economic Affairs; Wilson particularly wished to ensure that that department should be 'at least as powerful as the Treasury'.[1]

When Brown resigned from the Department of Economic Affairs to become Foreign Secretary, his successor at Economic Affairs, Mr Stewart, was given the title of First Secretary of State, although apparently Mr Brown was still the second man in the Government. Between 1967 and 1968 Mr Stewart was First Secretary of State, for a time with no departmental functions and then combining the office with that of Secretary of State for Foreign and Commonwealth Affairs. In April 1968 the title of First Secretary was given to Mrs Barbara Castle, together with the newly-created office of Secretary of State for Employment and Productivity. The significance of the title had be-become obscure, but Mrs Castle's standing seemed to be enhanced. All this time George Brown held the elective post of Deputy-Leader of the PLP, and he continued to hold it after he resigned from the Government in March 1968. In July 1969, when the Prime Minister raised the question of Brown's returning to the Government, Brown insisted that 'he could return only as Deputy-Prime Minister since he was still the Party's Deputy-Leader'.[2]

In November 1970 the new rules of the PLP provided that in future the office of Deputy-Leader of the parliamentary party would lapse on the party's coming into power. George Brown's position as elective Deputy-Leader of a party in power, yet not holding any office, in 1968–70, had clearly been anomalous, and the PLP's reform brought the party's rules into line with the constitutional assumptions, besides removing a possible source of difficulty for a future Labour Prime Minister.

When the Conservatives returned to power in 1970, Mr Heath made no appointment of First Secretary of State, and by this omission created a precedent which could be of some significance. As the new

[1] Harold Wilson, *The Labour Government, 1964–70* (M. Joseph, 1971), p. 3.
[2] *ibid.*, p. 708.

procedure for electing the party Leader had first been used in 1965, this was the first occasion on which an incoming Conservative team included a man who had been runner-up in an election for the Leadership. But Maudling was merely made Home Secretary, and the only mark of distinction conferred on him was the placing of his name immediately after the Prime Minister's in the list of ministers. The office of First Secretary of State was allowed to lapse. When Mr Maudling resigned in 1972 it was made clear that there was no second man in the Government.[1]

Now that both parties have clear rules for electing their Leaders and potential Prime Ministers, it seems more than ever constitutionally pedantic to object to the appointment of a Deputy-Prime Minister on grounds connected with the Sovereign's prerogative of appointing the Prime Minister. On the other hand, any Prime Minister is probably glad that there is no sign of any convention requiring him to appoint a deputy; constitutional pedantry may stand in the way of the development of expectations which could well be embarrassing, and thus set up a rather flimsy barrier which has quite a useful function.

---

[1] Cf. James Margach, *The Sunday Times*, 23 July 1972:
'If Mr. Heath is unable to be in the Commons for his question session, ministers will deputise for him according to the subject. . . . When Mr. Heath is not able to chair Cabinet meetings . . . the agenda will decide the chairman.'
When Mr Wilson returned to power in 1974 he announced that Mr Short, the Leader of the House of Commons, would deputise for him when necessary, taking the chair at Cabinet meetings and answering Prime Minister's questions if the Prime Minister should be absent; but no special title was conferred on Mr Short.

6

The Appointment and Choice of Ministers

THE PROCESS OF APPOINTMENT

There is no precise definition by statute of the Prime Minister's right to advise the Sovereign to appoint to ministerial offices. Although technically the Queen simply receives advice from the Prime Minister, and thus is apparently free to refuse to appoint a minister as advised by him, there is no doubt that in practice she must follow his advice. Queen Victoria did succeed in holding out against certain appointments, and King George V is recorded as having expressed strong opinions, though without effect, on a few occasions, but it is unlikely that the Sovereign would now think it appropriate even to seem to try to exert influence.[1]

The Prime Minister can decide more or less what offices he wants to have in his Government, and how many of his ministers he will have in the Cabinet. There are certain statutory limitations on the total number,

---

[1] The latest recorded instance of any kind of intervention by the Crown in a ministerial appointment is from the time when Attlee was forming his Government in 1945. According to King George VI's private papers, as recorded in Wheeler-Bennett's biography, Attlee told the King that he was inclined to ask him to appoint Ernest Bevin to the Exchequer and Dalton to the Foreign Office, and the King said that he favoured a switch between these two. In the event Attlee formally advised the appointment of Bevin to the Foreign Office and Dalton to the Exchequer in agreement with the King's suggestion. According to Attlee's own account, his mind was not made up at the time when he first discussed these two offices with the King, and although the King did say that he would like to see Bevin at the Foreign Office, he would have reached the same decision even without the King's suggestion.

The subjective interpretations which the two sides put on these transactions are of some constitutional interest. George VI did not lay claim to a positive role, but when he had scope for thinking that his role was positive, he apparently was ready to find a positive element in it.

but, as was shown in 1964, it is an easy matter for a Government to ask Parliament to pass legislation authorising an increase in the maximum number of ministers to be appointed.

The lack of written constitution has had interesting consequences in the matter of the Executive's patronage. The Bill of Rights laid down things that the King could not do without parliamentary approval, but this provision could be made of little value if Parliament contained a majority of members who were dependent on the King's favour. From 1660 onwards the Commons recognised the danger that the Crown could establish an effective control over the Commons by appointing numerous members to offices of profit, and several Place Bills were passed. Then in 1701 the Act of Settlement provided that as from the accession to the throne of the House of Hanover no office-holders whatever were to sit in the Commons; but even before that provision came into effect there were second thoughts. It was felt that something would be lost if ministers, being wholly excluded from the Commons, could not explain their policies and be attacked in the House. In 1707 the Succession to the Crown Act was passed, under which a member appointed to an old office (created before 1705) lost his seat in the House but could seek re-election. Later, further statutes allowed new offices to be created under similar conditions, and for a long time any minister could, in practice, continue to sit in the Commons provided that he resigned his seat and was then re-elected at the ensuing by-election. Much later, in 1919, a Re-election of Ministers Act exempted certain offices from the need to seek re-election, and another Re-election of Ministers Act in 1926 ended the need for re-election altogether.

The provisions of the Act of Settlement could have laid the foundations of a system based on separation of powers on the American pattern, if they had been allowed to survive – but they were not. Political reality took charge and the legislative and executive powers were firmly united.

For a long time the successive enactments setting a limit to the number of members of the House of Commons who could hold offices of profit kept the number so small that it could hardly be expected to have a serious effect on the result of divisions in the House. But by the 1960s it seemed that the existing restriction on the number was so fragile and impermanent that there might as well be no legislation at all. When Labour came into power in 1964 one of the Government's first acts was to introduce a bill to permit an increase in the maximum number of office-holders in the House of Commons. The House of Commons (Disqualification) Act of 1957, then in force, provided that no more than seventy persons holding specified offices might sit in the House of Commons. Also, the Ministers of the Crown Act, 1937, allowed no more than eight Secretaries of State, and the Ministers of the Crown (Parliamentary Secretaries) Act allowed a maximum of thirty-three Parliamentary Secretaries (or junior ministers). The new Prime Minister wished to increase the number of ministers in his Government, and he did appoint more than the existing law permitted. To comply with this law, twelve ministers served without salary for the time being. Meanwhile, a Machinery of Government Bill was brought in to permit the maximum number of office-holders in the Commons to be ninety-one instead of seventy; it also allowed the appointment of nine Secretaries of State instead of eight, and thirty-six Parliamentary Secretaries instead of thirty-three. It increased the maximum number of Ministers of State to eighteen. In doing this it showed some prescience. There had been eleven in the previous Government (eight of them peers), and the new Government included thirteen. Within three years the figure of eighteen was reached.

The bill was passed without difficulty, supported by the House of Commons majority. It showed that there is nothing to prevent a government from increasing the proportion of members of the House of Commons who are dependent upon it, and that the Opposition's objections can easily be disposed of. During the next few years, when the Government had difficulty in obtaining the support of all its House of Commons members for some of its proposals, the Opposition often referred to the 'payroll vote', a term which was not inappropriate though a senior minister suggested that it was insulting. By 1968 there were eighty-nine office-holders in the Commons (including all the paid whips), compared with fifty to sixty in the 1930s, and sixty-five in 1960. After 1970 the number was reduced again.

THE CHOICE OF MINISTERS

There is no statute requiring ministers to be in Parliament. In practice, although the only statutory provisions passed on this matter were those of the early years after the Bill of Rights, which attempted to exclude the ministers from Parliament, the present constitutional system absolutely requires that all ministers should be members of either Commons or Lords. This convention is a consequence of that which concerns ministerial responsibility. If ministers are to be responsible, they must be answerable, able to answer questions about, and able to explain in Parliament the actions of such policies for which they are responsible. A person who is not a member of either House may be appointed to a ministerial office, but only if there is a plausible expectation that he will shortly be in Parliament.

If a Prime Minister wishes to include in his Government some non-politician who has no seat in Parliament, he can easily do so and advise the Queen to confer a peerage on the person concerned; otherwise a member of the House of Commons must give up his seat in order that a by-election may be held at which the new minister may be a candidate. When Labour came into power in 1964, Frank Cousins, who was not a Member of Parliament, was appointed Minister of Technology. Mr Bowles, an elderly holder of a safe seat at Nuneaton, was persuaded to accept a peerage and thus to leave his House of Commons seat vacant. The constituency Labour Party of Nuneaton obligingly adopted Mr Cousins as its candidate, the by-election took place, and Mr Cousins was elected after a two-month delay which was tolerated because of the assumption thet he would shortly be in Parliament.

There is no formal limit to the number of people whom the Prime Minister may bring into his Government either by giving them peerages or by having safe seats found for them in the House of Commons, but political considerations suggest that he should only bring in two or three people in these ways at any one time. With few exceptions, service in the House of Commons or Lords is a necessary step in a person's career before he can aspire to ministerial office.

In theory the Prime Minister may choose anyone he wishes from among his party's supporters in the two Houses to form his Government. There are certain limits however in practice. In the case of the Labour Party when the party comes into power after a period of opposition as the result of a general election, there is a special situation because some members of the party in the House of Commons have in the previous Parliament been members of the Parliamentary Committee elected by all the members of the parliamentary party. There is no formal obligation on a new Labour Prime Minister to give offices to these people, but there is a clear expectation that he should give office to all but one or two of them. In Australia, where the situation is basically similar, the Parliamentary Labour Party formally chooses the persons from whom the Cabinet is to be selected, but there has never been any serious move in this direction in Great Britain.

About a dozen government posts need to be given to peers, if only in order to provide for adequate representation of the Government in the House of Lords, in addition to that provided by five holders of royal offices, who act in part as Whips. At least two high-ranking posts, carrying seats in the Cabinet, must in practice be given to peers; every peacetime Cabinet has included the Lord Chancellor and the Leader of the House of Lords. The post of Leader of the House of Lords has often been combined with a departmental office, but lately with the office of Lord Privy Seal.

Most of the peers in the Government can nowadays be expected to hold second rank or junior offices. As recently as 1951 there were seven peers in the Cabinet, but such a situation would be virtually impossible now. There is a rigid convention that the Chancellor of the Exchequer cannot be a peer; one can say with scarcely less confidence that by now a peer could not well hold any major post connected with internal administration. Lord Home (as he then was) was Foreign Secretary before he became Prime Minister in 1963. The Opposition complained, but to no avail. In 1970 the office of Secretary of State for Defence was given to a peer, Lord Carrington, and no great trouble ensued. A government office which requires its holder to travel during parliamentary sessions can usefully be given to a peer, because membership of the House of Lords demands less attendance in Parliament.

An easy reform that has been often proposed but always rejected would allow any minister to speak in either House of Parliament. One objection is merely traditional, another avers that the burden on ministers would be excessive.

Political prudence suggests the need to include members of the different elements in the party, such as those often designated as relatively moderate or relatively extreme in their views. No geographical region should be wholly overlooked. It is more important to get the right balance than to put the right man in the right job. Special qualifications do not count for much – too little, perhaps – and ministers are moved from one office to another quite frequently. When it comes to promoting members of his team to higher posts the Prime Minister is likely to be guided partly by factional considerations but mainly by his own assessment of a man's performance in junior office, which may be influenced by the opinions of the party as a whole, as reported by the whips.

7

The Cabinet and Prime Ministerial Government

THE SIZE, STRUCTURE AND ROLE OF THE CABINET

The Cabinet is the assembly of the principal ministers of the Crown, brought together by the Prime Minister at regular intervals, and for supplementary meetings as he may think fit, to deal with matters of high policy (including legislative proposals to be presented to Parliament), matters primarily concerning one department but involving broader issues, and matters involving several departments which cannot conveniently be settled without wider participation.

The principle of collective responsibility developed in part as a response to the need for coherence in decision making, but once it was established it brought its own reinforcement to the need for deciding collectively. If every minister shares responsibility for all the Government's decisions it is well that he should have a part in the act of choosing between major options.

Cabinet government is the form through which this need is satisfied. Something of this kind operates in most sophisticated political systems, with the degree of dominance exercised by the chief as the main variable. The British form has developed and adapted itself through practice in response to changing circumstances, with little formal definition. Long-standing convention requires that the processes should be kept secret; as decisions must be collective, the public agreement that is required would be weakened if the dissensions, bargains and concessions along the way were exposed for public judgment. But the secrecy restricts comment, not only on the choices of those who operate the machinery, but on the machinery itself. The membership of the Cabinet at any time is public knowledge, and so are the outcomes of its deliberations; but the memoirs of people who have been recently concerned in its working, however copious, are discreet where they are required to be. Thus any analysis of the role of the Prime Minister personally, or of the cabinet committees in relation to the full assembly, must be based on unsystematic information, some of which is supplied by people who are much concerned with presenting their own actions in a favourable light.

One common theme is that although we have 'cabinet government', the Cabinet as such, in full assembly, is not an effective body. One school of thought concentrates on the Prime Minister's supposed dominating position, with or without a group of favoured cronies, another suggests that the Cabinet's supposed powers have been dissipated among several groups of ministers. For fifty years it has been argued that modern Cabinets are too big. When judgements are attempted on the outcomes of the system's working plenty of evidence indicates that Parliament's control has slight effects, and that, as a corollary, ministers' powers, however they may be balanced within the cabinet system, are excessive – though much of what happened between 1964 and 1970 casts doubt on these assumptions. Other evidence suggests that, far from being too powerful, ministers are so bound to seek solutions that will work consistently with other solutions that they have little room for positive action, but merely react to each crisis which confronts them in the way that they hope will cause least immediate trouble.

During the period of cabinet government the Cabinet has tended to grow in numbers, from around five in the early eighteenth century, to a dozen or fifteen in much of the nineteenth, to twenty after 1900. The highest figure, twenty-three, has been reached at various times, with variations down to fifteen, and fewer in wartime, when one single objective – successful conduct of military operations – has taken such priority that the more positive and complex aims of normal government have been reduced to secondary importance.

One element has not changed. The Cabinet has never had an independent home of its own. The Privy Council has always met in royal premises, but Cabinets, less formal at first, met elsewhere. Since 1856 the regular meeting-place has been the Cabinet Room in the Prime Minister's official residence at No. 10, Downing Street, so other ministers came to him for cabinet meetings, which were run with little formality and no proper records until the Secretariat was first established during the First World War, accommodated in huts in the garden behind. The Secretariat survived the War, though was soon suspected of being a sinister centre of power; in 1922 it was defended as a body 'concerned purely with recording the proceedings of the Cabinet and its committees and communicating the decisions to appropriate bodies'.[1] Once established, it thrived; now the Secretary to the Cabinet is a

---

[1] J. P. Mackintosh, *The British Cabinet* (Stevens, 1962), p. 353.

civil servant of equal standing with the head of the civil service and the Permanent Secretary to the Treasury, but above all other permanent heads of departments; and recent improvements to the premises at 10 Downing Street, in which work is done to serve the Cabinet collectively, cost £2 million. You can say, if you wish, that the Cabinet has its palace, in which the Prime Minister for convenience is allowed free tenancy of a smallish flat; or that the Prime Minister has a palace with numerous minions, to which other ministers may come at his beckoning from time to time, sometimes to fulfil their collective role.

As government has undertaken more new functions, and new departments have been created, Prime Ministers have been faced with the difficulty of keeping the Cabinet's membership down to a reasonable number. Heads of departments of secondary importance have been left out; at some recent periods (the last in 1967) use has been made of a barely comprehensible formula by which certain ministers have been formally stated to be 'of cabinet rank' although not members of the Cabinet.

The commonest complaint, over many years, has been that at any cabinet meeting, whatever is being discussed, some members are ill-informed, because they are mainly occupied with their own departments and with problems of co-ordinating with others whose affairs impinge on their own. It is sometimes argued that the ideal Cabinet would consist of five or six people without departmental responsibilities, free to spend their time thinking about the big issues of policy. A variant of this plan is that each should have a general oversight over one of the main concerns of government: foreign relations, finance, social affairs. Two objections have stood in the way of such a solution: detached ministers would have too little contact with current business, and their answerability to Parliament, in relation to the departmental chiefs, would be unsatisfactory.

Churchill tried an experiment with two 'overlords', each co-ordinating the work of a group of related departments, in 1951, while each departmental head was responsible for his own department. The experiment might have been carried further until the Cabinet consisted only of co-ordinators, but it was not successful, and was soon dropped.

Reforms of the 1960s, grouping two or three departments so that they form a single one, with its head responsible to Parliament, but assisted by second-rank ministers, have made it possible to restrict the size of the Cabinet without leaving sections of the administration unrepresented in it. By 1968 the overseas and defence fields were presided over by only two ministers in the Cabinet, where thirty years before there had been eight.

Between 1964 and 1970 Harold Wilson reduced the number of

departmental heads by his amalgamations, but the size of his Cabinet remained between twenty-one and twenty-three because at times he made use of 'double-banking' (two ministers of the same department in the Cabinet) and included more than the minimum of members without ordinary departmental responsibilities. However, by the end of 1970 Mr Heath, with his latest amalgamations, had brought the number down to seventeen, and only one departmental head (Posts and Telecommunications) was left out, as compared with nine in 1957. But by 1973 the number had risen to nineteen, with the addition of a Secretary of State for Ireland, and of a Minister for Trade and Consumer Affairs. The former appointment was a response to the Northern Irish situation; the latter was a new extension of the device of double-banking (this time for the Department of Trade and Industry), to give a special voice in the Cabinet to a spokesman for the public as consumers. Early in 1974 a new post of Secretary of State for Energy was created, and maintained by the new Government.

The argument about numbers is not really very important or interesting. Detached wise men may be useful as advisers, but not for deciding policy above the heads of the people who must carry it out. But if the Cabinet must be made up mainly of people with departmental responsibilities there will always be some who have not had time to think about some of the matters which have to be decided; a reduction to ten members would not solve their problem – and might make it worse.

One relatively informal solution has been the extensive use of what have often been called 'Inner Cabinets', with the Prime Minister and some senior colleagues meeting rather frequently to look for solutions to major problems – though in most cases they have thereby merely strengthened their arguments to put before the full meeting. Also, there have been *ad hoc* groups formed to deal with particular problems, sometimes taking day-to-day decisions in the expectation of obtaining cabinet approval.

We have ample evidence that two major decisions of the 1940s and 1950s were made by small groups of ministers in such a way that the full Cabinet could only confirm them. One was the decision of the Attlee Government to manufacture atomic bombs; the second was the decision in 1956 to agree that Israel should invade Egypt, and that the British Government, in concert with the French, should then announce an intention to invade the Suez Canal area of Egypt if the Egyptian Government did not agree to withdraw its forces to the west of the canal zone.

It is thus evident that some of the most important policy decisions were taken by small groups of ministers and then presented to full cabinet meetings either when it was too late for them to be rescinded or on the assumption that rejection was out of the question. Such situations were not without precedent, and indeed something of this kind has happened, openly or secretly, in different forms since the sixteenth century. There is nothing unconstitutional about it; what the constitution now requires is that the Cabinet should be a united group, and that no one should continue to be a member of it and yet disavow any of the decisions made on its behalf.

Apart from the variable but long-standing use of informal 'Inner Cabinets' quite extensive use has been made of cabinet committees, so that for each of several areas of governmental concern a group of ministers, including some not in the Cabinet, has done the major work of co-ordination and of preparing decisions to recommend to the full meeting. It has for long been the practice not to disclose information about the existence of these committees, their membership or their functions, but there has been quite generous divulgence of the way the system worked under Harold Wilson in 1964–70. At the first meeting of his newly-formed Cabinet in October 1964 he laid down rules based to the best of his memory on those insisted on by Clement Attlee. 'Departmental disagreements should be threshed out before Cabinet met; where disagreement remained, this should be clearly stated and the arguments set out either in joint or separate papers.'[1] Early in 1968 he is said to have produced a new and clear definition of the role of cabinet committees; he also set up a new standing committee, 'the equivalent of an Inner Cabinet, or Parliamentary Committee, as it was officially called',[2] and he made known the committee's membership and purpose. It was at first composed of the Prime Minister, the Secretaries of State for Foreign and Commonwealth Affairs, the Home Department, Employment and Productivity, Defence, the Chancellor of the Exchequer, the Lord Chancellor and the Leader of the House of Commons. Here was a group of ministers with interests covering all the main areas of the Government's activity, meeting frequently to consider all issues of major political importance. It dealt with matters brought before it by the Prime Minister, and it deliberated after being fully briefed by the Cabinet Secretariat. It met twice weekly, while full cabinet meetings, normally only once a fortnight, received reports of decisions of the Parliamentary Committee. The rules for committees, described below, aimed at avoiding further discussion of matters about which the Inner Cabinet had agreed. The assumption appeared to be that the full

[1] Harold Wilson, *The Labour Government 1964–70* (M. Joseph, 1971), p. 17.
[2] *ibid.*, p. 524. On p. 649 he calls it 'the Management Committee (Inner Cabinet)' and again on p. 655 he refers to a meeting of the 'Management Committee' just before a full cabinet meeting, so it seems that the formal name was rather obscure.

meetings were mainly occasions for the whole team to be kept in touch with current problems.

Wilson's book (p. 649) records that in May 1969 Mr Callaghan, then a member of the Inner Cabinet, made a speech at a meeting of the Parliamentary Labour Party 'which was taken by a number of ministers as dissociating from cabinet policies, particularly on the Industrial Relations Bill'. The restrictions imposed on ministers by collective responsibility could hardly apply to a private party meeting, but the speech was leaked to the Press, and some ministers were 'incensed'. Wilson told Callaghan that he hoped there would be no question of resignation, but dismissed him from the Inner Cabinet 'which had to work on a basis of close trust in the very difficult situation we were facing'. Callaghan 'accepted this and devoted himself to his departmental duties'. There was here an interesting distinction between the degrees of solidarity required of inner cabinet and other cabinet members, in relation to discussions within the Party's private machinery.

Along with the establishment of the Parliamentary Committee went a strengthening of some other standing committees of the Cabinet. A new degree of publicity about these was allowed; a back-bench Labour Member, Mr J. P. Mackintosh, wrote an article in *The Times* for 21 June 1968, in which he gave the names of the chairmen of eight committees. The Prime Minister presided over the Defence and Overseas Policy Committee (whose composition had already been revealed, in an earlier form, some years before) and over the Economic Policy Committee. Mrs Castle, Secretary of State for Employment and Productivity, presided over another economic committee dealing with prices and incomes, and the Chancellor of the Exchequer over the Public Expenditure Scrutiny Committee. The remaining committees were those on Legislation and on Future Legislation (both under the Leader of the House) and on Home Affairs (under the Home Secretary). Mr Mackintosh indicated that the committees' powers had been increased:

'Mr. Wilson has given instructions that when the general opinion of the committee is clear and the chairman is satisfied, that is the end of the matter. A minister can then appeal to the Prime Minister, who may or may not put the question on the cabinet agenda. . . . Also committee chairmen may put before the Prime Minister or the Parliamentary Committee questions which are agreed but which, they feel, may cause political trouble.'

Mr Patrick Gordon Walker, who was himself in the Cabinet between 1965 and 1967, confirmed Mackintosh's account in a book which he published in 1970,[1] describing Wilson's new scheme as 'a major innovation'.

In a well argued commentary on the evidence up to 1970, Mr Colin Seymour-Ure has suggested that there were signs of what he calls 'disintegration', a tendency for the whole Cabinet to distribute its decision-making energies fortuitously.[2]

There would be cause for concern if each cabinet meeting simply endorsed the decisions or recommendations put to it by the departmental ministers, each in his own field. There is need not only for co-ordination between departments but for truly joint decisions (not merely confirmation) when substantial questions are involved. But the joint decision does not need to be taken jointly by all the departmental heads with each playing an equal part with every other. It is inevitable that on any particular issue some ministers are relatively ill-informed or indifferent. The practice of distributing the matters which require joint decision among a series of groups, each consisting of people who have a duty to be involved in the matters which come before them, is probably the best practicable solution, so long as there is scope for ministers outside any group to call into question the line that is being followed.

In the period of Conservative rule beginning in 1970, nothing of moment emerged about the Cabinet's committees. However, the White Paper of October 1970, *The Reorganisation of Central Government* (Cmd 4506) averred that departments should be organised 'by reference to the task to be done or the objective to be attained, rather than by reference to the "client group" involved'. More interesting was the setting-up of a central policy review staff, giving services common to all ministers and designed to give ministers in their collective role in the Cabinet a degree of support they had lacked in the past. The services to the Cabinet collectively were emphasised, and any suggestion that the staff would strengthen the Prime Minister's relative position was hotly denied. On the contrary, the staff would advise the ministers of the pros, cons and consequences of any course of action.[3]

PRIME MINISTERIAL GOVERNMENT ?

The most persistent argument of the 1960s revolved around the question whether or not the cabinet government of the British system is

---

[1] Patrick Gordon Walker, *The Cabinet* (Cape, 1970).
[2] *Parliamentary Affairs* (Summer 1971), pp. 196–207.
[3] Cf. Lords Debates, 10 November 1970. After two years at work the chief of the central policy review staff, Lord Rothschild, spoke of his work on television. The only salient feature was his insistence that he worked for the Cabinet collectively, and saw the Prime Minister rarely.

being replaced by prime ministerial government.[1] The old theory, well expressed by Bagehot, was that supreme power belonged to a collectivity, the ministers forming the Cabinet, with the Prime Minister as the 'first among equals'. His personal power was limited by three interlocking factors:

1. He had to keep the support of his close colleagues, who were to some degree his immediate rivals. If he displeased several of them at once the malcontents could well conspire together to remove him and replace him by one of their number.

2. He had to maintain the loyalty of the members of his party in the House of Commons. That loyalty was accorded not to him alone but also to the team of which he was the leader. To some extent, his dependence on his party in Parliament was bound up with his dependence on his close colleagues, as each of these would have a personal following in the House.

3. He and his ministerial colleagues were subject to well-known constitutional limits, by statute and convention.

Meetings of the full Cabinet may be ill-devised for taking all the decisions which go beyond individual departments, and it seems clear that the responses of the machine, through cabinet committees and less formal devices, have involved some decline in the Cabinet as such. To some extent the Prime Minister's office could be expected to become relatively more important in consequence. He can determine the shape of his Cabinet's committee system, he can make new committees and determine their functions, he can greatly influence the method and location of real decision making.

Meanwhile, it would be an exaggeration to suggest that cabinet business has become entirely formal. In Harold Wilson's own account of the difficulties between November 1967 and January 1968 over the attempt to improve the economic situation after devaluation, the Cabinet in full session appears as the central figure. Although 'Cabinets do not proceed by the counting of heads', Wilson admits that the review of public expenditure produced evenly divided views. 'It was the only time in six years that colleagues seemed to be keeping their own tally of the "voices". And such were the strains that I was reading day by day in the press that the "vote" was eleven to ten, or twelve to nine on this or that particular proposal.' Wilson mentions six cabinet meetings

[1] Cf. In particular Humphrey Berkeley, *The Power of the Prime Minister* (Allen & Unwin, 1968); and R. H. S. Crossman's Introduction to W. Bagehot's *English Constitution* (Fontana, 1963).

in the first fortnight of January; it is clear that the full assembly was not being by-passed at this time.[1]

Both Macmillan and Wilson have presented accounts of their prime ministerial terms (1956–63 and 1964–70 respectively) which do not support the theory of prime ministerial government.[2] The picture is of considerable respect for the Cabinet as such as a body to be involved in major decisions, with a good deal of delegation to ministerial committees as a response to the increasing quantity and variety of decisions needing to be taken; together with some selective personal intervention by the Prime Minister talking to individual ministers about problems immediately affecting their departments.

In this picture the one single element which could be taken to indicate the nature of the Prime Minister's power is the amount, nature and direction of his personal interventions, and there is room for a variety of subjective interpretations. Lord George-Brown cites particular instances when it appeared to him, at least, that Wilson took too much upon himself, or upon himself together with one or two other ministers, but these cases, in the light of the particular circumstances, do not add up to a proof that Mr Wilson was taking all power into his own hands. There is little evidence of any discernible trend towards concentration of power on the Prime Minister over the last few decades; Neville Chamberlain gave more evidence of this than any of his peacetime successors.

The Macmillan and Wilson memoirs do indicate a special involvement with foreign affairs, and perhaps there is evidence of a long-term trend towards an involvement in this field. During both these administrations the Prime Minister's choice of individuals for the office of Foreign Secretary may suggest a desire to maintain effective overall control of foreign affairs. As G. W. Jones has put it, 'A Prime Minister intending to play a major part in handling foreign affairs requires an amenable Foreign Secretary'. Jones then speculates, with some plausibility. 'This explains why Mr Macmillan kept Mr Butler out of this job, although Mr Butler cannot have pressed very hard for it, and why Mr Wilson was never keen for Mr Brown to take it on.' It explains also why Sir Anthony Eden substituted Mr Lloyd for Mr Macmillan: 'the former would be a better subordinate.'[3]

Mr Wilson's great personal activity in the foreign affairs field was in

[1] Wilson, op. cit., pp. 479–83.
[2] Wilson, op. cit.; Harold Macmillan, Memoirs, 3 vols. (Macmillan, 1971–3). Cf. G. W. Jones, 'Prime Ministers and Cabinets', Political Studies (1972) pp. 213–22, and 'Prime Ministers and their Advisers', Political Studies (1973), pp. 363–75.
[3] Jones (1972), op. cit., p. 215.

spite of the fact that, unlike his four Conservative predecessors, he had not been much concerned with this area before attaining the highest office. In this sense he could be compared with Chamberlain; but Chamberlain entered an international society which was at that time dominated by heads of government with unquestioned total power over the affairs of their several countries, including external relations.

Such evidence as we have for the period 1970–3, with the Foreign Office in charge of a politician who was a quasi-professional in this field, provides evidence of a rather different sort, with prime ministerial dominance more apparent in home affairs.

One possible indicator of personalised power in the head of a Government may be the presence in his entourage of an *éminence grise*. Since the time of Churchill there seem to have been no significant figures of this type. Jones[1] refers to various persons who might perhaps seem to have held such a position, but indicates that there is little hard evidence to show that any recent Paymaster-General or other non-portfolio minister has been the equivalent of Churchill's Lord Cherwell; and that no Cabinet Secretary or other civil servant or special economic adviser has appeared to exercise any special continuing influence beyond that which must be appropriate to his institutional role. Both Wilson and Heath appear as highly 'professional' Prime Ministers, giving full scope to the established institutional processes, even though they may have extended these by creating new offices.

Lord Rothschild, the head of the Central Policy Review Staff since this body was created in 1970, has insisted repeatedly that he is not the Prime Minister's man but the Cabinet's man, and there is no serious evidence to support a contrary interpretation.

In July 1973 Mr Heath went out of his way to blow a personal trumpet very loudly on behalf of the Maplin Airport project, along with the Concorde and the Channel Tunnel, thus apparently attacking those (certainly in his own parliamentary party and probably in the Cabinet too) who were urging circumspection rather than the blind commitment of resources to Gaullist *gloire*; but within two months Lord Rothschild made a speech which seemed to be a direct contradiction of the Prime Minister's July clarion call, and Maplin was deferred for two years with the option of abandonment plainly kept alive.

A Prime Minister's actual role is always difficult to measure. It may not be the same as it appears to be to the public, though the public appearance may in its turn influence the reality. It may be interpreted quite differently by two individuals who have immediate experience of it. But there are a number of factors which can be expected to have an

---

[1] (1973), *op. cit.*, pp. 363–70.

influence over both the appearance and the reality. There is always an interplay between the current structure of other political systems, including the dominance exercised by individuals, and public expectations both at home and abroad. While we may easily identify a number of influences making for concentration of power, we should also notice that the nature of the institutions of the EEC may well have a contrary influence.

Quantitatively there is no doubt that governmental functions have been steadily increasing all through the present century. At the same time, there are several plausible reasons why the increased power of government should be more concentrated, not less.

Improved communications make it possible, and therefore normal, for the most important international contacts to be made at the level of chief executive. Also some state constitutions give a clear supremacy of power to one man, who undertakes the major international business himself, and so there is an expectation all round that chief executives shall take personal charge. The President of the United States matches (more or less) the Soviet Party General Secretary; and since 1959 the French President has had an essentially similar role. The West German Basic Law invests the Chancellor with functions going beyond those of a 'first among equals', and practice has extended the Chancellor's role.

Public opinion has come to accept the notion that meetings below the summit level are not of so much significance as the hugely publicised contacts between effective heads of governments. The British Prime Minister, surrounded by effective monarchs, becomes more of a monarch in his turn.

The new process by which the Prime Minister is appointed, based on election by the whole of his parliamentary party, would seem likely to raise him above his colleagues. Instead of being the people obviously and clearly responsible for his choice, the other party leaders are now either defeated rivals or politicians who could have had no chance in opposition to the man who was elected. Freed from his old dependence on the top men of his Cabinet, he is more obviously their superior. He holds office because he has been elected by his parliamentary party, they hold office because he has appointed them.

We may also observe the weakening of the old doctrine that a Prime Minister was damaged by the resignation of an important colleague. Even if the resignation arises from dissatisfaction with the Prime Minister, rather than from a difference over policy, it can leave the rebel isolated. Harold Wilson was only a little perturbed when George Brown walked out, saying that he did not like Wilson's running of the Government – and Brown, whom Wilson had defeated rather narrowly for the party leadership five years before, was generally accounted the second man in the Cabinet. The departure of Ray Gunter, for rather similar reasons ('I no longer desire to be a member of your Government'), not long after, produced a stir of excitement but no harm to the Government. In 1962 Macmillan dismissed a third of the Cabinet in order to bring in new men. A decline in Macmillan's standing seemed to begin about this time, but there is little evidence that the decline was caused by the dismissals. The later trend, started by Macmillan and brilliantly exploited by Wilson, towards the creation, every year or so, of a new prestigious Secretary of State, emphasises the Prime Minister's power to dispose things as he thinks they should be.

Another factor which could seem to favour a growth in the Prime Minister's power is to be found in the trend towards the personalisation of politics, promoted by the new importance of the mass media. There is no doubt that nearly all voters really vote for a party, not for a local candidate. If a general election is to be interpreted as a choice between parties it is also a choice between potential Prime Ministers. As the public tends to identify a party with its Leader, so the Leader becomes particularly important in relation to the electoral process, and thus receives an accretion of personal prestige. In the 1966 and 1970 general election campaigns Heath and Wilson received more than half of the television coverage given to their respective parties.[1]

On the other hand, there is some contrary evidence. Both major parties resist the temptation to concentrate attention excessively on the Leader, thinking it to be in the long run electorally unhelpful. Also, opinion poll findings do not support a claim that party and Leader are identified. The great swing of opinion poll support from Labour to Conservative in 1967, confirmed by by-election and local election results, and maintained, with some fluctuations through 1968 and 1969, was not accompanied by any significant increase in responses expressing approval of Heath as Conservative Leader. At the same time Wilson continued to fare better than his party, though this fact might be used to support an argument that the party was dependent upon him personally. If the proportion of people approving of a Prime Minister in office is greater than the proportion approving of his party as a whole, his position in relation to his party is likely to be strengthened.

The main evidence for prime ministerial domination might be found in the ease with which governments in the past five years have fundamentally reversed their policies, even those involving party ideology, without facing overt ministerial revolts or resignations. Between 1971 and 1973 the Conservative Government began suddenly to support industrial 'lame ducks', and introduced measures for controlling prices

[1] David Butler and M. Pinto-Duschinsky, *The British General Election of 1970*, (Macmillan, 1971), p. 207.

and incomes. In both cases its actions were opposed to the doctrines and earlier policy orientations of the party; yet the changes produced no high-level resignations. On the other hand, Wilson tells us that, on a much less fundamental issue, he abandoned his plan to appoint an effective transport planner; '. . . it was an occasion on which I yielded to sectional cabinet pressure and, looking back on it, I was wrong'.[1] By early 1973 there was still no transport policy, no sign of a dominant spirit capable of overriding sectional pressures. It is perhaps on matters with some ideological content that a strong Prime Minister can best show his strength; driven to pragmatism by the ineluctable pressure of events he may be stronger in such fields than in those, like transport planning, in which a real national interest may have only weak advocates against the entrenched sectional spokesmen.

Where Prime Ministers have demonstrably succeeded in gaining support for new policies, their innovations have given little sign of being expressions of their own prejudices or preferences; rather they have been (at least since Suez) expressions of flexibility in confronting disagreeable and intractable problems.

[1] Wilson, *op. cit.*, p. 184.

8

Ministerial Responsibility

Ministerial responsibility to Parliament, or more specifically to the House of Commons, is the central principle of the political system. It is based on convention; the principle was not ordained at any time but can be regarded as a natural consequence of the relations between Parliament and ministers which developed in the eighteenth century.

The Bill of Rights could logically have produced a system based on the separation of legislative from executive powers. The constitutions of the several North American states, and that of the USA, gave separate roles, and above all separate legitimation, to the elected legislatures and to the elected chief executives.

The British solution was less deliberate. Within the relationship of Crown and Parliament established by the Bill of Rights, Parliament's power to refuse to grant money to the Executive was the foundation of Parliament's claim effectively to require the resignation of ministers who became objectionable to a parliamentary majority.

The principle has been modified from the beginning, but in changing degrees, by the collective nature of responsibility within the two-party system. In European countries which have adopted the expectation of ministerial responsibility, the power of the popular assembly to remove ministers has, for most of this century, looked convincing because it has been exercised from time to time. In Britain, whenever a single party holds a House of Commons majority, the ministers' collective domination over their majority has weakened their responsibility to the assembly as a whole.

Responsibility presumably involves some sanction in case of proven harmful error, particularly when shown to be due to malevolence, misjudgement, stupidity or negligence, as distinct from mere misfortune. For a long time misuse of public funds, discovered and reported by the Public Accounts Committee (or even, discreetly, through the auditing process) has been attributed to persons. Since 1968 the Parliamentary Commissioner for Administration has been available to examine complaints about decisions, taken normally by officials at various points in the administrative hierarchy well below the highest level, with the purpose of determining whether or not there has been maladministration. A large proportion of cases of maladministration have concerned decisions of tax officials in relation to individuals. As a protection of citizens against possible infringement of their reasonably accepted rights by officials, the ombudsman system is at least of some effect. But there is still no means of checking decisions which may harm the public as a whole after being taken merely to satisfy sectional pressures, or worse still to satisfy a body of demands within the bureaucracy itself, which may, for the dominant civil servants, attain a validity of their own mainly for the sake of proving that a controversial position, once taken up, was justified.

'Answerability', in the narrow sense of a minister's duty to answer questions and to give explanations, does not depend for its effectiveness entirely on the ultimate sanction of a power of dismissal. Ministers are not responsible to the House of Lords, but they must still give an account of their actions and policies there, both in replies to parliamentary questions and in debate. The operation of the duty in the Lords usefully illustrates the collective nature of the Government. There are usually hardly any heads of important departments in the Lords, and parliamentary questions in that House are directed to the Government as a whole. The reply is given by a peer who holds an office in the Government, and who has been briefed by the department with whose affairs the question is concerned. Often he has no personal involvement and no scope for answering in any way but so as to reflect established departmental policy.

The second meaning of ministerial responsibility is more fundamental. It assumes that the members of the assembly can not only require ministers to give explanations, but by a majority vote withdraw their support and thus their permission for those ministers to remain in office. It may reasonably be argued that the assembly's right to question, to receive explanations and to attack the explanations, is not worth much unless it is supported by the second right, that to dismiss, whose effectiveness depends in practice on two factors. The first is the party-composition of the assembly. If there are several parties with strong representation, or if there is little party discipline (for example, if the individual elected members depend for their election on independent local support rather than on support given to a national party), the Government will always be in some real danger of being defeated. If, on the other hand, the Government is based on the support of a single

E

well-disciplined party with an overall majority, and if almost all of its parliamentary supporters owe their seats to that party rather than to personal or local factors, then the likelihood of a defeat of the Government (or of any particular minister in it) will be smaller. This is the normal British situation.

The second factor is more technical, derived from constitutional provisions or conventions. If the interval between general elections, and thus the duration of each Parliament, is rigidly fixed, at exactly three, four or five years, the likelihood of a defeat of the Government will probably be greater than if the Government can, under constitutional provisions or conventions, arrange for a new general election in the event of a hostile vote.

In Britain ministerial responsibility was real, with several government defeats, for some thirty years in the mid-nineteenth century, but then the two parties became more distinct from one another and each became more strongly disciplined. Now defeat, as a result of withdrawal of support by an element among the Government's supporters, has seemed out of the question – except perhaps over entry to the EEC in 1972. If a Government is in serious trouble with an important group among its supporters the ministers tend to modify their policies until some compromise is reached.

The true meaning of ministerial responsibility looks rather hazy and uncertain. Illustrations of its effectiveness from the past twenty years are hard to find, and much comment has been sceptical about its value. Meanwhile it may be that the mere existence of the principle has promoted both compromise and restraints, half concealed in private party meetings – or even, when Labour is in power, in meetings of the party's National Executive Committee.

We may identify four aspects of the political responsibility of ministers, and look in some detail at the operation of each of the four. They may first be briefly stated:

1 Individual responsibility means that a minister must resign if the House of Commons votes no confidence in him. He must also resign, forestalling any such vote, if he acknowledges a serious error for which he is responsible, even of a personal kind.

2 Collective responsibility, as applied to the Government as a whole, means that if a vote of no confidence is passed the Prime Minister and his whole Government must either resign or ask the Queen to dissolve Parliament, in the hope that a general election will produce a House which will have confidence in him and his Government.

3 Collective responsibility, as it affects individuals, means that every minister (of whatever rank, in Cabinet or outside it) shares the responsi-

bility of the whole Government for every part of its policy, and for all its actions. By remaining in office a minister identifies himself with the whole of the Government's policy. If some policy is put through which a minister is not prepared to support, he should resign.

An individual minister who wants to put pressure on his colleagues in the Government to accept a policy which he advocates may threaten to resign if they will not adopt it.

4 A Government which wishes to put through a policy which is unpopular with some of its supporters can put pressure on the dissidents to support the policy by threatening to resign, or to dissolve the House. This threat is a powerful weapon.

INDIVIDUAL RESPONSIBILITY AND DISMISSAL FROM OFFICE

If a minister is criticised by a House of Commons majority vote he should be in danger of suffering some penalty. As impeachment can be said to be obsolete, the only sanction available to the Commons is a power to force him to resign. But when we come to look more closely at this supposed power, with respect to an individual minister, we see that it is not much less remote than the power of impeachment. Ministers do resign – at a rate of several per year – but not because a majority House of Commons vote calls upon them to do so. Individual ministers are protected by the collective responsibility of all.

If a motion critical of a minister were put to the vote in the House the outcome would be favourable to him if his colleagues supported him, because the parliamentary party would support the Government of which he was a part. He could in practice be censored by a House of Commons vote only if his ministerial colleagues, and in particular the Prime Minister, disowned him, but in this case he would be made aware of this withdrawal of support, and resign too soon for any vote of censure on him to be passed.

Scandalous behaviour or admitted personal error

The simplest cause of resignation is a minister's personal fault, through actions which cannot be justified by any argument, and which may or may not involve disgraceful behaviour. In 1935 J. H. Thomas disclosed part of the Budget to persons who then profited from the disclosure and rewarded him. The facts were discovered by a tribunal of inquiry which was set up because there was evidence suggesting that somebody had had advance knowledge of the Budget proposals. Thomas resigned in disgrace. Mr J. Profumo resigned from the War Office in 1962 when it became evident that he had had improper relations with Christine Keeler, though he had assured the House of Commons that he had not.

Both Thomas and Profumo resigned and withdrew from public life as soon as the scandalous facts became known.[1]

Hugh Dalton resigned as Chancellor of the Exchequer in 1947 because he carelessly disclosed part of his Budget to a journalist while he was walking to the House of Commons to make the speech. He made a mistake which caused no harm, and from which neither he nor anybody else gained anything whatever. He was technically at fault because, for good reasons, rigid custom requires that the contents of the Budget should be kept secret until the House hears them; but he was not disgraced, and he was given another office in the Cabinet.

Cases of this type present no difficulty.

Arguable errors of policy

Political actions of individual ministers are regularly attacked by the Opposition, with no great effect. The question of a possible resignation arises only when the criticism is not only from the Opposition, and when it is based on some action which Government supporters consider to have caused harm. When a minister is under attack the Prime Minister will either ask him to resign without a parliamentary vote, or support him so that any vote will be treated as a question of confidence in the Government as a whole – and it can be assumed that the Government's majority will be kept intact. The Prime Minister's decision whether to ask him to resign (or to accept his resignation if it is offered), or to stand by him, depends on calculations of political advantage. He may be influenced by the views of senior colleagues, by what he hears from the whips about the opinions of his own party members in the Commons, by newspaper comment, by his impressions of grass roots opinion in the party and among the public, perhaps with his eye on an imminent by-election.

The classical theory of individual ministerial responsibility expressed through resignation, by now threadbare, received a little reinforcement through the resignation of Mr J. Callaghan as Chancellor of the Exchequer in 1967. He had over a long period identified himself with the policy of avoiding devaluation, so when the pound was in fact devalued he felt that consistency required him to resign. Nevertheless he did not resign from the Government, but exchanged positions with Mr Roy Jenkins, who had been Home Secretary up to that point. Mr

---

[1] The resignations of Lord Lambton and Lord Jellicoe in 1973 fell into this category. Both had consorted with a prostitute, and in the case of Lord Jellicoe, who was Lord Privy Seal and Leader of the House of Lords, the disclosure of this conduct was alone a cause of resignation even in a permissive age. Lambton's resignation had more solid grounds, as he was a defence minister and thus vulnerable to blackmail.

Callaghan's personal standing in the Government and in his party did not seem to be affected. In no sense was his resignation a penalty for failure; he probably welcomed the change of office.

One source of weakness in the principle of individual responsibility arises from the vast scope of the operations of departments. The minister himself can only lay down broad lines of policy, and ensure that everyone concerned in its operation receives instructions which are effectively designed to implement the overall policy in detail. His civil servants should know how to apply his policies, and when to refer a particular problem higher up the structure to get a ruling. By constitutional convention, they are anonymous people; they cannot be questioned in Parliament about their decisions. But if one of them takes an action which causes trouble, the minister may have to answer for it. Does this imply that if a grievance is found to be legitimate the minister responsible should resign? It is possible to suggest an answer, based on an interpretation of the system, but it must be illustrated by a study of particular cases – though the evidence suggests that calculations of political advantage are significant.

Clearly, the minister should take responsibility for everything that has been done on the basis of a reasonable interpretation of instructions which have come down from the top. If they have been misinterpreted the minister may be blamed for failing to ensure that his wishes were adequately communicated. If, on the other hand, failure to carry out his instructions can be attributed to perversity or stupidity, it is reasonable for him to dissociate himself from the civil servant's action and apologise to Parliament for something of which he makes it clear that he disapproves. The prospect of being disowned by his minister should encourage a civil servant to ensure that he does not risk such a fate.

The best recent example of a resignation was the case of Crichel Down in 1954. Some private land had been taken over for wartime purposes. After the end of the war, civil servants of the Ministry of Agriculture went ahead with their own plans for the use of the land without regard to an earlier undertaking that its former owner should be given the chance of buying it back – as his heir wished to do. A long series of complaints led to the setting up of a committee of inquiry, which found that civil servants had indeed acted improperly. There was severe criticism in the press, and great indignation among Conservative Members of Parliament. The wrongs that had been done were particularly objectionable to Conservatives, because they were wrongs affecting property rights.

The minister, Sir Thomas Dugdale, could have pleaded innocence. The proceedings that were objectionable had been initiated before he came into office – indeed under the previous (Labour) government –

and for a long time he had known nothing about them. He could not reasonably be blamed for not knowing. However, at a fairly late stage, when he did become involved, he supported his civil servants – on the basis of the picture which they put before him. The Prime Minister accepted Dugdale's resignation because there was no reason why the Government should let itself be contaminated by identification with the offence; it was convenient to the Government as a whole that the minister should be sacrified. He resigned and did not again hold office; he received a peerage in 1959.

In one sense Dugdale's resignation can be compared with that of the Foreign Secretary Hoare in 1935: the Hoare–Laval plan to buy off Italian aggression against Abyssinia, by giving the aggressors a good part of what they hoped to win by force, also aroused much righteous indignation among Conservative government supporters. (Hoare resigned, Britain maintained a righteous posture, and the aggressors got all they wanted, by force.) But Crichel Down was different in many other respects, and highly influential in constitutional development. Parliamentary pressure was an important factor in Dugdale's resignation, but it operated most effectively in Conservative Members' private meetings, both in the Food and Agriculture Committee and in three meetings of the 1922 Committee. Yet the indignation of Conservative MPs was directed more at the civil servants directly responsible for the wrongful actions than at the minister himself. In the long run he felt obliged to identify himself with them when faced by back-bench MPs' attacks; he told the Conservative Members' Food and Agriculture Committee that if it wanted 'a head on a charger it must be his'.[1]

The Crichel Down affair was influential in another way. The injured party, Commander Marten, was well connected; both he and his cause might seem to be identified with the Establishment, and thus exceptionally well placed to fight against bureaucratic injustice. Yet the difficulty and delay in securing redress, even in these favourable circumstances, were so tremendous that it became blindingly clear that ministers' responsibility to Parliament for their departments' actions had become a poor safeguard against abuse of power. And in this case the minister could not plead complete innocence:

'A large part of the blame for the deliberate failure to implement a promise about placing the tenancy of the land open to public tender, the gist of Marten's grievances, must be assigned to the Commissioners of Crown Lands of whom the minister was the only one with responsibility for "matters of major policy"; the policy pursued, however, of granting

[1] G. K. Fry, 'Thoughts on the Present State of Ministerial Responsibility' *Parliamentary Affairs* (1970), p. 10.

the tenancy to a particular favoured farmer, was that preferred by the Permanent Commissioner, a civil servant.'[1]

In this case, then, the minister's personal involvement was more than formal, and that fact may have contributed to his resignation. But that resignation was not immediate or automatic; exceptional agitation among government supporters preceded it.

It should be noticed too that only the minister himself resigned. His two parliamentary secretaries were both involved in the transactions, but did not suffer from that involvement. One of them, Lord Carrington, had actually visited Crichel Down and supported the ministry's position. He not only did not resign but moved steadily up the ladder of promotion to high office, moving through several other posts. Dugdale was sacrified although he did not give the orders; others more directly involved, but in subordinate roles, paid no penalty.

Beside the Crichel Down affair we may cite the affair of Hola prison camp in Kenya in 1960, when the Colonial Secretary still had responsibility for the administration of Kenya. The guards used violence in their attempt to force certain recalcitrant Mau Mau detainees to work, to such an extent that they killed some of them. The guards had indeed been told to make the prisoners work, but the brutal treatment, causing death, was scandalous. Someone in the hierarchy above the guards apparently deserved to be blamed. Who? The Colonial Secretary? Or someone lower down? The Secretary of State, who clearly had not given the specific instructions to the guards himself, argued that the terrible events that happened were due to errors some way down in the hierarchy, and thus not to be reasonably attributed to him. If precedents suggested that resignation was appropriate, the reasonableness and fairness of the precedents was in doubt. The Opposition's censure was resisted by the Government, the majority party in the House of Commons supported the Government's defence of Mr Lennox-Boyd, and he did not resign.

There have been other cases in which departmental error was established, yet the ministers concerned did not resign. In 1961, after the Romer Report had shown that naval security had been inadequate, Lord Carrington offered to resign but the Prime Minister said that he should not, because he could not reasonably be blamed 'in modern conditions and this extremely complicated organisation'.[2] Mr Julian Amery refused to resign as Minister of Aviation in 1964 over the errors which an outside inquiry found to have been committed in the technical

[1] G. K. Fry, op. cit., p. 13. For more discussion of Crichel Down, cf. D. N. Chester, 'The Crichel Down Case'. *Public Administration* (1954), p. 394; S. E. Finer, 'The Individual Responsibility of Ministers', *Public Administration* (1956), pp. 393 f.

[2] H. C. Debs, vol. 642, cols 1685–7.

costs branch of his department in connection with excessive charges paid to the Ferranti Company under the terms of a contract.

In all these cases there was no doubt that there had been maladministration of some form or other, yet it was reasonable to argue that the minister's resignation would be artificial and unfair. But if ministers do not resign, while the officials who are blamed remain anonymous, except in so far as they may be identified in an inquiry's report, there is a gap to be filled in the system of public accountability.

The device of the appointment of the Parliamentary Commissioner recognises the inadequacy of the protection given by ministerial responsibility in such cases as Crichel Down. But there are still other fields, yet more important, which are not covered, particularly where error is clearly established beyond doubt only after an interval so long that the ministers, and even the civil servants most immediately involved, have moved on to other fields of activity, or to retirement.

In 1971 the failure of the Vehicle and General Insurance Company had serious consequences. Motorists, required by law to be covered for third party risks, were deprived of that cover. An inquiry found that there had been negligence in the Department of Trade and Industry, and it publicly censured the civil servant who had been responsible for the inadequacies. It explicitly exonerated the Secretary of State. Meanwhile, the impugned civil servant had retired, and received some public sympathy because his competence had been impugned in circumstances which made it difficult for him to defend himself.

More serious was the case of the Concorde aircraft project. In 1963 funds were allocated, on the basis of an estimated cost, for research and development, of £170 millions (of which £20 million represented an allowance for cost-escalation). The cost then escalated dramatically, stage by stage, during the next ten years. But the project was still pursued, having been begun under a Conservative administration, continued (with a mixture of misgivings, attempts to escape, and some trumpeted enthusiasm) by a succession of Labour ministers, and then under another Conservative minister. The civil servants involved had changed.

By 1973 it was certain that the total development cost would be above £1,000 million, and that there was little prospect of selling any of these aircraft except to the British and French airlines, who would then operate them with poor prospects of covering the costs of producing and operating even the aircraft which they would own. Even by 1973 the outcomes were not absolutely clear. Some were still arguing, against all the odds, that the venture would be a success. The evidence suggested a very high probability of financial disaster, but there was no means of attaching blame to any individual politician or civil servant, or even to any group. It is interesting to compare the docility with which this business has been received by the successive Parliaments with the vigorous reaction of the then Opposition to another unsuccessful, but far less risky gamble of the late 1940s, the East African groundnuts scheme. No minister resigned in either case.

The Concorde scheme illustrates the diffusion of responsibility in government, and the temptation to be irresponsible: features which appear to be increasing seriously.

We may note too that in 1967 the then President of the Board of Trade, Mr Douglas Jay, assured the House of Commons that a third London airport would be needed, to cope with increasing traffic, by the early 1970s. Two years and three ministers later an independent commission estimated that a new airport would not be needed before 1980. But there was no effective means of effectively calling to account either the minister or the civil servants who had been responsible for the estimate of 1967. Ironically, Mr Jay had been dismissed from his ministerial post very soon after his insistence on the need for a new airport by 1967, but for reasons wholly unconnected with the error, whose enormity had not yet been disclosed.[1]

RESIGNATION OF A GOVERNMENT

If a Government should be defeated on an important issue, either (a) it could resign and leave it to the Queen to try to find another Government which would obtain a majority (and this would be likely to happen only if the dissidents among Government supporters were ready to join the Opposition); or (b) the defeated Prime Minister could advise the Queen to dissolve Parliament.

A single well-disciplined party with an overall majority is unlikely to defeat its own Government. A Government with a small majority is vulnerable to chance or mismanagement – though the effects of a chance

---

[1] Cf. Harold Wilson, *The Labour Government 1964–70* (M. Joseph, 1971), pp. 426–7:

'I broke my journey at Plymouth, where I had arranged for Douglas Jay, who was on holiday in the west country, to meet me – I did not want to bring him all the way to London to hear that I was asking him to stand down.

'We met in the station-master's office and, understandably, he took it badly. He suspected that it was because of his clear anti-Market stance and some calculated indiscretions – which had won him press headlines at critical times – suggesting divided counsels among the economic ministers. This was not my reason. He knew how highly I regarded his great success in development area policy. But he was now over sixty, above the "retiring age" which I had informally laid down, except for very special cases. I was anxious also to bring Tony Crosland into the economic team.'

defeat would not be certain. In 1964 the new Labour Government was almost at once in danger when thirteen of its supporters were delayed in Scotland by fog. In fact they reached the House in time to vote, so the Government's majority was maintained, but the then Prime Minister has made it clear that if he had been defeated for such a reason he would not have resigned but 'put down a motion of confidence to give our underlying majority, small though it was, an opportunity to overcome the vagaries of the climate'.[1]

Every Government in 1931–72 had an adequate majority behind it, except in the short-lived Parliaments of 1950–1 and 1964–6. In normal circumstances a Government would be defeated only if a sufficient number of supporters voted against it or abstained on an important issue. In that case a new general election would be held. In such an election the dissidents would probably be opposed by official party candidates, and probably defeated; in some constituencies the split in the party would let the Opposition candidate win. If the split were seriously reflected in the votes, the Opposition party would win the election; either way, the dissidents would probably disappear from the political scene. An effective rebellion must look likely to bring disaster to the rebels, and the probable triumph of the Opposition party would be poor compensation. It is almost inconceivable that the House of Commons could defeat a Government, although there have been some serious alarms in the past ten years. However, until 1973 there had been no defeats in the two-party situation since before 1900.[2]

If a Prime Minister resigns his whole Government resigns with him, though a successor of the same party will normally advise the Queen to reappoint most of them, so that there is only a reshuffle. At any time there are some government supporters who would like to see the Prime Minister replaced by another of the leadership group, and advocacy of a change at the top is a favourite sport of political writers in the press; but the internal party machinery gives little help to plotters. A resignation because of age almost inevitably comes at the end of a period of dissatisfaction over failing leadership; Macdonald in 1935, Baldwin in 1937 and Churchill in 1955 resigned after clinging to office too long, and the same could reasonably be said of Macmillan, who resigned when he went into hospital for an operation. All these were personal decisions which came after discontent had been rumbling for some time without any formal outlet. The immediate occasion of Chamberlain's departure in 1940 was a division in the House of Commons in which he had a

---

[1] Cf. Harold Wilson, op. cit., (p. 30). A somewhat similar position was taken up in March 1974.

[2] The special situation with the European Communities Bill in 1972 is discussed in Chapter 22.

majority of 81, though his normal majority was 200. With 29 Conservatives voting with the Opposition (including respected elder statesmen) and more than 60 abstaining, he judged that he had received something like a vote of no confidence. The traditional theory of responsibility to Parliament was operated with vigour on that occasion – and Chamberlain's resignation was followed by the establishment of a Government of a new complexion.

Eden's resignation in January 1957 is difficult to classify. A particular policy, with which he was specially identified personally, had indisputably collapsed, and there were dark suspicions, later to be confirmed, that he had grossly deceived the House of Commons and the people. But in several votes during the period of the crisis he had been solidly supported by his party, with only a handful of abstentions. His resignation a little later, being due to bad health, settled nothing.

MINISTERIAL RESPONSIBILITY AS A WEAPON AGAINST DISSIDENT SUPPORTERS

By now we have looked at that aspect of ministerial responsibility which is expressed through Parliament's power to dismiss. But the principle works the other way round too. A Government in office can use the threat of dissolution as a device for securing the assent of a body of its parliamentary supporters who may be objecting to a particular policy. Dissident supporters have such pressing motives not to defeat their own Government that responsibility, instead of being a check on the Government, is a device by which it strengthens its position and safeguards itself against its own dissidents. In 1967–8 several of Mr Wilson's Government's policies were opposed by the Labour left wing, but the number of dissidents was never enough to put the majority in danger. However, if any of the Government's parliamentary supporters were somewhat tempted to desert their leaders they were brought to compliance by fear of a dissolution. There was just one apparent deviation from this pattern. In 1969 the Labour Government's measures to regulate industrial relations were opposed by trade union interests and by many Members of Parliament, and in the long run the Government abandoned its policy without risking defeat in a vote. But this was a special case. There is no other interest outside Parliament so strongly placed as the trade unions in relation to the Labour Party, which owes its origins, and in the last resort its continuing existence, to the unions. The affair illustrated the uniqueness of this relationship, rather than any general power of the House of Commons as such to check a Government.

INDIVIDUAL RESIGNATION

Every minister (including every junior office-holder) shares responsibility for everything that is done by the Government, so long as he continues to hold office. The rule covers all office-holders who receive payment in respect of their offices, whether they are in the Commons or in the Lords, whether they are in the Cabinet or outside it. It covers all decisions, and no office-holder can plead exemption from responsibility on the ground that he was not consulted. There might seem to be good reason to distinguish between cabinet members, who take part in the making of important decisions at cabinet meetings, and others who do not. However, the whole concept of the unity of government requires non-members to share responsibility equally with members, and there is no distinction between decisions which are made at cabinet meetings and those which are not. The Government's policy is to be seen as a single whole, including small and great decisions. Many ministers or junior ministers have resigned because they disagreed with decisions in which they were not personally involved. In recent years the rule has even been extended informally to Members of Parliament who are close to the Government without being part of it, and even parliamentary private secretaries have been required to resign because they have abstained in a division in the House.

If a minister personally disagrees with a part of his Government's policy but does not resign, convention requires that he should not make his disagreement publicly known. If his disagreement affects his own department he may show his discontent in Cabinet or cabinet committees but he must put through and defend the policy on which the Government as a whole decides. If he disagrees with some policy not affecting his department he is unlikely to be in any difficulty over speaking in the House of Commons, because ministers normally speak only on matters affecting their own departments. (There have been exceptions.) But he must vote with the party in divisions, and in any public speech he must avoid any indication of his disagreement.

All office-holders are now expected to show complete solidarity in public. A probable cause of this development is to be found in the modern practice whereby office-holders make speeches all over the country, mainly at weekends. As the main speaker on a public platform, any office-holder is a spokesman for the whole Government and for all its policies, not only for his own department. He must be prepared to answer questions about any aspect of government policy, without letting his answers indicate disagreement.

It would seem that a minister's attempts to persuade his colleagues to accept his views could reasonably include argument in private party meetings, because he can legitimately use evidence of party support when pressing his views on party colleagues. But Harold Wilson in 1969 produced a doctrine which the Cabinet accepted unanimously, imposing an element of restriction on such intra-party action by ministers. This statement was first made to the Cabinet and then publicly released; Wilson records it:

I felt it right to address a constitutional homily to the Cabinet about the position of a minister when attending a meeting in any other capacity, such as a member of party committees. I stressed that his duty as a minister, including the full acceptance of total collective responsibility for all government decisions, must transcend all other considerations and loyalties. Should membership of an outside body involve a conflict of loyalties, then that membership must be resigned. . . . In every action, speech and vote, a minister must act as a minister. Any minister not able to accept that doctrine must resign.'[1]

The immediate occasion for this homily was Mr Callaghan's vote against the Government's Industrial relations policy at a meeting of the Labour Party's National Executive, and his speech in the PLP which has been discussed above (p. 56).

Some resignations reflect departmental defeats in the Cabinet, as when the Chancellor of the Exchequer, Financial Secretary to the Treasury and Under-Secretary resigned together in 1957 when the other ministers collectively insisted on expenditure above the amount that the Treasury ministers were prepared to agree to. In other cases ministers have resigned over questions not in their own field. In January 1968 Lord Longford resigned from his post as Lord Privy Seal and Leader of the House of Lords because he could not accept the Government's announced plan to defer the raising of the school-leaving age in the interests of economy. In 1971 Mr E. Taylor resigned as Under-Secretary of State for Scotland because he could not support the Government's Common Market policy.

When a minister resigns because of a disagreement, convention forbids him to disclose any cabinet proceedings with respect to the matter, but allows him to make a statement in the House giving his reasons, and subsequently to attack the Government's policy in the House and on public platforms.

A minister who resigns over a policy disagreement may go noisily or quietly: the more nosily, it seems, the better for his future political career. Eden, Macmillan and Wilson all resigned in open disagreement with their Governments at early stages in their careers, but reached the

[1] Wilson, *op. cit.*, p. 640.

highest office later. The three Treasury ministers who resigned in 1957 all held high office again within the next four years, and Bevan (who resigned noisily in 1951 with Harold Wilson) would most probably have done so but for his death while his party was in opposition. All these were supported by their constituency parties, and by significant groups of parliamentary colleagues. The system does not impose mere obedience.

A minister who resigns is likely to find some support among his parliamentary colleagues, and his resignation is likely to cause his Government some embarrassment at least. A threat of resignation may be a useful weapon with which to support an argument, and if resistance is only lukewarm it may be successful. It was commonly assumed until comparatively recent times that the resignation of an important minister over a disagreement could be very damaging to the whole Government, and to the Prime Minister in particular. Experience since 1957 suggests that this is not necessarily true. The Macmillan Government weathered the resignations of Lord Salisbury over its release fiom detention of Archbishop Makarios, and of all the Treasury ministers together, without trouble. Mr Macmillan himself produced a new definition of such awkwardness with his memorable phrase 'a little local difficulty'. The Labour Government under Harold Wilson was faced with even more serious resignations of personalities in the front rank – Frank Cousins, George Brown, and Ray Gunter – and seemed none the worse.

The evidence of these cases, together with several others less dramatic, in the period 1957–68, suggests that a threat of resignation, even by a few ministers acting in concert, may not be a very powerful weapon with which to support a dissident argument against a determined majority led by the Prime Minister. No Government wants to collapse through its own disunity, so ministers have a strong motive for trying to sink any differences in compromise solutions.[1]

The Prime Minister has absolute authority to remove any minister from office. The form is always resignation, though the term 'dismissal' is often used colloquially, and it expresses the reality of the Prime Minister's power.

Most enforced resignations of ministers arise not out of particular actions which are impugned, but out of the Prime Minister's wishes to make changes in his team for political reasons. He may think a minister has been unsuccessful in some way, or want to bring in someone, probably a younger man, for the sake of making his Government more effective; but then someone has to be left out.

Dismissals are usually cloaked for public announcement by a letter from the resigning minister to the Prime Minister asking that he may

[1] For a useful discussion of this matter, cf. R. K. Alderman and J. A. Cross, *The Tactics of Resignation* (Routledge, 1967).

be allowed to be relieved of his onerous duties to return to the back-benches. His letter and the Prime Minister's reply, normally full of praise for the minister's good work, are then published in the press. The conventional politenesses have become less polite lately.

A minister who resigns, except because of a serious fault, is generally thought to have earned some reward for his services. There seems to be a convention that the Prime Minister should offer a peerage to a colleague who resigns, and when a Government is defeated at a general election the outgoing Prime Minister may recommend people, including ministerial colleagues, for peerages in a resignation honours list. In the changed social climate of the 1970s a peerage is a less delightful recompense even to Conservatives – even to Conservatives' wives – than it once was. Under Labour, between 1964 and 1970, only life-peerages were given, so that even the greatest of retiring ministers could not enjoy the prestige of a hereditary viscounty or earldom. There is little benefit in a peerage now except for the satisfaction of being able to take part indefinitely in parliamentary life, with some pay for doing so. No hereditary peerages were conferred under Mr Heath's administration in 1970–74, and by this time it seemed probable that none would be conferred in the future.

There is no provision for the payment of pensions to ex-ministers, except that an ex-Prime Minister has by statute the right to receive a pension for life, irrespective of how long he has served.

There is an ever-increasing number of non-political offices to which ex-ministers can be appointed if they leave the House of Commons. Also, many ex-ministers are much sought after for lucrative posts in private commerce and industry, and they can accept these without abandoning their House of Commons seats. Very rigid conventions forbid ministers from holding any outside position while in office, but there is nothing to stop them from accepting directorships on the morrow of resignation.

There is something magic about changes in the Government. Political journalists are always speculating about the next reshuffle. At intervals of about six to twelve months a few ministers resign and rather more change their jobs. It seems to be almost a political convention that shifts should take place periodically, though the main benefits sometimes seem to come merely from the very process of change. A new minister on entering his office for the first time may well have no experience of the field of government over which he is to preside. He has to take some time to find his way around his department, and can hardly be expected to contribute very much to it until he has obtained some understanding of its activities and problems. This fact might provide a strong argument for keeping a minister in the same job for a long time. On the other hand, the minister is supposed to provide a strictly political leadership as distinct from an executive or administrative one, and a newly-arrived minister may well be expected to produce new ideas which arise more from the freshness of his mind in relation to the tasks of the department than from experience in handling them.

9

The Administration

The ministers who exercise the powers of the Crown work through civil servants and military personnel, giving them orders and taking their advice. Various statutes (particularly Army Acts and Superannuation Acts, beginning in 1934) and internal rules and unwritten practices define aspects of their position such as conditions of appointment, promotion and removal, positive and negative duties, pay and recruitment. The statutes have no special status and are subject to repeal or replacement by the normal legislative process at any time; but there are some solidly-established assumptions about the working of the system. Non-industrial civil servants (of whom there are about 500,000) are appointed on the basis of assessed merit and potential suitability for the job, determined by persons not subject to the influence of politicians. The Crown's right to dismiss at pleasure has never been destroyed, but in practice dismissal is only for an offence against known rules, proved by a prescribed process. Civil servants are anonymous, mere servants of their ministers, but the anonymity rules have lately been modified in some degree.

A Royal Commission on the Civil Service, in its Report in 1953, gave an authoritative statement:

'We think it will be generally accepted that the community must suffer if the present tradition is impaired whereby a non-political Civil Service carries out impartially the tasks required of it by Governments of different political complexions. A corollary of this is that in the matter of recruitment and dismissal there must be no question of patronage or manipulation of appointments and that no improper influence should be exercised by tampering with the salaries of particular posts of individuals. The State as employer must therefore limit its freedom of action, in a way that a private employer need not, to secure, particularly in the higher Civil Service, immunity from political and personal pressures. This requires that recruitment procedures leading to admission to the

F

established Civil Service should be more formal than those outside and should not be changed at short notice; that there should be a greater degree of security of tenure than is necessarily found outside; that the salaries of all posts in the Service should be public knowledge and should not be susceptible of arbitrary variation; from which it follows that there must be a high degree of standardisation in pay and conditions of service. Thus the State must enter into relationships with its employees which are more formal than those in the generality of other employments, and it can have no secrets, either from the Service generally or from the public, about the pay and conditions it offers to any of its staff.'[1]

Attempts at defining just what is a civil servant have not been very inspiring. The Royal Commission on the Civil Service 1929–31 (Tomlin Commission) produced a definition which is commonly accepted: 'The following is usually taken as the working definition of civil servants, namely, those servants of the Crown, other than holders of political or judicial offices, who are employed in a civil capacity, and whose remuneration is paid wholly and entirely out of moneys voted by Parliament.' Let it be noted that this is only a *working* definition, a definition that tells us very little, and that needs to be amplified.

In the eighteenth century it was a common thing for people to be appointed to government posts because of their relationship with persons having power or influence in the political system. Changing needs and values in the mid-nineteenth century made the old system inadequate and objectionable. Reform seemed necessary, and as with other problems the Government decided to seek expert advice. Sir Stafford Northcote and Sir Charles Trevelyan were invited to prepare a report. In 1853 they did so, and advocated the establishment of an impartial body to recruit civil servants by open competitive examination. Reform came slowly and in two stages. In 1855 a Civil Service Commission was set up, with power to hold qualifying examinations. Not until the Order in Council of 1870 was the commission given the function of recruiting by means of examination as proposed by the Northcote-Trevelyan Report.

Civil servants were divided into three main classes, according to the different levels of discretion and responsibility required – administrative, executive and clerical – with the administrative class at the top. The division survived for 100 years. The Civil Service Commissioners made arrangements for competitive examinations, designed to be appropriate tests of ability for the different types of responsibility of the three classes. Candidates for the administrative class were until the 1940s examined by means of academic examination papers. Then they

[1] *Report of the Royal Commission on the Civil Service, 1953–5*, Cmd 9613 (1955–6).

were allowed to opt for tests of a more practical type, and this new more varied method was used for all candidates by the late 1960s. Increasing use was made of promotion from one class to the class above, but the Crown as employer always kept the power to operate the system through its own machinery without other devices for further adjudication.

In addition to these classes the civil service has also needed engineers, scientists, doctors, lawyers and other people with special qualifications for special tasks. They are also recruited through arrangements made by the Civil Service Commission, but in most cases without competitive examination. That safeguard was scarcely practicable in these cases, but it was felt to be unnecessary because the special classes were in the position of mere technical advisers; the assumption was that the administrative class, having benefited from the information supplied by their technicians, then evaluated it and were still responsible for giving advice to their ministers. Well before 1970 this essentially inferior role of the specialists had become outdated, but it persisted until the reforms which followed the report of the Fulton Committee in 1968.

Civil servants remain at their posts when a Government changes, and each is expected to serve the political chief of his department irrespective of the party to which his chief belongs, and to switch his loyalty to a new minister or a new Government. Ministers, who are politicians and who come to office with the intention of carrying through particular policies, develop their policies together with civil servants who give them advice. The civil servants are not supposed to be initiators, but rather to understand and interpret the minister's policies, and having done this to see the difficulties which might arise in implementing them, and possible ways of overcoming or meeting the difficulties. They have to give the minister a fair and accurate picture of the consequences likely to follow from the choice of this or that alternative, and in the long run to carry out his instructions. The more senior a civil servant's position, the more he may be involved in the course of his work in the business of policy making, the greater the emphasis on the necessity of his being, and seeming to be, politically impartial.[1] If he is involved with policy he may occasionally sit in the civil servants' box in the Commons or Lords, close to the Government front bench, silent and technically not present in the House. The civil servants' identification with their ministers, in the eyes of Parliament, is essential to the system of which they are a part.

---

[1] An authoritative and detailed statement of this position is to be found in the *Report of the Committee on the Political Activities of Civil Servants*, Cmd 7718 (1948–9). A Treasury Circular of August 1953 spelled out some particular rules. Cf. Geoffrey Wilson, *Cases and Materials on Constitutional Law* (Cambridge, 1966), p. 93.

One important exception to the rule of anonymity has been admitted. Each department's accounting officer, who is usually its permanent secretary, may be called on to appear personally before the House of Commons Public Accounts Committee to answer questions about its accounts. Also, civil servants give evidence before parliamentary select committees to explain administrative procedures, and the increased use of select committees in the 1960s has led to a vast increase in such appearances. But civil servants do not come to answer questions about decisions to which they have contributed. If they were to do this, their anonymity would be breached. A precedent upholding this rule was set in 1969 when the Select Committee on the Parliamentary Commissioner wanted to call a civil servant before it to answer questions about his part in a particular decision; the Attorney-General came instead to explain why such a proceeding would be improper.

British civil servants have been so successful in maintaining their professional norms of impartiality and incorruptibility, that they are often blamed for the defects of their virtues. There has been criticism of the service for being inward-looking, for having expertise in the business of being a civil servant but not in the real problems that have to be dealt with. The system has produced a bureaucracy which is on the whole cultivated, civilised and polite, not given to oppressing people, but with a propensity to develop a departmental view and hold obstinately to it, and a propensity also to prefer the solution that will cause least trouble among groups which are organised effectively enough to be capable of causing real embarrassment.

However, although civil servants must serve any government impartially, they can, after a general election has produced a change, serve a new Government well, only if, while still serving the old, they have prepared themselves to serve the new – a very awkward task, particularly as they cannot foretell the result of a general election. The rules of secrecy and anonymity prevent any civil servant from disclosing what has been done in the uncertain period before an election, and no minister could ask for clarification. Some general comment by ministers after the 1964 general election makes it possible to guess how such a situation may be handled, and it is worth quoting Harold Wilson on his new Government's approach to the legislative programme for its first parliamentary session:

'The civil servants responsible, under the leadership of the Secretary to the Cabinet, Sir Burke Trend, had anticipated our needs. Neutral and non-political though the civil service is, it is as sharp as any other body of men in recognising political realities. They had read the election manifesto, and studied every statement. The first draft of the Queen's speech was ready within days, perhaps hours, of the opening of the ballot-boxes; or was it, I wondered, ready even before? Had two drafts been prepared, on alternative election assumptions?'[1]

In 1965, following a recommendation of the House of Commons Select Committee on Estimates, a committee was set up under Lord Fulton to consider all aspects of the civil service. The committee reported in 1968 (Cmnd 3638); the Government accepted its main proposals, and quickly moved to implement them. There was no intention to change the civil service's constitutional role; from the constitutional point of view the main point of interest was the transfer of the Treasury's old supervisory functions to a new Civil Service Department, which came into existence on 1 November 1968. As proposed by the Fulton Committee, the Prime Minister took control of the department, with direct responsibility for senior appointments, machinery of government and security, though day-to-day responsibility was entrusted to the Lord Privy Seal.[2] The Civil Service Commission was integrated into the Civil Service Department. However, as Mr Wilson put it,

'We are ensuring that the Civil Service Commission shall continue to be independent in all matters relating to the selection of individuals. This independence derives from Orders in Council and the commissioners are appointed by Order in Council. These arrangements will continue. ... The First Commissioner has become a deputy-secretary in the new department responsible for recruitment.

'In matters of recruitment policy he is responsible to ministers in the normal way. He and his staff are working closely together with those in the department responsible for personnel management and training. In matters of selection – that is, when acting as commissioners considering individual cases – they will continue to have exactly the same independence as they had before.'

Thus the commission's status was changed, though it was intended that the change would not affect its manner of functioning.

The proposal to abolish the old classes could not be made effective at once. The removal of the barrier between the administrative class and the scientific and professional classes involved some weakening of the old constitutional device which was intended to ensure that only persons who had imbibed the special professional standards of the administrative class should be in a position finally to give advice to ministers.

[1] Harold Wilson, *The Labour Government, 1964–70* (M. Joseph, 1971), p. 420.
[1] Cf. the Prime Minister's statement, Wilson, *op. cit.*, pp. 539 f., and H. C. Debates, 21 November, 1968, col. 1548.

Even after Fulton we still have no clear definition of civil servants' legal status or functions, save that they act on behalf of the Crown, under the direction of ministers. The obscurity contrasts sharply with the position in France, where, because administration is necessary, and because it is desirable that the role of persons involved in it should be defined, the administration is a recognised and defined entity. A. V. Dicey made good use of a discussion of *droit administratif* to illustrate the situation in England. *Droit administratif*, he wrote, could be best described as 'that portion of French law which determines: (*a*) the position and liabilities of all state officials; (*b*) the civil rights and liabilities of private individuals in their dealings with officials as representatives of the State; and (*c*) the procedure by which these rights and liabilities are enforced'.[1] Under this system the rules regarding these matters form a body of law distinct from the ordinary law and the ordinary courts have no jurisdiction in disputes which arise out of it. The Council of State and tribunals inferior to it provide the means of adjudication in any such disputes, but the Council of State is itself part of the administration – that part of it which is concerned to see that the whole administration works as it should. It is the keeper of the administration's conscience.

Dicey extolled the British system under which 'no man is punishable or can lawfully be made to suffer in body or goods except for a distinct breach of law established in ordinary legal manner before the ordinary courts. . . . Every official, from the Prime Minister down to a constable or a collector of taxes, is under the same responsibility for every act done without legal justification as every other citizen.'[2] The protection of the individual, Dicey argued, was more effective under these arrangements than under any others. 'The general principles of the Constitution (as for example the right to personal liberty, or the right of public meeting) are the result of judicial decisions determining the rights of private persons in particular cases brought before the courts.'[3]

This was all very well a hundred years ago, but even by the time of Dicey's first edition a trend had begun which made his analysis inadequate. The increase in the activity of the State, in regulating types of activity, and in providing that certain classes of persons, or all persons in certain defined circumstances, should receive benefits from the State, created a need for a vast amount of adjudication for which the ordinary courts were not well equipped. The absence of a system of administrative law made it necessary to devise expedients to deal with these developments, and the adaptation of these to the new needs has had to

---

[1] A. V. Dicey, *The Law of the Constitution* (Macmillan, 8th ed, 1909), p. 189.
[2] *ibid.*, pp. 189, 193.   [3] *ibid.*, p. 195.

be kept as far as possible within the assumptions of the rule of law. The process has groped its way along, and is still doing so. The solution, in its essence, has been twofold.

1. *Adjudication*

When the State has taken power to regulate activities, or to confer conditional benefits, decisions about the application of the regulations to particular cases, such as those about the eligibility for benefit of particular claimants, may be of an essentially judicial character. Disputes inevitably arise. The task of adjudicating, for each particular class of decisions, has been entrusted to a specially-created body, somewhat akin to a court of law, staffed in part by persons having expert knowledge of the problems involved and in part by lawyers. One of these bodies may have, typically, a lawyer as chairman and two persons who have either expert knowledge or some qualification which should make them likely to have a good understanding of the problems involved.

Over a long period in the first half of the twentieth century successive Acts of Parliament have created new needs for machinery for adjudication, and each Act has created a device suited to the purposes which it has to serve. Failure to set up special tribunals would have entailed either a vast increase in the powers of civil servants, together with a huge extension of the ordinary courts to deal with complaints against them, or (if the courts had had to do this work themselves) an extension of the ordinary courts on a scale which could not have been achieved. Administrative tribunals were in fact the only practicable solution.

The great variety of these devices, and the lack of a single system of administrative law to ensure universal adherence to the principles of natural justice, caused disquiet, which led eventually, in 1955, to the setting up of a committee under Lord Franks, with the following terms of reference:

To consider and make recommendations on:
- (a) The constitution and working of tribunals other than the ordinary courts of law, constituted under any Act of Parliament by a minister of the Crown or for the purposes of a minister's functions.
- (b) The working of such administrative procedures as include the holding of an inquiry or hearing by or on behalf of a minister on an appeal or as the result of objections or representations, and in particular the procedure for the compulsory purchase of land.

The Franks Committee Report made an important definition of the role of administrative tribunals within the constitutional system: 'Tribunals are not ordinary courts, but neither are they appendages of government departments. Much of the official evidence, including that of the Joint Permanent Secretary to the Treasury, appeared to reflect the view that tribunals should properly be regarded as part of the machinery of administration, for which the Government must retain a close and continuing responsibility. Thus, for example, tribunals in the social service field would be regarded as adjuncts to the administration of the services themselves. We do not accept this view. We consider that tribunals should properly be regarded as machinery provided by Parliament for adjudication rather than as part of the machinery of administration. The essential point is that in all these cases Parliament has deliberately provided for a decision outside and independent of the department concerned, either at first instance (for example in the case of rent tribunals and the licensing authorities for public service and goods vehicles) or on appeal from a decision of a minister or of an official in a special statutory position (for example a valuation officer or an insurance officer). Although the relevant statutes do not in all cases expressly enact that tribunals are to consist entirely of persons outside the government service, the use of the term 'tribunal' in legislation undoubtedly bears this connotation, and the intention of Parliament to provide for the independence of tribunals is clear and unmistakable.'[1]

What is the status of this dictum? To what extent is it authoritative? The tribunals are part of the Constitution, but there is no statute defining their position within the system of government; paragraph 40 of the Franks Report should probably be accepted, until it is superseded, as the most authoritative available definition.

The Franks Committee proposed that a Council on Tribunals should be set up, and this was done by the Tribunals and Inquiries Act, 1958. Franks had proposed a separate Council for Scotland, but the Act provided only that there should be a Scottish Committee. Section 1 of the Act defines the council's functions:

There shall be a council, entitled the Council on Tribunals:
(a) to keep under review the constitution and working of the tribunals specified in the First Schedule to this Act (being the tribunals constituted under or for the purposes of the statutory provisions specified in that Schedule), and from time to time, to report on their constitution and working;

[1] *Report of the Committee on Administrative Tribunals and Inquiries*, Cmnd 218 (1957), para 40.

(b) to consider and report on such particular matters as may be referred to the council under this Act with respect to tribunals other than the ordinary courts of law, whether or not specified in the First Schedule to this Act, or any such tribunal;

(c) to consider and report on such matters as may be referred as aforesaid, or as the council may determine to be of special importance, with respect to administrative procedures involving, or which may involve, the holding by or on behalf of a minister of a statutory inquiry, or any such procedure.

The council makes an annual report to the Lord Chancellor, as required by Section 2(7) of the Act, and, apart from its general function as defined above, it may make general recommendations to ministers about the making of appointments to membership of tribunals; the minister must, in that case, have regard to their recommendations (Section 4(1)). The Lord Chancellor may make rules for regulating the procedure to be followed in connection with statutory inquiries held by or on behalf of ministers, and he is obliged to consult the council before he makes such rules (Section 7A(1)).

The 1958 Act thus imposed a degree of uniformity on these multifarious processes. It did not exactly create a system of administrative law, but it brought definition to the way in which the new processes of adjudication fit in with the constitutional system as a whole.

2. Checks on administrative action

Administrative tribunals and inquiries deal with only certain defined aspects of administration. The administrative machinery still produces vast numbers of decisions affecting citizens' interests which cannot conveniently be brought within the purview of any tribunals. Any citizen who believes that his interests are damaged by an unjust or silly decision of a government department has only one course of action open to him within the machinery provided under the Constitution: to complain to his Member of Parliament. The effectiveness of such a complaint would have to rest on the 'answerability' aspect of ministerial responsibility to Parliament. The Member, having heard and understood a constituent's story (often a process involving much patience and some insight), can ask the appropriate minister for an explanation and press for a remedy. He can do this either by asking a question in the House, or by putting the case to the minister directly, verbally or in writing or both. The minister can then take the case back to his department and have it looked into. The fact that the minister is involved ensures that the impugned decision is reviewed at a high level. The process of review may reveal some misinterpretation of the rules, through perversity or obtuseness, or because the rules were badly devised or badly communicated.

The system has many weaknesses. Its effectiveness looks likely to be haphazard, rather dependent on personal factors, including the knowledge, energy and persistence of the MP involved, the minister and possibly of some of the civil servants who do the business of reviewing. Some of these factors operate unseen. The MP has no access to papers in a department. There is always a possible suspicion that even if there is real ground for complaint, the department is covering up, relying on the inherently weak position of the MP who has brought the complaint, and even on the relatively weak position of the minister himself. If the MP decides to press his case by actually asking a question in the House he thereby increases the department's propensity to cover up, and his weapons for pursuit are not very effective.

The parliamentary question is a device of the last resort in such cases, for use when a Member has taken a matter up with a minister and failed to get satisfaction. It is useful in obliging a minister to make a public defence and justification of his department's position if he can do so; he does not like to offer an obviously unconvincing justification. A minister may, therefore, feel that he should make a concession in any case where his justification is likely to seem inadequate. But the process is really hardly a satisfactory protection against maladministration.

Ministerial responsibility, theoretically the means whereby protection for citizens is obtained, has in practice proved to be more of a barrier standing between the citizens and the administration than a means for ensuring really effective protection. The search for a new process has taken a long time. Under the system in France, the Council of State can be concerned with any complaint about malfunctioning of the administration, but this depends on the existence of 'the administration' as an entity in its own right, defined by administrative law. Such a concept could not be imported into England without a fundamental change in the status of the Crown; although ministers may be responsible for the acts of their civil servants committed under their direction, those acts are ultimately performed on behalf of the Crown.

Another solution was a length adopted, under the influence of Scandinavian experience.[1] Under the terms of the Parliamentary Commissioner Act, 1967, a Parliamentary Commissioner for Administration was appointed, and his office began to function in 1968. The innovation was made within the framework of existing constitutional assumptions, so the Commissioner's jurisdiction was restricted to those

---

[1] Cf. Frank Stacey. *The British Ombudsman* (Oxford University Press, 1971). T. E. Utley's *Occasion for Ombudsman* had been published as long ago as 1961 (Christopher Johnson).

fields of administration for which ministers are responsible to Parliament. Local authorities, the police, nationalised industries and the health service were all excluded; although they may in different ways perform functions which belong to public administration, constitutional assumptions about their relations with ministers and Parliament would make it inappropriate for their acts to be reviewed by process common to that used for central departments. The absence of any administrative law concept of 'the administration' requires that any review of their acts should be through different agencies. Personnel questions in the armed forces and civil service are also outside the Commissioner's jurisdiction; inclusion would have involved a change in the concept of the Crown as an employer.

The Commissioner is a servant of the House of Commons. His task is to receive and examine complaints of maladministration by central government departments, which must be submitted to him not by citizens, but by Members of Parliament, on their behalf. Thus his duty really involves the task of helping Members of Parliament in the performance of functions which in the nature of things it is difficult for them to perform adequately themselves. He is (normally) excluded from concern with grievances for which there are alternative remedies by way of proceedings in a tribunal or a court of law.

With the help of a staff of about forty the Commissioner on receiving a complaint first determines whether it falls within his jurisdiction; if so he makes his investigation (for which he may require the production of documents) and reports on the result of it to the Member of Parliament and the department concerned. His report may recommend redress; and he may make a special report to Parliament on any particular case, if he thinks fit. His annual report, which he is obliged to make by statute, inevitably contains statistics and summaries, and draws attention to problems of principle, whereas any particular case will be dealt with in a special report. The Commons has set up a Select Committee to consider his reports. Of the cases referred by Members of Parliament, about half have been found to be outside the Commissioner's jurisdiction, and about one-tenth have been found to have involved some maladministration.

As the House of Commons set up a Select Committee to consider his reports, any special report becomes the subject of an investigation by the committee. Although the Attorney-General soon ruled that junior civil servants should not appear before the committee to be questioned about particular actions which they had taken (*see above*, p. 84), a report by the committee may have an effect on the minister concerned, and on his department, which may be compared with that of a report of the Public Accounts Committee. 'Not only will a department's financial accounts be liable to thorough extraneous review, so will almost all its area of administration.'[1]

The Parliamentary Commissioner soon found that a weakness in his defined position needed to be cleared up. If he concluded that a decision had been made in accordance with established rules he could not report that there had been maladministration. He considered that he could do his work more effectively if he were empowered to consider and to report on the validity and good sense of the rules themselves. This point was put before Parliament in his annual report for 1968, and the Select Committee agreed that his powers should be interpreted as including the extension which he advocated.

In 1974 new arrangements were made for separate machinery for dealing with complaints concerning the National Health Service and the administration of local government. The old assumption that elected representatives could provide sufficient safeguards against misuse of official powers had given way to a new acceptance of a need for professional protection in matters outside the jurisdiction of the courts.

[1] G. K. Fry, 'Thoughts on the Present State of the Convention of Ministerial Responsibility', *Parliamentary Affairs* (1970), p. 15.

10

The Opposition

It is recorded that 'His Majesty's Opposition' was a term first used before the first Reform Act. In the words of Erskine May, 'the importance of the Opposition in the system of parliamentary government . . . has long received practical recognition in the procedure of Parliament'. The Ministers of the Crown Act, 1937, made a significant constitutional innovation by giving statutory recognition to the Opposition's existence through providing for its Leader to receive a salary.

The official Opposition is in the first place a parliamentary concept, and the rules and practices which determine how a party organises itself as the parliamentary Opposition must be of significance for the working of the Constitution. In the second place it is the party which hopes to win the next general election, meanwhile supporting and sustaining the alternative Government.

The election of the Leader has been dealt with elsewhere, because it may determine who is to be Prime Minister.[1] The Leader of the party which is in opposition appoints colleagues, some in the Commons and some in the Lords, to shadow ministerial posts, corresponding with the offices in the Government. A complete Shadow Government is named, with some non-cabinet shadow ministers, and sometimes a complete range of shadow junior ministers as well.

From the constitutional point of view the main activity of the shadow ministers is in parliamentary debates, though they also contribute, less formally, to building party policy and to expressing it through the mass media. In a debate on the second reading of a bill, the minister who sets out the arguments in favour of the bill, and the reasons for its presentation, is followed by an Opposition spokesman, whose speech is regarded as an authoritative exposition of the attitude of the Opposition as such. So too is the winding-up speech from the Opposition front bench. Both front-bench speakers are appointed by the Leader for each

[1] *See above*, p. 26 ff.

debate, and on a very important matter the Leader may himself make one of the speeches. But the appropriate shadow minister concerned with the matter in hand has a very solid expectation that he will be either the opening Opposition speaker or the winder-up.

As an Opposition front-bench speech expresses party policy, and is commonly regarded as doing so, it is important that its contents should be prepared in consultation with a group qualified to represent the party's views. For formulating party policy in relation to parliamentary business the Opposition party makes use of a Shadow Cabinet, a group of senior shadow ministers corresponding collectively with the Cabinet itself.

The Opposition Leader's rights in appointing his shadow colleagues are determined by internal party rules and practices, which are not quite the same in the Conservative and Labour Parties. A Conservative Leader in opposition is left with an absolute power to appoint and dismiss colleagues according to his own judgement, but a Labour Leader is under one important formal restriction. Membership of the Shadow Cabinet is not in his gift. It is determined for him. The Labour Party's rules were at first designed for an Opposition party, and they operate normally when the party is not in power.

At the beginning of each parliamentary session the whole Parliamentary Labour Party elects three officers, its Chief Whip and twelve other members of a Parliamentary Committee. In opposition, together with three Labour peers (Leader, Chief Whip and one representative), these collectively form the Shadow Cabinet, and the Leader cannot alter this fact. In distributing shadow ministerial posts he is expected to give a position to each member of the Shadow Cabinet, and as their membership of the group depends on the Parliamentary Party, not on him, he cannot dismiss any of them from it on his own authority. Similarly the Labour peers elect a Leader, a Chief Whip and one representative to the Parliamentary Committee, so there are sixteen Shadow Cabinet members who owe their positions to an elective process over which the Leader himself has no control.

But the total number of shadow posts exceeds the membership of the Parliamentary Committee, so the Labour Leader is not restricted to those who have been elected. In making junior shadow appointments or dismissals he has the same freedom as a Conservative Opposition Leader, or as he would have himself if he were Prime Minister.

A Labour Shadow Cabinet is subject to two formal restrictions on its freedom to determine its policy and to instruct its parliamentary spokesmen. First, its authority is subordinate to that of its creator, the full assembly of the Parliamentary Party, which meets at least once a week during parliamentary sessions, and determines its collective view on forthcoming business, by vote if need be. (In doing this it often confirms the opinions reported by the relevant party committee.) Its decisions are binding on the Shadow Cabinet as a whole and on shadow ministers individually. Secondly, the Parliamentary Party is subordinate to the supreme authority of the full assembly of the Labour Party, gathered together in conference. Normally a full conference is held only once a year (though very rarely, as in 1971, a special *ad hoc* conference may be called to deal with an urgent problem); so the conference resolutions in the nature of things can only lay down general lines for the Parliamentary Party to follow. The uncertainty of the effect of the conference resolutions was made evident in 1960, when Hugh Gaitskell, as Leader, announced that in the forthcoming parliamentary session, provided that the PLP re-elected him to his position, he would not consider himself bound by the terms of a resolution which had been passed against his wishes and against those of the party's National Executive Committee. Although his re-election was opposed, he was duly re-elected as Leader; he and the Shadow Cabinet, under the guidance of the PLP and in agreement with the party's National Executive, carried on the business of opposition in Parliament as though the awkward conference resolution had not been passed; and a year later the conference itself passed a new resolution which virtually rescinded the effects of that which Gaitskell had opposed in 1960.

The Labour Party's constitution was not changed as a result of these difficulties, and there have recently been signs of an attempt to strengthen the external party controls over the PLP and Shadow Cabinet in opposition (though not when the party is in power). In the early summer of 1971 the party was seriously divided over its attitude to the British application to join the European Economic Community. The Conservative Government was at that time pursuing a policy initiated by the Labour Government before the 1970 election, and doing so with energy and apparent success. But short-term arguments about tomorrow's pennies had produced doubts over the Common Market policy among penny-minded trade unionists, and opinion poll reports suggested that the same doubts were besetting the majority of the electorate. It looked as if Labour might gain some electoral advantage by reneging on its former policy. A special conference was called, and it passed a resolution which left it open to the PLP and its leadership to oppose the terms of entry, if it should seem advantageous to do so. By this device it seemed that the supposedly democratic power of the conference was restored to a position higher than that in which it had been left by the debacle of 1960.

When the party is in opposition the role of its National Executive Committee is also important, and its importance has lately been increased. All but three of the thirty-one members of the NEC are elected by the annual conference to form party policy in line with conference decisions during the ensuing year. Nearly half of the principal members of the Shadow Cabinet normally belong to it, though only the Leader and Deputy-Leader of the PLP are members *ex-officio*. Members of the PLP may constitute a majority, but some of these are back-benchers; front-bench office-holders are normally a small minority. Open differences between this body and the PLP are normally avoided, but the movement towards intra-party democracy in the 1970s has tended to enhance its real powers, derived from the party's own assembly, as distinct from those of the PLP. The process can lead to curious results.

After the 1970 general election the Labour Party made a technical change in its power structure when in opposition. Under the rules previously in force, when the party was in power and the elected Leader of the PLP became Prime Minister, the PLP elected a chairman to be its spokesman in relation to the Labour Government, but when the party was in opposition the Leader was also chairman of the PLP. On 4 November 1970, the PLP introduced new rules providing for separation of the positions of Leader and chairman in opposition. The reason for the change was that the Leader had responsibility, in opposition, for advocating policies recommended by the Shadow Cabinet, and that this responsibility involved a function essentially distinct from that of the chairman of the PLP as a whole.

This innovation seemed to emphasise the role of the Shadow Cabinet as an alternative government, rather than as the parliamentary mouthpiece of the collectivity of Labour members (any of whom can after all speak for himself). By it the PLP brought its organisation into a form which somewhat resembled that of the Conservatives, whose general assembly of Members of Parliament, the 1922 Committee, is always an assembly of back-benchers. Whether in power or in opposition it is seen as a vehicle for conveying information about back-bench opinion to the parliamentary leadership. Its influence on them may be substantial, but it is undefined and works informally.

The Shadow Government and Cabinet are nowadays reshuffled in the same way as the Government, and appointments to shadow posts are communicated to the Press which tends to report them very fully as major political events. Even announcements of minor changes in the Shadow Government are reported with almost as much prominence as changes in the Government itself.

It is commonly expected that every person who continues to hold a shadow post (no matter how unofficial such posts may be) should regard himself as identifying with the whole of the Opposition's policy no less than if the party is in power. Any speech which he makes outside

Parliament is regarded as an expression of party policy. At the party conference, when a party is in opposition, each discussion is about the party's policy in a particular field, and the shadow minister usually sums up.

There are resignations from the Opposition front bench over disagreements in just the same way as there are from the ministerial offices. The Leader may ask one of his Opposition front-benchers to give up his position if the person concerned has done something which is at variance with party policy. In April 1968, when Mr Enoch Powell made a speech outside the House, concerning immigration from the Commonwealth, to which his party front-bench colleagues took exception, Mr Heath immediately 'dismissed' him; that is, he informed Mr Powell that from then onwards he would no longer be invited to attend meetings of the Shadow Cabinet, and this message was communicated to the Press. Mr Heath's act of dismissal was based on the by now well-established assumption that the Opposition front bench is a collectivity whose members are expected not to deviate from one another in their public statements.

Thus in a sense the doctrine of collective responsibility of ministers has spread over so that it applies to shadow ministers also. But it is not quite the same; the Leader does not have to explain deviations from the official line. In 1968, when the Conservatives decided in a body to abstain from voting on the Labour Government's bill to allow only 1,500 Kenyan Asians to migrate to Britain per year, Iain Macleod, then Shadow Chancellor, was one of thirteen Conservatives who voted against the bill, and his independent action was tolerated.

In 1971 several members of the Labour Parliamentary Committee voted in the House of Commons against the decision of the PLP (in its turn reflecting a conference decision) on the principle of British membership of the EEC. They had made known their intention to support EEC entry at the time of the election of the Parliamentary Committee at the beginning of the session, and had been elected notwithstanding. On this issue there was a public agreement to differ: unremarkable in itself but a reversal of an apparent previous trend. Mr Jenkins, the Deputy-Leader, and some others resigned from the Parliamentary Committee in March 1972, when that committee's majority successfully recommended to the PLP that it should support a Conservative rebel's motion asking for a referendum on the issue of membership of the EEC on the terms negotiated. In this case the party's National Executive Committee played a part. The Shadow Cabinet had already decided against a demand for a referendum, but a little later the NEC voted in favour of such a demand, and the new position of the Shadow Cabinet and PLP followed the NECs decision.

G

In 1970 Mr Wilson stated that minor front-bench spokesmen would be free to speak for themselves, as though they were back-benchers, on matters outside the fields of responsibility of their shadow departments. This was not an innovation; rather it was an explicit check to a drift towards rigidity which seemed to be built into the system. Rigidity had not yet set in; in 1962 Mr Christopher Mayhew had been shadow deputy-spokesman on foreign affairs and also spokesman on matters concerning broadcasting. When the Pilkington Committee's report on broadcasting was published Mayhew wished to support its proposals favourable to the BBC, but the PLP had reservations. Although ten years before it had bitterly opposed the introduction of commercial television by legislation passed by a Conservative majority and government, the PLP was by this time aware of its supporters' predilection for the more trivial outputs of the commercial media. Mayhew was allowed to give up his job as broadcasting spokesman, so that he might be free to give his own opinions on that topic, but to continue with his job on foreign affairs. Wilson's statement of 1970 was in agreement with the spirit of the 1962 arrangement concerning Mayhew. It should be noted, though, that Mr Wilson gave this relief only to minor party spokesmen. It should be remembered too that when the Conservatives were last in opposition there was a period, in 1965, when there was no published list of minor party spokesmen at all. A Government must require all its office-holders to be identified with all its functions and they have more and more closely defined tasks, some by delegation. The Opposition can afford two levels of commitment without weakening the role of its main leadership as the alternative Government.[1]

[1] For a new and full discussion of this whole subject cf. R. M. Punnett, *Front-Bench Opposition*, Heinemann, 1973.

Parliament in the Constitution

Elected assemblies are commonly called 'legislatures', as though their function were to make laws. Written constitutions assign the law-making function to them either implicitly or explicitly, and the French 1958 Constitution even attempts a definition of the proper domain of 'law-making'. Montesquieu's concept of a legislative assembly, separate and distinct from the Executive, may have been derived in part from his observation of eighteenth-century Britain, but even then the British Parliament's functions were better described by Aristotle's term 'deliberative', and the same is still true now.

The bicameral Parliament of today is the direct descendant of the old assemblies of the King's court which medieval monarchs summoned for the purpose of discussing affairs of state. These old assemblies were in the strict sense parliaments, or, as that word implies, talking-shops. Their basis was feudal and hereditary. From the thirteenth century onwards, as the feudal revenues became inadequate for the needs of the state, the kings gradually developed a practice of summoning representatives of local communities or counties (the Commons) to whom they could explain the need of money and from whom they could get agreement about various impositions on the community. The Commons assembly became gradually more selfconscious and confident, and was eventually not just a body supplementary to the gathering of feudal lords, but a separate body with its own claim to be heard. Processes which were at first developed because they were convenient and appropriate came to be accepted as normal, then insisted upon, then, after controversy, defined if necessary by statute or standing order. Henry VIII found it useful to ask Parliament to agree to his policies, confident that approval would be forthcoming. Elizabeth found it more self-confident, but respected it. When the early Stuarts tried to act without it, there was soon an explosive difference over the interpretation of the constitutional rights of King and Parliament, and the settlement of 1688 was the solution.

Meanwhile, the Houses had claimed various privileges, both for themselves collectively and for their members; members' freedom from arrest in Parliament-time, and freedom of speech in the assembly, go back to the fifteenth century. Procedural forms developed, and were embodied in standing orders, some of which, with various resolutions and speakers' rulings, provided the only basis of some of the most important elements of the constitution.

Regularity in summoning Parliaments was slow to come. Elizabeth's ten Parliaments sat for only 140 weeks in 45 years. It was the behaviour of the Stuart kings that led to the demand for periodical elections and annual meetings. From 1688 onwards two basic principles have survived: there must be regular elections, and the King can do nothing of which Parliament disapproves. 'Parliament' in this sense has come more and more to mean in effect the House of Commons alone. The scope and effectiveness of its power to control the executive have all along been greatly influenced by the extent to which its majority in its turn has been identified with the people it is supposed to be controlling. But the procedural forms have been built up on the assumption that the control is real.

Along with the procedure regarding taxes the Commons in time came to demand that they should be informed about the purposes to which the tax money had been devoted, and from this they succeeded in claiming control over the whole process of expenditure: no money collected from the people was to be spent except for purposes approved by Parliament. A regular procedure for legislation was established, so that every new statute was debated in principle and in detail in each House before being finally approved by both and sent to the King for his signature. In other fields new practices were tried, objected to or approved of, adopted for regular use or ruled out of order. After 1832 the parties gradually became more rigid and monolithic, until by 1940 the ministers' dominance over their own party virtually assured them of a majority at every vote. The scope of government increased, and a time-table of business became regularised, giving the ministers control over the distribution of time.

Substantial changes in procedure have been made since 1966, but they have not altered the essential purpose of the standing orders, which involves striking a balance between two opposites: to allow adequate discussion of all aspects of public affairs, and yet at the same time to enable ministers to put their business through without undue delay. 'Adequate discussion' and 'undue delay' are relative terms. There is no single unquestionable right balance.

Much of the constitutional definition of Parliament is connected with the relations between the two Houses. There is a very old convention to the effect that taxation and expenditure are matters for the Commons; this is accepted as reasonable because they represent the whole people whose money is involved. The convention is expressed in various resolutions and precedents. As long ago as 1417 an ordinance of Henry IV stated that subsidies were 'granted by the Commons and assented to by the Lords'. In 1671 a resolution of the Commons claimed that the Lords had no right to amend a financial provision made by the Commons, and in 1678 another claimed that the Lords could not amend an authorisation of expenditure. The Lords did not register agreement to these resolutions, but did not contravene them, and their silence amounted to assent. There was no cause to embody them in legislation for a long time.

Until 1911 there was neither statute nor even Commons resolution to prevent the Lords from *rejecting* a financial measure. In 1860 the Lords did reject a bill repealing a duty on paper, and in reply the Government instituted a practice of putting its whole range of tax changes in a single bill. When the Lords rejected the whole Finance Bill in 1909, the Government reacted by introducing legislation; in 1911 the Parliament Act was passed to provide that money bills should go for the royal assent a month after being passed by the Commons, no matter what the Lords should do.

The main rules concerning the relations between the Houses, still in force in 1974, are based on statute, mainly the Parliament Act of 1911, as modified by that of 1949. Under the 1949 Act any bill (except one dealing with money) may still be introduced in the first place in either House (and recently more than a quarter of all bills have been introduced in the Lords), and every bill goes through both Houses. Each House can reject or amend any bill, but if the Lords reject a bill passed by the Commons, or insist on amendments to it which the Commons find unacceptable, the bill can go to the Queen for signature in the next session of Parliament, even without the Lords' consent, provided that the Commons pass it again without substantial change. In the case of a bill certified by the Speaker as a 'money bill' (a technical term defined by the 1911 Parliament Act) the Lords can interpose a delay of no more than one month. But these provisions are only the formal part. Since about 1945 it has apparently been accepted that the Lords should not reject, or insist on amendments to, any government bill. There is however still a feeling that they should reserve a right and a duty to

interfere, as a last resort, with a bill striking at the roots of the constitutional system, and in 1969 this question seemed more real than might
have been expected; they did amend a bill interfering with parliamentary constituencies, and the bill was dropped and replaced by other
measures.

When we look at the constitution as it affects Parliament it is most
convenient to look at the House of Commons first and at the Lords
separately. In looking at the Commons it is also convenient to divide the
study into sections, first the procedure as a whole, secondly its role with
respect to taxation and expenditure, third legislation, and fourth the
general function of checking upon, or supervising, the ministers in the
exercise of their tasks.

12

The Rules of the House of Commons

The role of the House of Commons in the Constitution can be understood only through an analysis of its performance. But that performance depends first on an institutional framework of rules and their interpretation, and on practices and conventions in the management of business in accordance with the rules.

The rules are set out in standing orders, as interpreted by successive Speakers. Within the rules and interpretations business is managed for the Government by a minister, the Leader of the House, in conjunction with party whips. Standing orders include some major constitutional principles, including processes expressing the intentions of the Bill of Rights regarding Parliament's rights over taxation and public expenditure.

Being addressed by the House to itself they do not require approval by the other House or royal assent, and new orders or changes to existing orders can be made by a simple process. It would thus be in theory possible for a government to have big changes made for its own advantage by using its majority; but it now seems to be recognised that no major change in standing orders ought to be made except by a free vote of the House on the basis of a report from a select committee on procedure, which should not be dominated by the Government.

From time to time the House appoints a select committee of its own members to consider possible changes. A select committee on procedure is composed of back-bench members, with each party represented in proportion to its seats in the House. It receives memoranda from other Members, including ministers, from officers of the House, and from other persons who may wish to offer ideas for its consideration, and it may invite people to appear before it to give evidence. The sessions at which evidence is given are usually open to the public (as with other select committees) and the stenographic record is published. The committee can thus take note of written and oral statements advocating or opposing reforms, or explaining likely consequences. After the hearings the committee prepares its report, which may contain recommendations upon which the House takes its decisions after debate.

Procedure was on the whole static during the fifty years up to the return to power of a Labour Government, with a substantial majority, in 1966. Then a great surge of enthusiasm for change produced many new practices, and some major revisions of standing orders.[1] The aim was partly to improve the ability of the House to perform its long-accepted functions, partly to bring ancient forms up to date, partly to find new processes to deal with the need to check the Executive's actions in their new breadth and variety, within the constraints of the two-party system.

Important aspects of the working of the House are provided for by sessional orders, applying only to the session in which they are passed. Their *ad hoc* nature gives room for flexibility without capricious innovation.

The standing orders tell us only a little about the working of the House, which is specially influenced in different ways by three agencies: the Speaker, the Leader of the House, and the Chief Whips of the parties. Even looked at narrowly, the standing orders give us only a skeleton of the rules. They are filled out by conventionally-acceptable short-term departures from their provisions, by sessional orders, and, more important, by rulings of successive Speakers. The sum total of the procedure and practice of the House is contained in Erskine May's *Treatise on the Law, Privileges, Proceedings and Usage of Parliament*. This volume was first published in 1845, and successive editions have been published since that date, the eighteenth in 1970. Each revised edition is now prepared by the clerk of the House, helped by members of his department.

Much of Erskine May consists of a record of decisions given by Speakers with reference to particular problems. When a Speaker gives a decision he creates a precedent, which is recorded for the guidance of himself and his successors on future occasions. The precedents are not absolutely binding, but just as common law pays much attention to precedent, so the Speaker, like judges, tends for the sake of consistency to follow the principles of previous rules. He is assisted by the clerk and his large and highly qualified staff, all of whom hold permanent

---

[1] Instead of setting up a Committee on Procedure about once in fifteen years the House set up one each session between 1965 and 1972. The changes up to 1969 are well summarised by C. J. Boulton in *Parliamentary Affairs* (1970), pp. 61–71. Professor Bernard Crick's book *The Reform of Parliament* (Weidenfeld & Nicolson, 1964) was highly influential in stimulating thought and action.

appointments. Their whole concern is with the working of Parliament, and they have to avoid any activity which would even appear to involve partisanship – though they, like the Speaker, may give advice to a select committee on procedure, and such advice may include advocacy of changes in the rules.

In some assemblies the presiding officer is concerned with managing the business in the interest of the majority, but since the eighteenth century the British Speaker has been expected to be an impartial servant of the House as a whole. When first appointed he is normally taken from among the more experienced members of the majority party. He is a person who has originally convinced a constituency party that he is enough of a party man to be adopted as a candidate; he has fought several elections as a partisan, and he has spent many years as a party man in the House of Commons. Yet as soon as he is appointed as Speaker he must be, and appear to be, totally detached from his party, concerned only to ensure that the rules of the House are observed, and that within those rules the business is conducted so as to secure the most effective practicable balance between the claims of the Government, the Opposition collectively, and members as individuals. Experience with the people whom the House has chosen as Speaker suggests that the transformation can be perfectly well achieved.

In exchange for lost personality as a party politician, the Speaker receives substantial prestige and financial benefits; becoming Speaker is in some ways a little like becoming President of a republic with a parliamentary system. Convention has established that once a person has become Speaker he will never again sit in the House of Commons except as Speaker, and it has been the practice for a retiring Speaker to receive a peerage immediately on retirement.

The Speaker has three deputies who take turns at presiding over committees of the whole House and who also take turns with the Speaker himself in presiding over sittings of the House. A Deputy Speaker has to be impartial while in the chair, and normally does not take part in debates or votes while holding office, though his abnegation of party politics is not final; if he resigns his appointment, or is not reappointed by a new Parliament, he may return to the political activity of an ordinary member.

Although a Deputy Speaker does not accept a commitment to abandon party politics for the rest of his life, holders of this office have shown themselves well able to abjure partisanship in the chair – and the same may be said of the far more numerous members who accept similar offices as chairmen of standing committees. Each session a chairmen's panel of ten members is set up, including Government and Opposition supporters, and each of these must be prepared to be an impartial chairman of a standing committee on two or more mornings a week, while he becomes an ordinary party member, asking questions, speaking and voting in the House, going to party meetings and dealing with constituents, for the rest of his time. Experience shows that the transition is perfectly feasible.

The strength and stability of the assumption that when a new Speaker is needed, it will always be possible to find a person who is both adequately equipped for the office, and ready to accept this great change of role, provide a good illustration of the nature of Parliament, and of the respect for institutions which enables the political system to work.

The appointment and term of office of a Speaker is clearly a sensitive matter. One firm convention is that a Speaker is reconfirmed in his office after a general election, even if there has been a change of governing party. Another, which once seemed to be established, that a Speaker should not be opposed at a general election, has now been broken several times, but only twice by the main Opposition party. It has been argued, fairly enough, that a Speaker, by the nature of his office, could not represent his constituents in the normal way, and that at an election they ought to retain the right to choose between party candidates. The democratic experiments involved some unfairness to the incumbent Speaker, who could not campaign for re-election as other candidates do. The last case was in 1974 (though Speakers have been opposed by independents). The Speaker's constituents will have to be content with being represented by a non partisan until a new device is found.

By 1950 some processes had been repeated so often that several practices concerning the appointment of a new Speaker seemed to be moving towards convention. Successive Speakers had retired during the life of a Parliament. On each occasion the Government in office had thought of a suitable successor and one or two alternatives among its own back benchers, discussed the plan with the Opposition leadership, and reached agreement by an informal process, in which the Chief Whips played an important part after sounding back-bench opinion. The agreed name was then formally proposed to the House and agreed to. The preference for a back bencher, in agreement with a dictum of Gladstone's, seemed to be near to becoming a convention, fortified by the obvious consideration that a minister is likely to be strongly identified with his party. Furthermore, on several occasions the first Deputy-Speaker (Chairman of Ways and Means) had been promoted to the Speakership, and there were signs that this promotion might become a regular and expected process.

The continuity was broken in 1951, when Speaker Clifton Brown retired, not in the usual way during the life of a Parliament, but by not seeking re-election at the general election. As that election produced a change of Government, and the former Chairman of Ways and Means was now an Opposition member, a new solution had to be found. The new Conservative Government favoured Mr W. S. Morrison, who, in addition to not having been Deputy-Speaker, was a former minister. The Opposition would not agree, and Morrison was voted into office on a contested vote. But he held office successfully for seven years, and was succeeded by a former Solicitor-General.

In December 1970, when Speaker King let it be known that he intended to retire, new problems arose. It was soon accepted that the choice should lie between two former members of Conservative Cabinets. The abandonment of Gladstone's principle against front-benchers was by now complete, though both the ex-ministers concerned had been on the back-benches for a long time. The Government and Opposition front benches came to an agreement that they would put forward Mr Selwyn Lloyd, but there were objections from the back benches on the ground that there had not been wide enough consultation. The new claim that the Speaker should be chosen by a genuine vote of the whole House, with a contest, instead of unanimously on the basis of informal discussions, is in agreement with the new preference for open contests instead of choices through elite networks, but a Speaker chosen in this way might well find the strain of adjustment to his new role all the greater.

The whole question was taken up by the Select Committee on Procedure in the session of 1971–2. In its First Report for that session, published on 3 February 1972, and approved in principle by the Government,[1] the committee rejected the device of a secret ballot but suggested that the essential requirement for an adequate solution was adequate time for consultation. A Speaker deciding to retire should therefore make his decision, if possible, in mid-session, giving at least ten days' notice of his intention. If this should not be possible, or if a Speaker should die in office, the chair should be occupied automatically by the Chairman of Ways and Means and a new Speaker chosen without undue hurry.

A ruling by a Speaker or deputy, or by a chairman, may be challenged only by a substantive motion expressing disapproval. Such a motion must be debated and voted upon (unless withdrawn), and such motions are moved occasionally, though hardly more than once in a year.[2] No such motion has been carried for many years, but the authority of a ruling is increased by the fact that it may be challenged.

[1] H. C. Debs, 3 July 1972, written answers col. 38.
[2] For example, in 1972 the Opposition put down a motion objecting to the chairman's ruling that many of their proposals to amend the European Communities Bill were out of order, as they purported to alter the very principles of the bill, to which the House had already given approval on second reading.

13

The House of Commons Today

The House of Commons is a collection of (in 1974) 635 persons[1] each elected by a relative majority vote of the adult inhabitants of a geographical division of the country. They are the body from which most ministers are chosen. Those who are not ministers may question ministers. They receive, discuss and decide upon requests from the Government to collect taxes and to spend the proceeds of the taxes for particular purposes; they discuss, in principle and in detail, bills which may be proposed by any of the Members, and decide whether or not to pass the bills, with or without amendment to the texts as originally proposed; they discuss and vote upon motions approving or disapproving of ministers' actions and policies; and the Government of the day remains in office only for so long as the House of Commons does not reject it by a majority vote.

This formal account is inadequate: when, as is normal, one party has an overall majority and forms the Government, while the other major party forms the Opposition and alternative Government; other factors have more real importance – and this was so even in 1974, with a minority government and the first factor absent.

1. Virtually all the Members belong to one of two political parties; each has been elected because his local party has chosen him as its candidate, and because more voters in his constituency have voted for him (as a party candidate) than for the candidate of any other party. Some have been chosen for safe seats; others owe their election to a nation-wide trend favourable to their party, and face a serious risk of

[1] As a result of a new arrangement of constituencies, approved by Parliament in 1971, the number was raised to 635 at the next general election. Previous numbers had been 615 from 1922, 640 from 1945, 625 from 1950, 630 from 1955.

defeat at the next election, which no personal action of their own is likely to avert.

2. As it is assumed that the Government in office will not be defeated, because its supporters share its interest in survival, the function of the debates has to be considered apart from the decisions which are to be made at the end of them.

3. The Prime Minister holds his office because he has (since 1965) been elected as party Leader by majority vote among the members of his party in the House of Commons. They have thus collectively a function as a convention, in the American sense, when a new Leader is required; they have to choose someone from among their own number, and in practice from the few whom the previous Leader has at some time invited to join him in the leadership group.

4. As the House is dominated by the Government, its main function is to discuss what the Government has done, or intends to do: to oblige the Government as a whole, or individual ministers, to explain and justify their choices between the options before them; and on occasion to persuade them to modify their policies. The supposed sanction of withdrawal of majority support is scarcely likely to operate, but on the other hand the actual process of questioning and debate is itself a sanction of a kind. If criticism is effective and well made, then the ministers must be successful in justifying themselves in open argument; otherwise although they may win the vote their position is an unhappy one.

The process of discussion and criticism works well only if the conditions and occasions for them match the essential character and relative importance of their objects; and the government decisions which are the objects may be classified, not only as legislative, financial or current policy, but on several different planes: general and particular; matters of principle and technical matters; ideological issues and issues where efficient performance is the sole and agreed aim; questions involving detailed knowledge backed by facts and statistics, and questions in which prejudice or intuition can be the only valid guide.

5. Although the most obvious part of the work of the House of Commons is in the context of a clash between Government and Opposition, there is also a collection of functions related to current decision making, which cannot sensibly be interpreted in party terms. Government policies are related to party preferences in infinitely variable degree. Controversy may be over principles, or method, or over the manner in which choices are made or the validity of the information on which they are based. Given the Government's dominating position, one of the most worthwhile of Parliament's potential contributions is to ensure that options are fully weighed and motives fully explained and

justified: that particular interests are neither neglected nor unduly favoured, that particular policies do not acquire a momentum on which good new arguments or changing circumstances can make no impression. For the task of probing, asking why and how, pressing for information and explanation, summarising arguments, proceedings in the Commons Chamber may be ineffectual unless based on painstaking and detailed inquiry outside it – and such inquiry, by its nature, must be delegated to small groups of Members.

6. On some matters the parties leave their Members to vote as they think fit, without party instructions. These matters are defined by their nature (e.g. question of conscience), or by the fact of their being outside the realm of government policy, or otherwise suitable for decision in isolation, on their own distinct merits.

Free votes are sometimes criticised on the ground that a chance majority is irresponsible, because it lacks coherence and has no need to consider the consequences of its choice. Members do indeed respond to pressure from their constituency associations, or from influential individuals or groups. Many, when freed from the requirements of their whips, find it convenient or politic to stay away.

7. Although the parties are not in a formal sense recognised by any constitutional provision, the constitution is a mere skeleton without them. It is only in form that they are private organisations. The House of Commons consists of parties, which have their own procedures for defining agreed party policy and settling differences before any matter comes to a debate and vote in the House. Each of the parties has a regular weekly meeting of all its members, and each also has about fifteen committees connected with particular fields of governmental activity. The private party meetings have become steadily more important in recent years, and their importance reflects the expectation that in any vote all the members of a party vote together except on some rather infrequent occasions. Labour Members are expected to vote in accordance with decisions taken by the Parliamentary Party, and Clause 5 of the party's constitution requires the MPs to give effect, as far as may be practicable, to the principles from time to time approved by the party conferences. The conference of 1970 took this a little further, by approving, by 3,085,000 votes to 2,801,000, a resolution to make conference decisions binding on the PLP. However, there are such difficulties in applying these rules precisely that their effect on Parliament is not easy to define.

THE IMPORTANCE OF PARLIAMENTARY TIME

Just as the physical shape of the Commons Chamber expresses the function of Parliament, with the party leaders facing each other across the clerks' table, and their party supporters on the benches behind and alongside them (all called back benches, including the two which are in front), so the order of debate expresses the balance between the straight opposition of the parties and the contribution of ordinary members. A typical full day's debate on a single topic takes about six hours – the first hour (or may be more than an hour) and the last hour being each divided between Government and Opposition front-bench spokesmen. About four hours in between are left for others.

A little more than a tenth of government time is used by ministers explaining the policies they have formed to give effect to their political objectives, after consulting civil servants and interest groups; another tenth is used for their replies to debates. An equal amount is used by Opposition spokesmen expressing their party's view, trying to carry Members with them either in their attacks on the Government, or in their partial or total support. Back-bench speeches are often partisan, but they express differing views within each party, extreme views or moderate views, views informed by regional or local considerations or by sectional interests which may be local or nationwide.

The distribution of time is prescribed in part by standing orders, in part by week-to-week and day-to-day decisions, in which the Government has the last word. A session, lasting a year, provides about 32 weeks for business; about 160 or 170 days, of which about 32 are short sittings before weekends or holidays, allowing members to get back to their constituencies or to other places where they may have engagements. An annual session has some fixed elements: the opening five days on the Queen's Speech, discussing the Government's programme for the year; the twenty-nine supply days, guaranteed as days on which the Opposition chooses the subject of debate; the Budget and Finance Bill debates; the twenty to twenty-four private members' days when back benchers, chosen by ballot, decide the subject of debate. Adjustments are made when the normal annual rhythm of sessions is broken, as in 1974.

Within each day there are fixed points provided for by standing orders. On Mondays to Thursdays the House meets at 2.30 p.m. and proceeds after five to ten minutes to question-time which ends at 3.30 p.m. After this any of several topics may occupy a little time, most notably ministers' statements and questions about them, or questions of privilege or personal statements, and every Thursday the announcement of the next week's business, which may produce a brief discussion. After all this, at 3.35, 4 or 4.30 p.m. as the case may be, the main debate on the motion begins. Under Standing Order No. 1 it must end at 10 p.m. unless the House has decided by vote, at the beginning of the main business, to allow an extension beyond that time.

This time is Government time in that the Government has ultimately decided on the business for the day; however, it does not greatly care how the time is distributed provided that its programme of legislation and other proposals can be carried out. The arrangements are worked out by the party Chief Whips, by a process of bargaining in which they engage after finding out what their members wish to discuss, and at what length. The processes are not defined by statute or standing order, but they are of the essence of the Constitution. The parties may disagree over policy, but they must try to accommodate one another and agree over the use of time for parading disagreements at different levels.

THE MEMBER'S CAREER

It is not necessary that a Member of Parliament should have no other occupation besides his membership. Until the late nineteenth century many Members were either working lawyers or country gentlemen without identifiable employment, deriving a comfortable income from the ownership of land, but having a role in their local community which involved expenditure of much time and energy for which no specific remuneration was expected. After being elected to Parliament the country gentlemen still continued to devote much of their energies to the country gentleman's duties and pleasures.

By the beginning of the twentieth century democratic ideas had made it seem unacceptable that people should depend on other sources of income before they could be Members of Parliament. The payment of a salary to each Member of Parliament was introduced in 1911, and it has continued since then. There was some opposition to the principle of payment, on the ground that it would be destructive of Members' independence, but that argument is now quite dead. The salary has been increased in keeping with the fall in the purchasing power of money.

Once payment was accepted in principle, the rate has been about two or three times the median earnings of all men in remunerative employment, an amount corresponding with that earned by a man pursuing a middle-class career at the age of 40 with slightly above average success. Allowances in addition to the salary have been added since 1964 so as to cover the costs peculiar to Members of Parliament, and from the 1960s onwards the rate of the allowances has been calculated so as to cover the needs of an efficient Member. From the beginning of 1972 the pay was raised to £4,500 a year, plus travel allowances for provincial Members, and a further allowance of up to £750 a year to cover their expenditure for staying in London. Limited expenses could be claimed to cover payments to secretaries and research assistants. In 1971 the principle of regular review was established, when a committee under Lord Boyle made recommendations on the pay of MPs together with that of ministers, higher civil servants and military officers, and holders of public posts subject to ministerial appointment. A suggestion that MPs' salaries should be linked with those of assistant secretaries in the civil service has been rejected as constitutionally undesirable.

The payment of a salary which is meant to be adequate still does not imply that Members should refrain from other remunerative employments. Many Members do in fact do other work, most commonly in the law courts, in commerce and industry at directorial level, and in journalism, public relations and the like. There is disagreement over the question whether such outside employments are really compatible with an MP's functions. The argument that, through sharing the activities and responsibilities of non-parliamentarians, Members can share more effectively the problems of ordinary people, is vitiated by the restricted nature of the types of work practicably open to them. Business director-ships align their holders with particular interests, and the Member's duty to declare his interest in any particular matter is only a partial safeguard. Again, if a Member of Parliament is to perform his function as such really effectively, he cannot well afford the time to do anything else. If Members were to become specialists in particular fields of governmental activity and exercise a more effective supervision over the workings of government, they would indeed find it difficult to combine parliamentary duties with other activities.

Opinions among Members of Parliament on this question appear to differ considerably between the parties. A majority of Conservatives have been found to favour outside activities, while a majority of Labour Members think that an MP should give all his time to his work. There is probably a trend towards Members of Parliament becoming full-time, though they can never become really professional in a career sense, because of the insecurity of their position – unless they have safe seats.

Nearly every Member of Parliament in one of the major parties is a potential minister, and at any given time a number of members of the House of Commons are ministers. This fact has an undoubted influence on the MP's role. Most people who seek election have a desire to exercise power and influence, and calculations about his prospects of attaining ministerial office may influence a Member's behaviour, including the extent of his readiness to oppose his party leaders. But subservience is by no means a necessary condition for preferment.

When a Member of Parliament is a minister most of his energies must be devoted to his ministerial functions. But he still represents his constituents just like any other Member. Being part of the ministerial team he is unlikely to harass a particular ministerial colleague whose department has caused a grievance to a constituent; however, he may be able to secure redress fairly effectively just because ministers can talk

H

together in an informal way about particular problems, so that there is every encouragement for any minister to take special notice of a grievance raised by a colleague.

PARLIAMENT, NATIONS AND REGIONS

Constitutional theory provides no scope for the representation through Parliament of the nations of the United Kingdom as such, and still less for the regions of England. However, Scotland and Wales are commonly said to be distinct nations, and national consciousness is tending to grow. Scottish and Welsh MPs have for a long time been expected to think of themselves as having a Welsh and Scottish national role in addition to their United Kingdom and constituency roles. However, the reality of this third role varies with individuals. Some Englishmen are elected for Welsh or Scottish seats, and an Englishman representing a Cardiff constituency is obviously less of a Welsh Member than a native Welshman and Welsh MP – and an Englishman who represents a Scottish constituency and is also head of one of the ordinary Departments of State has to relegate his Scottish role (as distinct from his constituency role) to a small corner of his political consciousness.

Since 1900 parliamentary procedure has given Scottish Members increasing scope for acting as such. By 1970 there were already three arenas in which they could work in relation to Scotland. First the Scottish Grand Committee consists of all Members for Scottish seats, together with some other Members added to correct the party balance in case of a vote. This body may consider the second reading of any bill relating exclusively to Scotland, provided that there is no objection in the House. It also meets half a dozen times a year to discuss Scottish administration. Secondly, any bill relating exclusively to Scotland is sent for its committee stage to a committee consisting wholly of Scottish members. Thirdly, since 1968 there has been a Select Committee on Scottish affairs, which examines Scottish administration. For Wales there are also committees of the first two types, though bills relating exclusively to Wales are rare.

Up to 1970 there had been no provision for any of these committees to deliberate in their own nations, though such meetings had sometimes been advocated.

A NEW ROLE PARTLY FULFILLED

The increasing scale and complexity of modern government impose on Parliament demands of a new order, if it is adequately to perform its traditional function of safeguarding the public interest and in particular the public's money. Major objectives are defined in party programmes, refined by the Cabinet, explained, attacked and defended in the normal process of parliamentary debate. The attempt to attain those objectives involves a careful process of identifying and measuring options, and that process may affect the objectives themselves in some degree, at least in detail. There is a danger that the options may not be adequately identified or measured; that prejudice or mere laziness may distort the options, that decisions may be taken on the basis of biased or partial information. The vast power entrusted to government demands a countervailing force, capable at least of posing questions to determine whether the power is being used with fairness, good sense and competence.

There is nothing novel in the claim that Parliament should provide the countervailing force. That claim rests on the role of Parliament from its earliest origins. It is only the nature of the role that has changed, so that the means employed to achieve the objective need to be adapted to new demands as they now present themselves.

Four conditions need to be fulfilled if Parliament is to respond adequately to the new form in which these old demands present themselves: information must be adequate; those who receive it must be able to understand, digest and analyse it adequately; procedural devices must provide for adequate communication of the results of that examination. Therefore there is a need for people with sufficient time, capacity and dedication to use effectively the opportunities provided by those procedures.

Some progress has been made, particularly in the 1960s. MPs obtain information from the Government itself, from interest groups, from independent sources, including the Press, and from casual contacts.[1] Some of the information comes in structured form, some not. The House of Commons Library, which is a means of channelling these sources, has been considerably expanded, and its staff increased – though this service is still on a small scale compared with the ideal.

MPs ability both to obtain and to process information has been improved by the provision to them of modest funds to enable them to procure assistance with their researches, but these funds do not enable an individual MP to hire a team of people – and the variation in the demands between Members, and between one period and another for a particular Member, create obvious problems, and in any case adequate assistants are not likely to be available just when they are needed.

One procedural innovation of the past ten years has been through an extension of the ancient device of the select committee. This is a means whereby a small group of MPs gathers evidence about some matter, then

[1] Cf. A. P. Barker and M. Rush, *The Member of Parliament and his Information* (Allen & Unwin, 1970).

produces a report summarising the facts and making recommendations. The report may or may not form the basis of a debate in the House; the recommendations may or may not be followed.

Not much has been changed in the way select committees do their business. A committee receives documentary material relevant to a problem, then hears 'evidence' from 'witnesses'. It may hold five or ten or twenty sittings of this kind, spread over several months. Then a draft report is prepared, usually by the chairman or by the committee's clerk, or by both together. Finally the committee considers the draft, section by section; members may propose amendments, and if necessary their proposals for change may be decided upon by votes.

British practice has never made use of the device, common in European parliaments, of appointing one member of a committee as *rapporteur*. This is presumably because a British committee does not run several inquiries at once – though it may divide into sub-committees, each to undertake a separate inquiry.

Ad hoc select committees have been used for a very long time. A normal committee to examine the government's accounts has existed continuously for more than a hundred years, and another, to examine the estimates, from 1912 to 1970, when it was replaced by a more ambitious Committee on Public Expenditure.

The reaction to new needs has been slow. In 1947 a committee was set up to examine statutory instruments (order and regulations made by ministers, by virtue of powers conferred by legislation) to see if there was any unexpected use of powers, or any charge on public funds, or any creation of a new offence.

In 1956 a committee was created to examine nationalised industries, and since then it has studied a minimum of one industry per year. It has at least succeeded in obliging ministers to think carefully about the nature of informal directions which they may give to the industries' boards, and it has contributed to some extent towards the setting of standards of efficiency for the industries – though little towards any deeper revision of the view of the industries' place in the whole national economy.

Between 1965 and 1970 several new committees were set up. One on agriculture and one on education were short-lived. Others have continued: one on race relations, one on the Parliamentary Commissioner, one on science and technology, and one on Scottish affairs. Committees may now hire experts to advise them.

Together these committees cover only a small part of the field of government, and since 1970 the new Public Expenditure Committee, through its seven sub-committees, has taken on the major part of the task of investigation. But the scope for further development is limited by two main factors. First, Governments are not enthusiastic for more effective interference with their processes. Second, there is a dearth of MPs ready or able to give time and skill to the work. For the average MP his role as a constituency member, and as a member of his party, concerned with one crisis then another, and with day-to-day problems as they arise, committee work such as this is not very rewarding. The work must inevitably take second place to the main parliamentary functions; the gap has not been adequately filled.

14

The Constitution and the People's Money

There is something sacred about the role of the House of Commons in relation to money. When the State wants to take money from the people and use it for state purposes the people expect that their interests should be protected by their representatives in Parliament.

The principles are two-fold. First, the Government is not to spend any public money except as authorised by Parliament. Therefore, Parliament has a right both to consider requests to spend money for particular purposes, and to authorise or refuse each item, and also to check afterwards that the money has indeed been properly spent for the purposes for which it was obtained.[1] Second, as the money has to be obtained through taxes, Parliament has the right to consider, and to authorise or refuse, each particular tax that the Government proposes. What Parliament does not claim to do is to attach the proceeds of particular taxes to particular parts of the Government's expenditure. But (with some exceptions) all money is voted for one year only. This rule has become embarrassing, but there are strong sentimental objections to changing it.

The United States Constitution provided that taxes might be imposed, with the authority of the Congress, to pay the debts and provide for the common defence and general welfare. That definition imposed a limitation, so that when on some occasion a particular tax, approved by Congress, has appeared to have some other purpose, such as the penalisation of factories employing child-labour, aggrieved people have refused to pay, and have successfully argued before the

---

[1] The process of audit was a gradual development, not made comprehensive until the passing of the Exchequer and Audit Departments Act of 1866.

courts that the tax was unconstitutional. New interpretations of the Constitution have allowed regulatory taxes, but the scope for difficulties remains.

Such difficulties have not arisen in Britain, because the sovereignty of the Queen in Parliament leaves us without any definition of the proper objects or limits of taxation. It is possible to think of taxes which would be said to be unconstitutional because unprecedented and wholly contrary to accepted practice or reasonable expectation, but there is no general definition to deal in advance with problems which might hypothetically arise, and the consent of Parliament would make any tax lawful.

During the past hundred years taxes of new kinds have been imposed without serious difficulty – death duties and progressive taxes on incomes in particular – and in one year the rate of tax on large incomes actually exceeded 100 per cent, so that there is in effect a precedent for a tax on capital. More important, during the same period new purposes of taxation have emerged, both regulatory and redistributive. Executive policies have, rather slowly, responded to new theories of economic objectives. It is now considered perfectly normal to budget deliberately for a surplus or a deficit in the nation's accounts for the good of the economy as a whole, though forty years ago the dominant opinion would have condemned any such policy as constitutionally improper. The laws and conventions of the Constitution have not stood in the way of the new development, but a vigorous and effective parliamentary contribution to fiscal policy as an instrument of social policy is inhibited, both by the rule that only the Executive can propose taxes and by the role of the Treasury. For each new development all that was needed was a decision by the House of Commons in confirmation of a proposal by the Government in office at the time.

Concern with taxation and the expenditure of public money has been central to constitutional development, and was a major factor leading to the turmoil of the seventeenth century. The settlement which was eventually reached still survives in essence. Certain broad principles have operated continuously since that time, though their details had become rather artificial, because of the development of the party system in Parliament, well before 1900. Many ancient and sacrosanct practices were swept away in 1967, but their disappearance created no public stir. The most obvious reason for the lack of interest in the changes was that they merely adapted the procedures to modern needs, in agreement with the spirit of the ancient principles. A less obvious reason, but more fundamental, is to be found in the changed character of public spending. Formerly it was devoted mainly to non-defensive military purposes and to the cost of carrying on an administration full of nepotism and political jobbery. Now the military purposes absorb only one-eighth of the total, and one must be very suspicious indeed if one doubts their essentially defensive character; the administration is generally believed to be free at least of nepotism and jobbery; and most of the expenditure is devoted to public welfare purposes which are generally approved, such as education, therapy and care for the sick and the aged, and transfers of purchasing power to groups of persons defined by their economic weakness, not by any particularistic values.

The great principles underlying financial procedure are that no proposal to impose any tax or to spend any public money is in order unless it emanates from the Government; that every financial proposal must be submitted to Parliament, which must have an opportunity to discuss it before voting on it; and that the House of Commons is paramount. To find authoritative statements of the principles we must look to some statutes and parliamentary standing orders. Those currently in force are an amalgam of old and new, informed in recent times by the purpose of allowing the Government to carry through its policies, subject to a rather limited amount of parliamentary discussion.

EXPENDITURE

More important than any of the written rules concerning finance is one overriding principle which is not written down at all, but which appears to be unchangeable and wholly rigid. This is that when the Government asks Parliament for authority to spend money for any purpose, it says in effect 'we are prepared to accept responsibility for carrying on this service only if we are allowed to spend on it the money which we consider to be necessary for its adequate performance.' Thus any reduction in the estimates by Parliament would be taken as a defeat of the Government and equivalent to a vote of no confidence, entailing its resignation or a new general election.

Although for a long time up to 1967 it was the regular practice for the Opposition to propose reductions in some of the sums of money requested by the Government for particular purposes, Parliament in fact always defeated the proposals for reduction, and gave a majority vote in favour of each item of expenditure which was proposed. The last exception to this was in 1895, when Lord Rosebery's Government resigned after a motion to reduce a minister's salary was carried in a 'snap' vote – and this was not in any meaningful sense a proposal to reduce an item of public expenditure, but a device, now extinct, for censuring a failure by a part of the administration.

The Government still has to ask Parliament for approval of its proposals to spend money, and Parliament votes on the proposals. Motions to reduce particular spending proposals may be moved and voted upon, but as they are sure to be defeated, and the Government's requests are virtually sure to be approved, Parliament's real control through this process has become almost entirely unreal. For this reason supplementary devices have been created over and above the time-honoured and essentially formal procedures, which were themselves realistically modified by a decision of 14 December, 1966.

The Government presents its estimates of expenditure for a financial year (beginning on 1 April) in great detail, so that the House of Commons may consider the heads or sub-heads one by one if it wishes. Each 'head' is presented as the subject of a vote. On the basis of these votes, an Act of Parliament each year authorises the specific expenditure of particular amounts for particular purposes. A second Act authorises further unforeseen expenditure, and there may be further Acts. These authorisations are made in most cases for one year at a time, though there are a few items of public expenditure which are provided for by permanent legislation, such as the Civil List or sums of money paid to members of the royal family, and the salaries of judges.

Until 1967 the House resolved itself into a Committee of Supply to consider the votes. Originally, the purpose of going into committee of the whole House was to enable all members to participate without the inhibiting presence of the Speaker, who was in the seventeenth century thought to be under the King's influence. This fear has been absent for 200 years. The procedure had been highly artificial for a very long time. By 1902 the attempt even to discuss the financial details of proposed expenditure had been largely abandoned, and the supply days were recognised simply as a fixed number of days in the session on which the Opposition chose the subject of debate. The Opposition could if it wished discuss details of expenditure, but on nearly every occasion it did not wish to; instead it wished to discuss the general administration of a particular service being carried on by the Government. So instead of each of the estimates being taken up one by one and made the subject of debate in the Committee of Supply, the process was done the other way round. If the Opposition wanted to have a debate about some topic or other it would be arranged that one of the supply days was used for the purpose, and those items of expenditure which happened to relate to the topic they wished to discuss would be put down and made the subject of debate. There were certain technical inconveniences, and in the course of time some ingenious devices were brought in to overcome them. The overall effect was that the sacred constitutional rules about supply had become little more than a lot of mumbo-jumbo.

In 1966 a new standing order abolished the Committee of Supply. The change was like a constitutional amendment, but it attracted little public attention, because it did no more than discard forms which had become obsolete. What is retained is the guaranteed right of the Opposition to choose the subject of debate on twenty-nine days in each session, or about one-sixth of the days on which Parliament sits during the year. If the Opposition wishes to discuss details of government expenditure it may do so, but the assumption is that normally it will not. There is still legislation authorising the expenditure of public money each year, but this does not mean that there is any real control over the details by Parliament as such.

A special problem concerning public expenditure arises from the old practice of voting money for one year at a time. Nowadays a very large part of government expenditure involves operations each of which has to continue over several years, and is meaningless when seen as a single year's operation. The expenditures are now put to the House of Commons informally on a long term basis, but the practice of approving each year's expenditure by legislation for the year still continues – and it is difficult to see how any other device could be invented. At any given time Parliament is liable to be dissolved long before the end of a three-year period, and a new House of Commons after a general election could not properly be bound by long-term decisions made during the time of its predecessors.

Having abandoned its ancient claims to control government expenditure through a committee of the whole House the House of Commons has developed other devices. The first of these in point of time was control of the accounts. In 1861 the House of Commons established a Committee of Public Accounts to examine the accounts of government spending in order to ensure that all money had been spent without waste for precisely those purposes for which it had been voted and for no other purposes.[1] This committee consisted of fifteen members of the House of Commons, and it soon received the assistance of the Comptroller and Auditor General, a servant of the House of Commons who may only be removed from his office by a resolution of the two Houses.[2] This device has continued to the present day. The modern Public Accounts Committee has fifteen members and its chairman is a prominent member of the Opposition. The Comptroller and Auditor General works with a staff of about 500. Each year the Public Accounts Committee receives his report on the expenditures of

[1] Standing Order No. 90; cf. Erskine May, *Treatise on the Law, Privileges, Proceedings and Usage of Parliament* (Butterworth, 18th edn, 1971), p. 682.

[2] His appointment was provided for by the Exchequer and Audit Department Act, 1866. Cf. Erskine May, pp. 257 and 682.

each of the departments. The accounting officers of the departments appear before it to explain the accounts.

There are obvious inconsistencies in all this. The Public Accounts Committee is supposed only to ensure that the money has been used, without extravagance, for the purposes for which it was voted, and is not concerned with the policy which led to the expenditure. Why? Because the policy is a matter for Parliament itself, and Parliament has already approved the policy by its act in voting the money. But as it voted the money automatically, the reply is unconvincing. Parliament leaves the detailed work of control over the estimates almost entirely to the Executive's own internal procedures, and these procedures are known to be reasonably thorough. It is in deference to Parliament's constitutional right that the Executive takes great care over the form of the estimates. Encouraged by the Public Accounts Committee it does its best to present them in a form which makes them understandable and which facilitates the task of checking the accounts. The charge of inconsistency is not wholly unanswered, but it arises, ultimately, from the overall dominance of Parliament by the Executive.

In recent years this process of control has had a few minor victories, however weak it may look. At least it has discovered excessive amounts paid by government departments for work undertaken on their behalf by private enterprise companies. On some bigger issues the system has failed. In July 1969 the Public Accounts Committee, observing that up to that point 'escalation' had raised the cost of developing the Concorde aircraft project from £170 million to £730 million (with a prospect of a further increase in the future), complained that not enough information had been supplied to Parliament. But the complaint did not stop the project. The official reply was simply that so much had been committed already to this scheme that it had better be continued, however valueless its ultimate objective. All that can be said in defence of this outrage is that the British machinery was less slow to produce criticism of expenditure on supersonic transport than the French or the Russian.

One of the weaknesses of control by the Public Accounts Committee is that it operates after the money has been spent. In an attempt to fill this gap the House of Commons set up a Select Committee on Estimates in 1912, to examine the estimates. This committee developed its effectiveness rather slowly, but became more useful after 1945. It was replaced in 1971 by a new Committee on Public Expenditure, with extended objectives (see below), but the same mode of operation through sub-committees.

Each sub-committee works in the manner common to select committees. The appropriate government department provides the sub-committee with papers setting out the grounds for the expenditures proposed, and describing the relevant administrative arrangements. The sub-committee holds a series of meetings at each of which one or more civil servants, or others who might be useful, appear before it to be questioned – up to a total of several dozen, usually on the basis of written submissions. Meetings may be held away from Westminster. The proceedings during these hearings are recorded verbatim and sold (not very cheaply) to the public by the Stationery Office. After a sub-committee has completed its hearings it prepares a draft report[1] which may be anything from ten to fifty pages long, which is bound to be partly descriptive, but which may contain criticism and proposals for changes in the administrative process which has been examined. The draft report is then discussed in a full sitting of the committee at which amendments to the draft may be proposed and voted upon. Eventually when the report as a whole and each of its paragraphs have been agreed (by majority vote if necessary, but probably not on party lines), the report is presented to Parliament and published. A report has no formal authority. It may be debated in the House, though such debates are rare.

It is unlikely that any great savings on details of expenditure were achieved as a result of the old committee's work, but its reports were useful as descriptions of administrative forms and practices. Civil Servants presumably derived benefit from having to think about their practices in such a way that they could explain them to Members of Parliament, potentially capable of seeing the weaknesses in routine methods and approaches with which the civil servants, through habit or inertia, might have become identified.

Committees of the United States Congress working in this field are more effective. But there is a fundamental difference between the constitutional assumptions in Britain and those in the United States. The United States Congress cannot dismiss the Executive, but it can, and often does, provide less (or more) money for a particular service than the Executive has asked for, and it often follows committee advice. In Britain, because constitutional principles do not allow Parliament to increase a sum requested by the Executive – and constitutional realities, arising from the nature of the party system and from the implications of ministerial responsibility, do not effectively allow it to make any reduction – no parliamentary committee can usefully propose to cut any estimate; it can only report an opinion in more general terms.

Within these limitations there is not much scope for any increase in

[1] The actual work of writing the first draft may be done by the Chairman or the Clerk to the committee, working in consultation.

real parliamentary control, but some attempts to improve its effectiveness have been made since 1965. First there was a provision for each sub-committee of the Estimates Committee to work regularly within the same field of governmental activity, then, more important, was the replacement of the Estimates Committee by a Committee on Public Expenditure.

In 1971 the House of Commons set up, under standing order, a new Select Committee on Public Expenditure[1] with a task going well beyond that of the Estimates Committee, which it replaced. The new committee could consider not only annual estimates but any papers on public expenditure presented to the House of Commons. The committee's membership, forty-nine, was a little larger than the Estimates Committee's had ever been. It set up six functional sub-committees in addition to a steering committee. These were: public expenditure (general); defence and external affairs; trade and industry; employment and social services; education and arts; and environment and Home Office.[2]

Its third report, published in October 1971, on the theme of two recent papers on public expenditure, is an important contribution to constitutional development with respect to the nation's finances. It suggested the direction in which Parliament's future debates might go: 'The House should seek to debate . . . the realities upon which the figures are based – that is the programmes themselves, for example what they are estimated to cost, what their objectives are and whether alternative programmes would or would not represent a better allocation of resources and money. . . . The basic issue before Parliament is the examination of the Government's whole choice of priorities.'

Thus the new committee can look at the whole development of a series of functions, and discuss the balance of priorities envisaged for the middle-range plans. The new scheme assumes that the Expenditure Committee's work should be linked with an annual two-day debate on a white paper setting out reasoned plans for public expenditure up to three years ahead, together with projections to the fourth and fifth years. As the forward plans are not yet wholly rigid, and cover all public expenditure (and not only the amounts of the annual votes), there is scope for these parliamentary proceedings to contribute to the formation of ministerial policy in a way that has not been possible in the past. The House has not much valued its new opportunity. The first three annual debates were tame affairs, reduced to one day, and at the opening on 7 February 1973 only five Opposition back-benchers were present.

[1] H. C. Debs 21 January 1971, cols 1045–7.
[2] Special Report from the Expenditure Committee, 23 February 1971.

TAXATION

Whatever may have happened with control of expenditure, the procedure for taxation has remained closer to the original constitutional conception of full parliamentary control. Perhaps the most important issue of the seventeenth century was the insistence of Parliament that no tax should be imposed except with parliamentary authority, and the House of Commons has continued to insist on having ample and real opportunity to discuss each of the taxes which the Government wishes to impose. Authority to impose taxes is given by legislation, some of it permanent and some requiring to be renewed each year. But even with those taxes which are based on permanent legislation any change requires new legislation.

The normal practice is for one Finance Act to be passed in July each year stipulating the objects which are to be taxed and the rate at which the taxes are to be collected. From the seventeenth century until 1967 the House resolved itself into a Committee of Ways and Means for the purpose of considering the Government's requests before taking the legislation through the usual stages of three readings and a committee stage. The Chancellor of the Exchequer presents his proposals in the so-called Budget speech in April. Since the reforms of 1967 this has been done in the House, not in a committee of the whole House. The Budget resolutions are then passed on the basis of a debate lasting about four days. Then the Finance Bill is prepared, and its details discussed in the committee stage, taken (until 1968) on the floor of the House of Commons. Members may propose reductions of particular taxes in the form of amendments to the bill, with decisions being made by vote if necessary. The Government can ensure that it gets its way on any particular point by means of the party whip, as with other legislation; but, just as with other legislation, the debate is conducted in the expectation that on some points the Government may let itself be persuaded to make concessions.

Of the changes in the procedure introduced between 1966 and 1968 the abolition of the Committee of Ways and Means was really only a technical readjustment. More important, the House gave up the hallowed right of each Member to take part in all stages of the discussions. The committee stage of the Finance Bill was taken away from the floor of the House, and the detailed discussion took place in a committee of only fifty Members. For many years detailed discussions in the committee of the whole House had been very burdensome, occupying six to ten sittings on matters of interest to small numbers of Members. A voluntary time-table had been tried in 1967 without success. The change of 1968 was thus defensible, though it aroused much controversy.

To a constitutional purist this change could appear dangerous, however pragmatically sound. If taxes are dealt with by a small committee, what becomes of the principle that no tax is to be imposed without the consent of Parliament? In each of several previous years, between 100 and 200 Members had participated in the detailed discussions on the Finance Bill, but for much of the time a handful of Members were actually present in the House, because the technical and detailed nature of many of the discussions was uninteresting to the great majority. The sacrifice of the principle that each Member should be able to participate was accepted in the interest of giving the House as a whole more time for discussion of matters other than taxes; it would really be rather pretentious to deny that a small committee could adequately deal with most of the points which the annual taxation proposals raise.

It happened that the Finance Bill of 1968 contained a large amount of controversial material, and the new small committee celebrated its existence by devoting even more time to the Finance Bill debates than had previously been devoted by the committee of the whole House. The committee had to sit for long periods, sometimes while the House as a whole was in session dealing with other business. Eventually a guillotine was imposed, so some sections of the bill were just not debated in the committee at all.

In 1969 a compromise was adopted, and this has been followed since then. Only the more technical and detailed parts of the Finance Bill are sent to a small committee, while the more important parts are dealt with, as before, by a committee of the whole House. This arrangement appears to be sensibly devised for the main objective, which is to distribute the House's time as effectively as possible for purposes determined by the balance between the parties.

Up to 1974 Parliament's contribution to taxation policy was still limited by the ancient rule that only ministers may propose taxes. Modern social policies, including particularly those which will be needed for protecting the ecology and combating environmental pollution, must depend on fiscal programmes if they are not to rely wholly on distasteful compulsion. Some scope for parliamentary initiatives will be necessary to offset the Executive's dependence on established commercial interests and administrative habits. Recognising this, the Select Committee on Procedure proposed in 1971 that the new Expenditure Committee should extend its functions into the area of taxation, and such a development would be an appropriate response to a new challenge to the political system.

15

The Legislative Process

In English the words 'parliament' and 'legislature' are virtually indistinguishable, and have been so for more than 200 years, but it would be wrong now, and it would always have been wrong, to suggest that 'law making' is Parliament's essential function. The United States Constitution assigns the law-making power to Congress, without defining law or law making. Erskine May attempts no such definition, nor does Dicey in *The Law of the Constitution*. According to Walkland, in a companion book to the present one, 'a conceptual definition of legislation which is often attempted is that it consists, to quote one authority, "of the making of determinations which are issued to indicated but unnamed and unspecified persons or situations".'[1] Walkland also quotes Davis again that legislation normally 'affects the rights of individuals in the abstract and must be applied in a further proceeding before the legal position of an individual will be touched by it, whilst adjudication operates concretely upon individuals in their individual capacity'.

The French Fifth Republic Constitution actually attempts to define legislative power, and though the definition applies to France only, it is worth quoting:

Art. 34   Laws are voted by Parliament.
Laws determine the rules concerning:
— civil rights and fundamental guarantees accorded to the citizens for the exercise of public liberties; the national defence obligations imposed upon the persons and property of citizens;
— the nationality, status and legal capacity of persons, the law of matrimony, inheritance and gifts;
— the determination of crimes and offences as well as the punishments applicable to them; criminal procedure; amnesty; the creation of

---

[1] S. A. Walkland, *The Legislative Process in Great Britain* (Allen & Unwin, 1968), p. 9, quoting K. G. Davis, *Administrative Law* (St Paul, 1951), p. 54.

new orders of jurisdiction and the rights and duties of the judiciary (*statut des magistrates*);
— the basis, rate and methods of collection of taxation of all types; the system of issuing money.

The law also determines the rules concerning:
— the electoral system for the parliamentary assemblies and local assemblies;
— the creation of categories of public corporations (*établissements*);
— the fundamental guarantees accorded to civil and military employees of the State;
— the nationalisation of undertakings (*entreprises*) and the transfer of the property of undertakings from the public to the private sector.

Laws lay down the fundamental principles:
— of the general organisation of national defence;
— of the free administration of local government units, of their powers and their resources;
— of education;
— of the status of property, real estate laws and civil and commercial obligations;
— of the law pertaining to employment, unions and social security.

Programme laws determine the objectives of the State's economic and social activities.

Art. 35   The declaration of war is authorised by Parliament.

Art. 36   The state of siege is decreed in Council of Ministers. Its extension beyond twelve days can be authorised only by Parliament.

Art. 37   Matters other than those which are in the domain of the law fall within the rule-making sphere.

There is no equivalent definition of the domain of law in Britain, and could not well be, within the existing constitutional structure. We should have to begin by saying that in England part of the law is common law as discovered by the courts and developed through the creation of precedents by their particular decisions, and the other part is statutory law, as set out in the statutes voted by Parliament and approved by the Monarch.

In the modern world there is a hierarchy of governmental decisions, in descending order of generality, from 'there shall be a national health service' down to specific prescriptions about the forms of the service. Within this hierarchy there is a borderline, above which are matters within 'the domain of law'. The place of that borderline is determined not by any absolute standard but by past practice and the need for

I

consistency. In British practice the borderline is drawn rather low, so that the statutes themselves contain many detailed prescriptions, all open to parliamentary discussion during the law-making process. French laws tend to be much shorter than English laws with similar objects.

The French list includes within the law-making power the process of laying down fundamental guarantees accorded to civil and military employees of the State. Here is one real difference between the two systems. In Britain this, like the declaration of war, is within the sphere of the royal prerogative – though it is suggested that by convention 'A Government shall not advise the Crown to declare war, make peace or conclude a treaty unless there is ample ground for supposing that the majority of the Commons approves the policy.'[1] In 1972 Mr Heath signed the treaty of accession to the European Economic Communities after both Houses of Parliament had approved the principle of accession on the terms agreed – and in that vote, exceptionally, the Government supporters in both Houses had been allowed to vote without instructions from their whips. But the bill providing for changes in British law as a consequence was short, leaving large tracts of decision making to be settled ultimately by ministerial orders; and, as is almost inescapable with legislation consequent on treaties, the legislation included elements through which the Parliament of that time was effectively binding its successors.

The nature of the laws of England, including the relations between common law and statute law, has been well illustrated by comparing the common law to a wall to which bricks are constantly being added (in the form of new decisions by courts creating precedents), and on which notices are stuck (representing the statutes). By now most of the wall is covered by notices, and additions to it are usually in the form of new statutes rather than new precedents.[2]

The written law of the land is contained in the statute book. Every new law passed is an additional 'chapter', and each year about fifty to eighty new laws are added. Some are very short, others a hundred pages long. Each statute has a short title (for example, the Transport Act, 1968) and consists of sections. From time to time a new and revised edition of the statute book is published, running to over thirty volumes.

The making of statutes is the most evident of the sovereign functions of the Queen in Parliament. There is no constitutional restriction on the subject-matter to be included in the statutes, nothing to prevent the

[1] O. Hood Phillips, *Constitutional and Administrative Law* (Sweet & Maxwell, 4th edn. 1967), p. 88.
[2] Christopher Hughes, *The British Statute Book* (Hutchinson, 1957).

passing of any statute, even of obviously unreasonable content, provided that it has passed through the proper recognised procedure in the two Houses of Parliament and been signed by the Queen. Once a statute has been passed and added to the statute book the courts are obliged to follow it in dealing with any cases that may come before them to which the statute is relevant. They interpret it, and interpretations create precedents, but they cannot find it invalid. It is therefore very important that there should be no conflict of meaning between one statute and another. If a new statute alters the effect of some older statute already in the book, the new statute must clearly include a repeal of whatever in the old one is inconsistent with the intentions of the new. The task of ensuring that the courts are not confronted with conflicting parts of the statute book is a difficult and technical one.

Although the statute-making power belongs to the Queen in Parliament, a statute may grant power to a minister or to any other person to make prescriptions of the character normally included within the statutes. There is nothing to stop Parliament from delegating part of its legislative power, and this is often done. In the 1920s there was much concern about this practice, which was then growing rapidly, owing to the increase in the total volume of the activities of government and thus in the volume of the matter which needed to be defined in statutory form. The disquiet of the 1920s has by now been largely dissipated, and is often argued that more delegation could be accepted without real damage to the democratic system because of the nature of the processes by which governmental decisions are made, and because the Government dominates the parliamentary process even with respect to the making of statutes. The final danger is that Parliament could delegate all of its legislative power. There is nothing to prevent this, but such a step would be regarded as revolutionary.

TYPES OF LEGISLATION

There are two kinds of statutes. Public acts are directed to the community as a whole. Private acts alter the law with respect to particular localities, or give special powers or functions or rights to particular bodies, such as individual local authorities, corporations, universities, or even persons. A few bills, which have both 'public' and 'private' characteristics, are known as 'hybrid' bills.

Private legislation

It is convenient to deal briefly with private legislation first. Before passing any private Act, Parliament is concerned to judge for itself that the special benefit conferred does not unduly harm either the public interest or any other particular interest.

The standing orders relating to private bills give scope for parliamentary debate and decision on the principles of any private bill, but they also recognise that in most cases there is no need for debate. After being presented, a private bill is brought up for approval ('second reading') at the beginning of a day's business, before question time. Such approval is taken to mean that nobody finds the bill objectionable in relation to the national interest. If even one single Member objects no progress is made, but the bill may be brought up for a general debate in the whole House, and before a vote is taken a minister may explain the Government's attitude.

The committee stage of a private bill is somewhat similar in form to proceedings in a court of law. If a bill is promoted by a local authority which wants a new power, its spokesman states the reasons why it wants the new powers, and any objectors may state the contrary view. The arguments are heard by a small committee of members of one or other House of Parliament, and the committee eventually recommends to Parliament what should be done. It is not only the national interest that is considered at this stage, but the extent to which legitimate private interests may be damaged through the passing of the bill. To that extent the process is by its nature judicial rather than legislative in the normal sense of the term. The task of the committee is to secure an equitable balance between the interests of the promoters and those of other parties who claim that their rights or interests would be adversely affected.

The committee has a majority of government supporters in its membership, but their actions in the committee are not subject to party discipline. The central Government can afford to leave its party members free because if a point should arise with serious implications for national policy, the Government could protect its interests by other means.

Public legislation

Public bills affect the community as a whole. Any Member may propose a bill, and there is provision, albeit limited, for debate on private members' bills (*see below*, p. 137). Bills proposed by private members may slightly outnumber Government bills, but Government bills enacted into law outnumber private members' bills by four or five to one. In total length, in importance and in time devoted to discussion the difference is far more than this.

All public bills, whether proposed by the Government or by private members, pass through the same procedure, first in one House, then in the other; then the first House considers the second's amendments. Each bill must pass through the two Houses successively. Important bills, and bills whose implementation will involve expenditure, go through the Commons first. Other bills may start in either House, and the Government finds it convenient to start about a quarter or a third of its bills of a session in the Lords.

In each House every public bill must be given three 'readings', and its details must be considered in a committee. The first reading is in practice merely an announcement of an intention to bring a bill forward and have the text printed in time for Members to study it before the debate and decision on the second reading, which takes place on the floor of the House.[1]

The second reading is the stage at which the House decides whether or not to approve the principles of the bill, after debate. After the second reading, the House entrusts the discussion of details to a committee, which normally consists of a small number of members, appointed, as the standing order says, with regard to the composition of the House. This cryptic formula is a way of saying, without using the word 'party', that each party must have a proportion of seats in the committee equal to its proportion of seats in the House as a whole. It is possible to propose that the committee on a bill should be a committee of the whole house, and such a proposal is normally voted upon, with the Government sure to get its way. Parliamentary convention suggests that bills affecting the constitution should be dealt with by committees of the whole House.

The committee proceeds by considering the clauses of the bill one by one. Any member may propose to amend any part of a clause, and the amendments are discussed and decided upon one by one.

The process may take sixty or seventy hours or even more on a long bill. Then comes the report stage, at which the House as a whole (or a committee) may go through the details again in the same way as was done at the committee stage. Finally the third reading is a decision on the bill as it has been amended in committee and on report. Here speeches are restricted to material contained in the bill.

Government bills. Government and private members' bills go through the same procedure, but the working of the procedure differs.

A Government bill is sure to pass second reading. If it were not, the

[1] Since 1967 Standing Order No. 67A has allowed the second reading to be taken in a committee, provided that no more than twenty Members object. This device is used only for uncontroversial Government bills, including those relating solely to Scotland, and its purpose is to save time on the floor of the House.

Government would be aware of the danger of defeat, and would not bring the bill forward. It can tolerate some abstentions or even contrary votes among its own supporters on second reading, but the whips can tell the ministers in advance how many rebels there may be, and only if there are not enough then to endanger the bill will the bill be brought in for decision.

So when a Government bill comes up for second reading the main purpose of the debate is to provide an opportunity for the minister concerned to describe its purpose and explain how he expects it to work, and for the Opposition front bench and other Members, both on the Government side and on the Opposition side, to state their views. A second-reading debate may be important for its effect on public opinion, and for the public reactions which it provokes.

The committee stage is that at which changes may be introduced. Spokesmen for the Opposition as well as ordinary Members may advocate changes in the text, so long as they neither alter the main purpose of a bill as defined in the long title, nor involve new expenditure. With some exceptions[1] every amendment that is proposed is voted upon, but given the nature of the party system it is almost always the minister in charge who decides whether a proposed change is to be accepted or not. He has beside him a majority of the committee, and party discipline discourages his supporters from voting against his wishes. Some thousands of amendments to government bills are proposed each year but it is unusual to find more than two or three occasions in a year on which a vote goes against a minister, even on a matter of detail. If this happens the Government is not defeated, and can usually ensure the cancellation of the amendment at a later stage of the proceedings. Now and again it gives way.

Although the minister has little need to fear defeat, he is expected to listen very carefully to the arguments, and if he can see a way to meet them wholly or in part without damaging his original purposes he will do so. In fact great numbers of amendments are made to the text of Government bills in committee with the ministers' agreement. Thus this parliamentary stage is not a mere occasion for debating and making partisan points.

If debate about any proposed amendment continues for a very long

[1] The committee's chairman decides which proposed amendments are in order, and when several different proposals are related to the same matter he may 'select' only one for discussion and decision. Also, a very substantial and controversial bill is apt to provoke so much discussion in committee that it could not be dealt with in the time available without some restriction on debate. With such bills the Government may ask the House to agree to a notion setting a time limit to discussion. One effect is to prevent discussion of some amendments, and of some whole clauses.

time, the closure may be moved, and if the chairman considers that there has been enough discussion, the closure motion is likely to be carried. As a safeguard it must be approved not only by a majority but by at least a third of the committee's members. More drastically, a guillotine motion may be passed in the House, setting a time limit to the committee proceedings. This was first done in 1881, as a response to Irish members' obstruction. On average, about one bill per year has been guillotined since 1946, and the procedural reforms of 1967 strengthened governments by providing that, when a time-table is proposed, only two hours shall be spent in debating that proposal. Once a time limit is imposed, the Opposition is allowed the main influence in the detailed decisions about the use of the time.[1]

One development of recent times has been the ever larger contribution to discussion of legislation made by groups of people organised as interests in the community outside. There is no statutory requirement that in preparing a bill a minister should consult groups whom it will affect, but prudence suggests that it is wise for him to engage in very wide and thorough discussion. Before introducing his bill the minister has probably heard the opinions of numerous interest-groups about its potential effects on them, and made changes of detail in response to preparatory informal discussions.

By convention the draft text is not publicly disclosed before it is actually printed after the first reading in Parliament. Therefore the informal discussions have been based upon the Government's plans, so far as they are disclosed, rather than on an actual text. When the outside interests finally see the printed bill they can continue to put pressure on the minister, sometimes with success. Ministers themselves propose many amendments to their own bills, sometimes as a result of continuing private discussions outside Parliament. But apart from this many of the amendments proposed by Members of Parliament during the committee stage have been fed to them by outside bodies in furtherance of their own interests, and Members have been plied with information and argument from outside in support of suggested changes.

Two points arise from this. First, the parliamentary stages are only a part of the total of discussion which takes place. They are like the part of an iceberg which can be seen above the water. Second, each member of the House of Commons is in a sense a representative of the community as a whole, and can thus represent a number of sectional interests – though preferably not if he is financially involved. It has often been proposed that there should be an additional House of Parliament composed of representatives of interests. What in fact happens is that

[1] Cf. John Palmer, 'Allocation of Time: the Guillotine and Voluntary Time-tabling,' *Parliamentary Affairs* (1970), pp. 232–47.

the views of the interests which might be expressed in a special House of Parliament receive expression indirectly through individual Members who take up their cause.

Having passed through the Commons the bill goes through the same stages in the House of Lords, and here too the committee stage is effectively the most important. There appears to be a convention that the Lords should not reject on second reading any bill proposed by a Government (unless there is a good reason for arguing that the bill is against the spirit of the Constitution); thus the second reading is an occasion for stating opinions and little more than that. The committee stage is like that in the Commons, though until 1971 it was always taken on the floor of the House. A peer representing the Government may introduce amendments on behalf of the minister, and when other amendments are proposed he uses arguments supplied by the minister (or his civil servants) in reply. His reply may be favourable or unfavourable. Not infrequently the House of Lords amends a bill against a minister's advice, particularly when Labour is in power, and the Opposition is in a majority. But then the bill goes back to the Commons for the Lords's amendments to be considered. Occasionally a compromise is worked out, but more often the Government insists on having Lords's amendments rejected in the Commons, and the Lords finally acquiesce.

The committee and report stages in the two Houses provide four occasions on which amendments to a bill may be proposed and voted on. With a major bill the first of these occasions, the Commons committee stage, is usually the longest, and the most striking thing about it is that the vast majority of proposals for amendment are withdrawn after discussion. This fact illustrates the essential nature of the legislative process more effectively than the less typical occasions when partisan points are decided by divisions on party lines; it also shows the value of the lengthy procedure allowing four stages for considering the text. Having heard arguments in committee the minister may well feel persuaded that there is indeed a case for some change, though not necessarily for exactly that change involved in the new form of words which has been proposed. He then asks for the proposal to be withdrawn in order that there may be a thorough examination of the problem in his department, and probably some consultation directly with interested groups. The amendment may come up again for final decision at one of the later stages – possibly even as a government amendment moved and accepted during the proceedings in the second House.

Some amendments are withdrawn because the minister explains that the objectives of the proposer will be attained through the application of the text as it stands; or he may be able to demonstrate that some suspected danger is unreal. Much of the discussion of details is thus constructive and not partisan; it involves a search for possible ambiguities, absurdities, contradictions, or injustices which might arise from the application of the text as originally introduced, and there is ample scope and time for the exchange of ideas between the minister, with his civil servants, and the groups who will be affected, or whose cooperation will be needed to make the bill work. The MPs are important in the process because they can oblige the minister to reply publicly to their arguments, and to make a public justification, in respect to each amendment proposal, of the decision which he ultimately recommends.

The whole process is long by the standards of legislatures in other countries; the British Parliament is exceptionally thorough and painstaking. Two features, found in various forms in other parliaments, are lacking. There is no opportunity for direct confrontation between interest-group spokesmen and MPs in the context of the actual proceedings of Parliament. (Select committees, which can examine 'witnesses', are occasionally used but not for ordinary public bills.) Such confrontation might conflict with the principle that the minister bears responsibility for the recommendations which he makes (or imposes). The other lack is opportunity for MPs to specialise in particular fields of legislation through the formal committee structure. Although the committees to which bills are sent for detailed discussion are called 'standing committees', these groups are really even less 'standing' than 'public schools' are public. This misleading nomenclature survives from a time when there was an element of permanent membership in these committees, which are still designated Standing Committee A, B, C, etc. In fact there is an *ad hoc* committee set up for each bill. Members are appointed by the eleven-member Committee of Selection, which may take some advice from the party whips but does not need to follow it. Its independence is important, because the whips might wish to prevent the appointment of a Member known to disagree with his party. Following recent changes in the direction of flexibility of numbers, membership of a standing committee may be anything between fifteen and fifty, depending mainly on the number of Members who wish to serve. The system allows for a standing committee to include people who have in fact chosen to specialise in the field covered by a bill (probably through membership of their party's subject committee), as well as others who may have a special interest in some particular aspects of it.

Private members' bills. That little corner of Parliament's work in which it deals with private members' bills is an expression of the pure function of a 'legislature'. A generation ago quite diverse elements in the Labour Party, notably Herbert Morrison, were inclined to dismiss this activity as an irrelevance, and no time was provided for it in 1945–8. But private members' time was then restored, and the Labour Government of 1964–70 extended it slightly. It was mainly from the Labour side, though not from the Labour Government, that some really significant – and successful – initiatives came in 1964–70.

There are some issues, including important ones, with which a Government in office cannot conveniently deal in its legislative programme, but which can well be dealt with, on the basis of individual initiatives, by Parliament acting as a collection of independent persons elected by the public.

Standing Orders (*see above*, p. 120) prevent private members from proposing bills involving public expenditure, and (since the 1930s) common sense has excluded major partisan causes. These bills usually deal with questions affecting private morals, the family, and social reforms which can be treated in isolation from government policy. Although a minister may express an official opinion, there is a parliamentary convention that the party whips should not be put on.

The right of private members to introduce bills is unlimited, but the right to have bills discussed is restricted in practice by the Government's control over the time-table. For a long time before 1939 the standing orders of the House of Commons laid down that a fixed number of days in each year should be available for private members. For the past thirty years the number of days (always Fridays) available has been determined for each session by a fresh sessional order. Near the beginning of a session a ballot for priority in the use of time on each of the first eight Fridays is held. On the later Fridays priority is given to third readings and Lords amendments.

During 1940–8 no days were provided at all. From 1948 onwards ten Fridays were provided each session, and in 1967 the number was increased to sixteen. This increase was given in exchange for some of the things which private members collectively had given up – notably the right to be present at all the debates at the committee stage of the Finance Bill.

There are many procedural obstacles.[1] On a really controversial bill opponents are likely to be so prolix in committee that by the time the House of Lords has finished with it all the time allocated for private members' bills in the current session is exhausted. If this happens the Lords's amendments can only be dealt with if the Government provides time – and if it does so the opponents may well argue that the Government has virtually adopted the bill, and ought to have included it in its own programme.

[1] P. Bromhead, *Private Members' Bills in the British Parliament* (Routledge, 1956) describes these in detail, and the system has changed little since that time.

Such an argument rests on a disputable interpretation of the working constitution. Another interpretation would seem to be more soundly based. The Government has been responsible, at the beginning of the session, for asking the House to agree to a motion to give some days for private members' bills. Thus, if within the time provided the House has approved the principles and a committee has looked at the details, the final passage ought not to be frustrated simply by the inadequacy of the time-table. The Labour Government of 1964–70 followed this interpretation, by getting the House to sit in the morning or late at night so as not to sacrifice its own business, but the Conservatives after 1970, having criticised Labour's method of dealing with the problem, decided not to provide any time beyond that given in the sessional order.

A private member's bill involving complicated administration may well be opposed by the Government on the ground that its implications must be thoroughly worked out, perhaps with a royal commission to collate facts and opinions before any action can be taken – and royal commissions are not only excuses for inaction or delay. Substantial legislation is so linked with executive action that it cannot be treated in a legislative ivory tower. Nevertheless, there is scope for quite substantial legislative reforms which do not heavily involve the administration, and it is surely fair to say that one of the major reforms of 1964–70 was the introduction of an elementary charter for a permissive society, mainly through six private members' bills (on capital punishment, censorship of plays, abortion, homosexuality, divorce and Sunday entertainments). These measures were not suitable for introduction as part of government policy (and on any of them a Government might stand to lose some votes, as a party, if the party were identified with them). Although both parties were divided in the free votes on the principles of all these measures, there was a clear party consistency, with more Labour Members voting for permissive reform than against, and more Conservatives voting to defend the *status quo* than to amend it.[1]

[1] Cf. P. G. Richards, *Parliament and Conscience* (Allen & Unwin, 1970), p. 180. Richards's book is mainly concerned with the story of these bills.

16

The Commons and the Executive

'Redress of grievance before supply' has an archaic ring, and 100 years ago a motion to go into committee of supply was regularly preceded by a debate on some 'grievance'. After Irish members had over-used this procedure to the point of obstruction, the procedure was changed. The raising of 'grievances' was not stopped, but other devices were developed, with distinct procedures appropriate to identifiable categories of grievances, general and particular, political and administrative. And the content of the debates on 'supply' changed so that by the time a minimum number of supply days per session was guaranteed virtually all the supply days were being used for grievance debates.

It is in the 'grievance' procedures that there have been the biggest and the most significant changes in the past few decades, and the changes express some quite fundamental developments in the conception of the role of Parliament. Grievances may arise from action or inaction, and in the latter case may involve positive proposals for action. But if the standing orders exclude MPs from proposing new taxes or expenditure, and the Government's programme leaves them collectively only a few days a year for proposing legislation, it may seem that there is not much scope for any positive role. Indeed there is not; but the traditional word 'grievance' is quite useful to identify the functions of Parliament that are neither legislative nor financial, but concerned with the Government's choices from the policy options open to it, broad and narrow.

In this broad sense we can list five types of procedure under which private members can raise grievances, and four others which are available to the Opposition (see Table). Together they account for about 35 per cent of the time spent in session.

	No. per week	Average no. of occasions per year	Approx. duration each occasion (hours)	Total duration per year – long session (hours)
Private members' occasions				
1. Question to ministers, with supplementaries	4	130	0·9	115
2. Daily half-hour 'adjournment debates'[a]	5	160	0·5	80
3. Holiday adjournment debates[a]	—	4	5·5	22
4. Private members' motions[a]	—	4	5	20
5. Urgent or topical adjournments[b]	—	4[c]	2·5	10
Opposition's occasions				
1. Supply days	—	29	6	170
2. Queen's speech amendments	—	3	6	18
3. Questions on ministers' statements	—	50	0·2	10
4. Various	—	10	6	6

[a] Balloted
[b] May also be Opposition-inspired.
The number '4' relates only to time since 1966.

The table indicates broadly the distribution of time among various procedures through which the House attempts to provide for the discussion of the immense variety of matters that individual members, or groups of members, or the Opposition, may wish to have ventilated, by a means roughly appropriate in each case. At one extreme we have the question asked by a Member on something of concern to his constituency, at the other extreme a motion of censure proposed by the Opposition, with a major debate on some matter of high inter-party controversy.

These devices have been changed and refined many times, particularly since 1965. Together they enable the House of Commons to perform a variety of roles quite effectively within the two-party situation, but they need to be supplemented by other devices, in some degree linked with, and dependent upon, the proceedings on the floor of the House, and some progress has been made lately with the refinement of these other devices.

Although we have had to classify these various procedures on the floor of the House as non-financial and non-legislative we must recognise that pressure on the Government to remedy some alleged omission may involve pressure for new legislation or for new expenditure. Some of the recent changes in procedure have been aimed at making such pressure permissible without infringing traditional rules.

Of all these devices the parliamentary question is the most widely known and admired; it is imitated in many other parliamentary assemblies. The story of its development, spontaneous and unplanned, is typical of the history of parliamentary procedure and of the Constitution as a whole. In 1721 a peer wanted information about a rumour, and he wanted to ask about it publicly. So, quite irregularly, during a sitting of the House of Lords, he asked a question, and a reply was given.[1] Other questions followed as the years passed, at long intervals, in both Houses. In 1783, after a question to Burke (then Postmaster General) had led to a long discussion, Speaker Cornwall ruled: 'Conversations are disorderly, but any Member has, in my opinion, a right to put a question to a minister or person in office, and that person has a right to answer or not as he thinks proper.'[2] Questions sometimes produced 'conversations', which became respectable when they were disciplined into the form of supplementary questions.

Successive Speakers' rulings defined the types of questions that were permissible, and those that were out of order. The essential rule was soon established that a question must relate to the field of responsibility of the office-holder to whom it is addressed. In the 1850s it became the practice to assign a definite place in each day's business to questions, and in 1869 the practice was confirmed by a formal resolution.[3] Later, when the time-table of the sitting needed to be defined more precisely, a fixed period was set, before the beginning of the main business.

For a long time now question-time has begun between 2.35 and 2.40 p.m. on every normal day of sitting except Fridays, after prayers and some non-discussable and mainly formal items, and has continued until exactly 3.30 p.m. when the Speaker must bring it to an end.

Within the question-hour the problem of supplementary questions has caused difficulty. A minister's reply is unlikely to be complete, and so Speakers have allowed further questions to be put for the elucidation of a reply. The less the Speaker restricts supplementaries the more effectively can Members pursue ministers. On the other hand, too many supplementaries restrict the number of original questions capable of being dealt with before 3.30 p.m.

In 1972, after it had been disclosed that some government supporters

---

[1] Patrick Howarth, *Questions in the House* (The Bodley Head, 1956), p. 14.

[2] *ibid.*, p. 43.

[3] D. N. Chester and Nora Bowring, *Questions in Parliament* (Oxford University Press, 1962), p. 25.

had put friendly questions to a minister, suggested by civil servants, to protect him against hostile questions from Opposition members, a committee reviewed many aspects of the system. It inevitably condemned question-planting, but it also looked at the extent of refusal to answer.

The Select Committee gave a list of ninety-five subjects about which governments habitually refuse to supply information. These included attendance records at the Council of Europe, the administration of the House of Lords attendance allowance, and instructions to research councils. The cost of renting part of the Piccadilly Hotel for the Roskill Commission was kept secret because 'it was not the practice to disclose information of this kind'.[1]

The report also dealt with wider issues concerning questions, and particularly with the effects of ministers' refusals to answer. Persistent denial of an answer to a particular type of question should not be held to make questions of that type out of order; such a question should be allowed once in a session, so that the Government would be obliged to review the policy which had led to the denial of an answer in previous sessions; and a single refusal to answer should render further questions on the same matter inadmissible only for a period of three months, instead of for the remainder of the session. Mr Prior's written statement of 6 December 1972 gave general approval to this plan.

The committee noted that only about one-third of the 15,000 questions for oral answer tabled in 1971 had in fact received oral answers. It suggested certain new restrictions on individual MPs, notably that no Member should be allowed to put more than one question to any one minister on any particular day; also it suggested that an experiment might be made with a question hour on Fridays, between 10 and 11 a.m.

The committee suggested the first invasion of the time for other business; on Tuesdays questions to the Prime Minister might be allowed to go on up to 3.45 p.m.

The Government, after considering these proposals for extending question time, decided not to advise the House to accept them.

At every sitting the last half-hour is set aside for a short adjournment debate initiated by a private member chosen by ballot (or on two days a week by the Speaker). A Member has about ten minutes in which to set forth an argument and a minister is expected to reply. This procedure is useful for a Member who has been fobbed off too easily at question time. Further devices such as the use of the last day before each recess for the four annual holiday periods, for three or four short private members' debates, provide similar opportunities.

[1] Cf. *The Observer*, 1 October 1972.

The debates on the supply days, and on some other days, are occasions for discussion of policy within a given field, usually fairly broad. They allow the ministers to explain their policy, the Opposition front-bench spokesmen to attack it, and the back-benchers to make their individual contributions.

Questions and adjournments do not provide a complete means of checking the Executive's work. There are some obvious weaknesses. It is accepted that questions are never asked by ministers or by the Speaker or his deputies, and very rarely by Opposition shadow ministers – though they often ask supplementaries. Question-time is seen as essentially a back-benchers' occasion, and one of its functions is to provide scope for MPs to raise matters of concern to their constituencies. In so far as this is so, it seems anomalous that a sixth of all constituencies are represented by members who are debarred, more or less rigidly, from asking questions. In fact the anomaly is not serious. Not very many questions are about constituency matters – though a Member who puts down a question involving the affairs of another's constituency may well be accused of trespassing. Also, about half of all Members who are not debarred from asking questions make little or no use of their rights, and surveys at various dates (the first in 1933) have found that about half of the questions were asked by one-tenth of the Members.[1] Questions serve many purposes, local, regional and nation-wide; opinions on their usefulness may differ but the ministers' duty to deal with them is some safeguard against arbitrary action anywhere in the central government's machinery.

In practice, if a Member wants to obtain a remedy for a grievance, he normally deals with the appropriate minister directly. The exchanges in the House of Commons are best seen as the public part of a much greater mass of unseen transactions by letters, telephone conversations, meetings and deputations. Collectively these contribute much more than the parliamentary exchanges to the decision-making process, but their importance in its turn depends in part on the thought which is constantly in the mind of ministers and civil servants, that if they leave a grievance unsatisfied the matter may be raised in the House. We see a reasonably sophisticated machinery for processing demands fed into the political system, in which members of Parliament have a role to play. One of the most striking characteristics of their contribution is its amateurishness, and although this has its strong points its weak points

[1] A study of the tabulation in the *Political Companion* for January–March 1971 (Political Reference Publications) shows that in the last half of 1970 the most active fifty-five Members asked between them 55 per cent of nearly 1,800 questions for oral answer – an average of seventeen each – while some 200 back-benchers asked no questions at all.

are more evident. As they become more widely recognised some attempts to remedy them have been made, though there is ample scope for more.

Questions for written answer, published in the official report, provide a useful means of obtaining information and getting some publicity for it, and the number of these is greater than the number of questions for oral answer. A minister who wants an opportunity to make some information public may well get a party supporter to ask a question, oral or written – though this must be done discreetly. In 1971 much embarrassment was caused when material concerning the 'planting' of questions came to light.

At the other end of the scale the supply days and censure motions, and various other occasions, provide for set debates, on topics of many kinds and varying levels of controversy, with Government and Opposition spokesmen stating their parties' positions, and back-benchers making their points. Sometimes the press and television give them prominence, sometimes not. The main value of these occasions is that they oblige government spokesmen to listen and respond to views which may be far from their own, and justify their decisions in public argument.

Apart from this, Standing Order No. 9 has provided a means by which the weekly plan of business could be interrupted for a debate on 'a definite matter of urgent public importance' – a device to enable a debate to take place suddenly, or at a few hours' notice on some immediate problem which had arisen suddenly, such as a decision to deport somebody by the next available plane. Since the 1920s successive Speakers' interpretations of the words had established precedents so strict and narrow that hardly any topic could satisfy the requirements. In three years 1960–3 the Speaker refused forty-nine motions and accepted four; in the next three (1963–6) he refused nineteen and accepted none.

In December 1966 the Select Committee on Procedure, after seven meetings, proposed a new form of words: 'a specific and important matter that should have urgent consideration'. The House agreed, and such debates have recently been less rare.

At about the same time reforms of financial procedure confirmed the real status of the twenty-nine supply days per session as occasions on which the Opposition chooses the subject for debate. The old rules imposed some tiresome limitations, based on tradition. With ingenuity it was usually possible to circumvent them, but esoteric skill was required, and it was relevant only to the bending of time-honoured rules to suit modern needs. Now there is no special problem. The Opposition managers know that they have their twenty-nine days in the session, or on average nearly one per week, and the days are taken so as to follow general convenience and the needs of the bargaining process.

K

Private members' motions supplement the supply days, on a non-partisan plane. After the gap of 1940–8 the sessional order giving major priority to government business has provided for a certain number of Fridays (about six) in each session to be set aside for motions moved by private members. It would be hard to find a party-free device for allocating the time, so a ballot is used for each of these days. Every member who is enthusiastic enough puts his name into the ballot, and the winner for the day has to decide to move and argue for a motion expressing a definite opinion about some matter. If he has no strong idea of his own he may act on the suggestion of colleagues, or of his party whips who know of topics that groups within the party wish to have discussed.

The nature of debate in the Commons chamber has inherent defects. Few people but the minister involved stay throughout the six hours or so that a full day's debate lasts, and public reporting can only be fragmentary, but the series of speeches which make up a debate, even though publicly reported in fragments only, provides a volume of argument of some value and appropriateness. All the same, the parliamentary contribution to decision making could be enriched by other processes, making provision for more solid argument than is likely to be produced through the clash of Government and Opposition, and the new committees of the past seven years have groped a little way towards the achievement of a better-informed and more coherent critique.

17

Parliament: Conclusion

Each of the procedures which we have discussed, on legislation, finance and current policy, is merely an expression of the overall purpose of Parliament, with respect to a particular object. The House of Commons votes by division, with the names of those voting recorded, about 300 times each year. On a small proportion of the divisions the Members are left free to vote as they think fit, but the great majority of votes are rather artificial because the Government is sure to obtain its majority. Now and again there is great excitement over a few abstentions by government supporters, but even then the decisions are not made just by the fact of more people voting one way than another way; they are made by ministers who then get their decisions confirmed by the parliamentary majority. Things that are said in Parliament may influence a minister, but other factors influence him more. An individual member of the Government's party may have more influence over the decision through speaking in a private meeting of a party committee, or the weekly full party meeting, than through speaking on the floor of the House, but his words in the party meeting are influential only because they are spoken in a parliamentary context.

How, then, should we assess the role of the individual Member of Parliament in the Constitution? The role of Parliament as a whole includes the sum total of the individual roles, but it is also much more than this.

THE MEMBER AND HIS CONSTITUENCY

First, an MP represents the people of his constituency; he provides for their participation in public affairs at second hand. He learns about their needs through making himself accessible for individual contact and by meeting groups and spokesmen of groups. He also learns from his own local party people, who themselves have further contacts. When necessary, he tries to get things sorted out by himself making contact with ministers, and at some points, particularly when a minister has failed to give satisfaction, he may raise matters in the House itself. He has then a role to play as an intermediary in the processes of public participation in public decisions. Some Members find all this rather irksome, because they prefer to devote their energies to larger questions of policy. Also, Members are not particularly well equipped for making themselves sufficiently knowledgeable about the vast variety of particular and unrelated local problems with which they have to deal. The creation of the office of Parliamentary Commissioner is a response to this valid complaint. It should both get the problems handled more effectively and relieve the Member of a burden under which he must inevitably flounder.

THE MEMBER AND THE NATION

The second main function of all Members of Parliament is to represent the whole United Kingdom. Burke's doctrine, that no Member is a mere delegate of his constituency, is scarcely relevant in modern conditions, in which the MP may think carefully about some national issues but votes with his party, save on very rare occasions when he is sure that his party is wrong. This is not a very demanding task, but related to the party's own internal communications it is not merely futile. More significant is the MPs contribution through discussion, formal and informal, to decisions which are not inherently partisan. The procedures which have been described give him little scope for such contribution. Other procedures, designed to increase that scope, have been persistently advocated for sixty years, but with virtually no success before the 1960s, and with only moderate success since 1965.

Proposals for specialised committees have always been opposed by strong elements of parliamentary and governmental opinion. The oldest objection has a constitutional basis. It has been claimed repeatedly that as each minister is responsible for his own field of affairs his overall responsibility would be damaged if a parliamentary committee became closely involved with it. This argument rests upon an assumption that once a transport committee (for example) was established it would begin to be a rival to the minister in the decision-making process. There is not the slightest reason why this should happen A transport committee would bring together a number of Members of Parliament who could spend part of their time making themselves thoroughly knowledgeable about matters concerned with transport, so they they could collectively contribute well informed and positive ideas, as well as more effective criticism, to the minister's decision making. A transport committee would probably increase somewhat the influence of Parliament on the eventual decision making, in relation to the influence already exercised by interest-groups, but such a development would be in no way in conflict with any new or old constitutional principle. A minister's responsibility could be made more meaningful and real, not less, if Parliament were more effectively equipped.

The second objection to the institution of committees comes from those who still like to see Parliament as essentially a place in which great political battles, arguments over major principles, and a continuous election campaign are carried on. In the Parliament interpreted in this light there is plenty of room for rhetoric and debating skill, extended even to conflicts within parties.

It can be replied that a continuous battle on this level is unlikely either to influence the actions of a Government during its term of office or to interest the public, however much it may gratify the self-esteem of the parliamentarians engaged in it. A Member's individual success or lack of it at this business may be measured by the increase or decrease of the population of the Commons Chamber itself during his speech, but if a speech has no effect on the vote when the House divides, and no effect on the ministers' decisions, the public may well feel that a Parliament so engaged is being merely self-indulgent.

Speeches on the floor of the House of Commons are unlikely to lead to the replacement of a minister by a new one who will produce new or modified policies. A series of speeches in any particular debate could conceivably contribute to a modification of a large and complex policy, but only if the speeches were based on study and analysis profound enough to expose the inadequacy of the foundations of the policy currently being promoted. Even so, the parliamentary speech is, by its nature and its whole environment, a feeble device in a complex argument. Almost any serious discussion of a contemporary problem demands close argument over tables of statistics, which the participants must all have thoroughly studied. Without such study there can be no effective criticism. Without an opportunity for close argument about the tables, between people who have the equipment to see the significance of the figures, there can be no meaningful discussion. Skill, time and enthusiasm are needed if the gaps, inconsistencies and distortions in the statistics are to be exposed. A study of debates in the Commons gives little evidence of any dedicated application of such skills, and it is doubtful whether the floor of the House is really a forum in which such skills could practicably be deployed. But if Parliament is to provide a counterweight to the undeniable dangers of bureaucratic decision making, there is a need for an informed parliamentary contribution, with procedures and facilities adapted to the task. The new growth of the scale of government suggests that, if the constitutional system is to be true to itself, there is a task for Parliament to perform, and to which Parliament has not yet adequately adapted itself.

To take some examples, it is clear that the decisions on Concorde, Maplin Airport and the Channel Tunnel were presented to Parliament by ministers who had not studied the options available, on the basis of answers (however expensively produced) to only some of the questions involved; and that Parliament approved these projects without adequate information or discussion.

It seems likely that a system of committees, through and in which some Members of Parliament could take the necessary time and trouble to study adequately the long- and short-term problems of the time, would be the most promising foundation upon which to build a more effective parliamentary role. This does not mean that it would be enough merely to set up committees; their forms, procedures and conditions of work would determine their effectiveness, and it is doubtful whether committees such as have been used up to the early 1970s are altogether suitable for the new tasks. It is not even certain whether adequate committees would be built within the existing House of Commons structure; the Second House of Parliament might well have a role to play. But it seems fair to say now that some kind of extended committee structure is a first requirement for the filling of a serious gap in Parliament's effectiveness.

The new committees set up between 1966 and 1970 were an attempt to respond to the new needs. Some with fields of interest corresponding with government departments were short-lived; some dealing with very special continuing aspects of the national life have been recognised as useful devices for dealing with their special fields. One with a broad field of interest, science and technology, has taken up a series of important questions and has perhaps come nearer than any other to success in responding to changed conditions. But the experience of all the committees at that time showed how much innovation was necessary if any committees were to become effective.

If the MP is to become an expert in a particular field, able to talk on equal terms with ministers backed by the mass of information obtained from their civil servants, both directly and through what the civil servants learn from outside contacts, he requires substantial material facilities, not merely secretarial assistance, but assistance with research and in the management of the documentation which is now necessary before a person can be really knowledgeable about any topic.

After the change of government in 1970 the only committees of this type to continue were those which were not connected with departments (race relations, the Parliamentary Commissioner, and Scottish affairs).

On the other hand, the conversion of the old Select Committee on Estimates into one on expenditure was designed to produce at least some of the objectives of the movement for reform. The new Expenditure Committee has sub-committees working in designated fields, with the intention that some at least of their members should serve for long terms. Also, the committee can now consider broad issues of policy, long-term as well as short-term, and is freed from the ill-defined constraints from which the old Estimates Committee suffered. It is provided with more assistance than its predecessor. It is too small to bring any great new features into the working of Parliament, but it has kept the new trends alive in a still modest form.

Several strands in the functions of Parliament can be identified, but there is no general agreement about the balance of importance between them. The three obvious functions of approving taxes and expenditure, making laws, and checking on current policy are all to some degree formal. These functions need to be redefined in terms of Parliament discussing the Government's economic policies, its proposed reforms, and its stewardship of public affairs (including above all its handling of crises), and all of them at several levels, short term and long term, broad and narrow, general and particular. Constitutional forms determine three main roles for the individual Member. First, he represents all the people in his constituency, and speaks for their particular local interests. Second, he is a member of his party, which for the time being is either the party of Government or the party of Opposition, striving to win the next general election, engaged in a series of clashes which bring excitement and publicity. Third, he is either already in his party's leadership-group, a minister or potential minister or shadow, or he is an aspirant to such a position, or he has no personal hope; but in any of these cases he is one of about two or three or four hundred members who collectively contribute in various ways to the choice of the leadership-group.

But the Government's ability to win every division imposes other demands on Parliament too: that with every decision of substance there should be a parliamentary process capable of bringing into the open every prejudice or bureaucratic immobility, or failure to plan or calculate with adequate care. The House of Commons does this fairly well, but not thoroughly. The recent reforms have improved the opportunities for such relatively unexciting work, but five years' experience suggests that enthusiasm for it is not widespread. Perhaps the more traditional roles are too absorbing to leave much room for anything else. Constituency work may be petty, the party battle artificial, and the leadership selection inward-looking, but they are not too dully laborious, and they are on the whole convivial tasks, besides being the ones prescribed by normal expectations. It may be that another House of Parliament, a reformed upper House perhaps, could really be better equipped for a continuing function of looking at the numerous administrative processes which modern needs have so greatly multiplied and inflated.

It may be that the best solution would be through use of the second House of Parliament, probably by the addition of some 200 salaried elected Members. Election in big constituencies (one, two or three constituencies per nation or region, each with about three to ten or even fifteen seats) by proportional representation would have several advantages. It would create a meaningful representation of regions, which is now lacking; it would introduce to Parliament an element reflecting national opinion more soundly than the Commons (where the overall majority always reflects a minority of the national vote). The restrictions on the Lords' powers through the Parliament Act would preserve the constitutional balance. The prospect of serving on serious committees would not only attract aspiring politicians of high calibre, but give them better preparation for ministerial office than life in the House of Commons can provide. If ministers were allowed to attend debates and speak in either House they might then continue to seek election to the Lords. Otherwise some of them would probably switch to the Commons, enriched by the apprenticeship which committee service would afford to them. A second House so constituted, with an elected element added to life peers, would be outside the main party battles and its members would be freer than Commons MPs to give their time and skill to that thorough study of concrete problems and choices which is needed if Parliament is adequately to check a modern Government's processes.

18

The House of Lords

The House of Lords, as it is in 1974, is a rather unimportant part of the British constitutional system, and it is tempting at this point to spend a couple of pages in giving only a minimal description of its composition and powers. We might then have added that it is likely to be reformed before long. But there are two good reasons for looking at this slightly embarrassing survival at some length: first, the Constitution at any given time is a product of its past; and second, there are many factors about the development of the Upper House, even during the twentieth century, which illustrate particularly well the character of the Constitution, and the ways in which it responds to socio-economic change.

The medieval assembly of barons and church notables, from which the House of Lords developed, may be said to have had a representative role in the society of that time, and that role did not become meaningless when elected knights and burgesses were summoned to Parliament in addition. Even up to the nineteenth century the great lords' prestige was sustained by universal deference to them, so that they still had a proper part in a body representing the nation.

In Bagehot's deferential society a hundred years ago, the House of Lords was still complementary to the Commons, but its legitimacy (in terms of accepted values) began to be seriously eroded after 1886. By the mid-twentieth century there was no longer any societal justification for a non-elected House. Aristocratic assemblies had disappeared from parliaments in all developed societies, and the egalitarian movement was stronger, both socially and economically, in Britain than in many of the countries which had abolished formal hereditary power. However, the House of Lords has survived till 1974, with its hereditary element intact (though modified), because it is still performing a useful function and because no urgent need for fundamental change has yet appeared. Meanwhile its powers had been restricted by legislation, and the ultimate ability of the Government to flood it with new peers, so as to gain a majority, forced it to take care.

THE LORDS' POWERS

An early restriction of the Lords' functions can be traced back to a Commons resolution of 1671: 'That in all aids given to the King by the Commons, the rate or tax ought not to be altered by the Lords.' This was followed by another in 1678: 'That all aids and supplies, and aids to his Majesty in Parliament, are the sole gift of the Commons; and all bills for the granting of any such aids and supplies ought to begin with the Commons; and that it is the undoubted and sole right of the Commons to direct, limit, and appoint in such bills the ends, purposes, considerations, conditions, limitations, and qualifications of such grants, which ought not to be changed or altered by the House of Lords.'

It was already established practice that proposals for taxation and expenditure should originate in the Commons, and the Lords made no demur. An expression of purpose of the Commons, though not embodied in legislation, provided an important constitutional definition, and it is still effective. Along with this went an assumption that the Lords should not *reject* any financial proposal; there seemed to be a convention that public money concerned the Commons alone. Apart from this there was no statutory definition of the relative roles of the two Houses of Parliament. Meanwhile the formal power of the House of Lords declined as the convention of Government responsibility to the Commons grew, and its real power declined when its members could no longer influence elections to the House of Commons.

The present century has seen a succession of statutes giving definition to the powers and status of the House of Lords, corresponding with the changing values of society. The old ascriptive basis under which a person deserved great respect because of who he was, and particularly if he was a peer, has given way to a set of values which rejects inherited position as a valid basis for political power.

The first statutory definition of a reduced power for the House of Lords did not come until the passing of the Parliament Act of 1911. Every bill had to pass through both Houses, and until then there was nothing to stop the House of Lords from rejecting a bill. Under the 1911 Act, if a bill passed the House of Commons in three consecutive sessions in essentially the same form, it was to go to the King for the royal assent even if the Lords rejected it each time. The same applied if the Lords introduced amendments which were unacceptable to the Commons. In 1949 a further Parliament Act was passed reducing the Lords' delaying power from three sessions to two, or effectively from about two years to about one year (or in practice rather less).

These statutes could almost be regarded as constitutional amendments, extended by what appear to be conventions which still further restrict the powers of the House of Lords. By 1945 it was clearly accepted that the Lords should pass any bill which had been included in a party's programme at the time of a general election, and that they should not insist upon amendments which the Commons rejected. Apart from the 1948–9 Parliament Bill, which was passed over the Lords' veto, no government bill was rejected by the House of Lords between 1914 and 1973 and the Lords did not insist on any really substantial amendment against the Government's wishes between 1945 and 1972, except over the timing of steel nationalisation in 1949; also their amendments to the bill on parliamentary boundaries in 1969 were equivalent to rejection.[1] Thus the Lords, having been deprived of the power of veto by the Parliament Act of 1911, have in fact chosen not even to use the power of delay that is left to them in so far as it concerns legislation proposed by the Government.

It has been suggested that the House of Lords should make a distinction between a bill foreseen in the governing party's election programme and a bill not so foreseen. But this suggestion depends on the doctrine that a party which wins a general election has a mandate to carry out the measures foreseen in its election programme, but no mandate to carry out any other measures. This doctrine was accepted by some around 1910, but is manifestly unrealistic because circumstances change within the life of a Parliament. The governing party's election programme can only indicate *some* specific intentions and an intended approach to policy. We cannot rely on so imprecise a definition. All we can say now is that it seems improbable that the House of Lords, as now constituted, would reject any Government bill, or insist on unacceptable amendments. The most likely occasion for an exception would be under a Labour Government, if a Conservative Opposition calculated that it would gain long-run political advantage from such action.

The 1911 Parliament Act was at the time intended to be provisional, to last until some major reform should resolve the problem of irreconcilable differences between the two Houses. The imaginable devices were all thought of: joint conference committees of the two Houses, joint sessions, or the submission of a disputed issue to a referendum. Fifty years later none of these had been adopted. The formal power of delay still survives, and now seems likely to be maintained, although the period of delay could well be further reduced and possibly hedged about.

There is a sound constitutional argument against any other device. In any issue of political importance any conflict between the two Houses is really a conflict between the Lords and the Government. But the very

[1] *See below*, pp. 157 and 179 ff.

foundation of the modern constitution is the Government's power and duty to form policies and carry them out, with the House of Commons majority as a consenting partner. Any outside interference by another House of Parliament, or by the public through a referendum, would be inconsistent with this principle, and its effect would be now little short of revolutionary. So the real issues now are no longer concerned with the formal powers of the Lords, but rather with the still narrower restrictions within which the House has worked, and with the possible adaptations of its functions within the formal and informal limits.

During the first years after 1911 the Lords made some use of their power to reject bills and thus to delay them for two years. They rejected or severely amended four important measures, and it so happened that the implementation of three of these bills under the Parliament Act was delayed, through the beginning of war in 1914, for longer than the two years. Their rejection of Home Rule for the whole of Ireland in 1912 actually led to a delay of ten years, and to the division of Ireland.

No similar conflict arose between 1918 and 1945, because except for the two short-lived minority Labour Governments the Conservative Party was in power, alone or as a dominant partner, all through the period. By the time a Labour Government entered office with a solid majority in 1945 the atmosphere had changed, and the Conservative majority did not use even its delaying power, except with the 1948–9 bill to cut its own formal power, and with the nationalisation of steel – and in this case it did no more than put off the vesting date for a short time, pending a new general election.

Between 1964 and 1970 the Conservative majority, faced again with a Labour Government, stayed well within its formal powers. Between 1964 and 1968 they agreed to many unpalatable bills sent from the Commons, and on the permissive society legislation of the period the Lords 'assisted rather then impeded reform'.[1] They made some amendments to Government bills against the Government's wishes, but did not insist on the amendments which the Commons rejected. Back-bench peers of the Conservative Party, together with Liberals and Independents, voted with the Opposition leadership to reject the section of the War Damage Bill of 1965 which amounted to retrospective legislation, but the amendment was not insisted on the second time round.

It was only in 1968–9 that the Lords really did make use of their surviving powers. The Parliament Acts had left untouched the Lords' power to reject a statutory instrument requiring the approval of both Houses of Parliament. The Lords rejected the Rhodesian Sanctions Order in 1968. They did not interfere with the Government's policy by

[1] P. G. Richards, *Parliament and Conscience* (Allen & Unwin, 1970), p. 203.

this action, because the order was simply made again, and passed. But they did cause irritation. In 1969 they introduced wrecking amendments to a Government bill which had to be passed at once, if at all. This was the bill to relieve the Home Secretary of his statutory duty to lay before Parliament the changes in constituency boundaries proposed, in accordance with the existing law, by the Boundary Commissioners. The Lords took this exceptional action on the ground that the bill was an interference with the electoral process for the advantage of the Government party. It was difficult to say that the bill was unconstitutional, but it was certainly against the understandings of the Constitution, and it maintained gross and outrageous inequalities of representation. The United States Supreme Court had found that much smaller inequalities deprived American citizens of their right to proper representation in the House of Representatives. Thus the Lords seem to have been 'right', in a constitutional sense, in mutilating this bill, though their action had no effect because it was circumvented.[1] So we have now a precedent for action by the Lords in support of citizens' rights against improper invasion by an unscrupulous Government supported by a House of Commons majority. But it is unlikely that the precedent is of any long-term significance.

JUDICIAL FUNCTIONS

One archaic part of the House of Lords' work that survives is its function as the highest court of justice. In the fourteenth century it was possible to appeal from the Court of King's Bench to Parliament, and in 1485 the judges held that for such appeals 'Parliament' meant the House of Lords. The thread of continuity in the Lords' appellate jurisdiction is thin; there have been many changes. The appellate role as it exists today is mainly quite modern. Appeal from the Court of Criminal Appeal to the House was provided for as recently as 1907.

By 1844 it was recognised that only those peers who had appropriate qualifications ought to attend the meetings of the House which performed judicial functions.[2] The Appellate Jurisdiction Act, 1876, allowed the Crown to confer peerages for life only on a number of judges, and thus recognised the distinct quality of the House's function as the supreme court. For a long time every sitting of the House of Lords as a court has been attended only by persons appointed to high judicial office, either as Lords of Parliament or as Lord Chancellor.

Until 1950 the judicial sittings were held in the Lords' debating

[1] *See below*, p. 179.
[2] Cf. Hood Phillips, *Constitutional and Administrative Law* (Sweet & Maxwell, 4th edn, 1967), p. 128.

chamber, although that arrangement was most inconvenient in every way, and made it necessary for the legislative sessions to begin inconveniently later in the day. In 1950 building operations made it almost impossible for the judicial sittings to be held in the main chamber, and the House agreed to allow them to be held in a committee room upstairs. The majority view insisted that this must be regarded as a temporary expedient, because the Constitution required that the House of Lords as a court should be obviously the House of Lords and not some sort of small committee sitting in another place. However, the temporary conditions lasted for two years, and the arrangement was found to be so convenient and rational that when the special need for it disappeared the judicial sittings continued to be held separately.

The House of Lords' judicial functions are thus now performed for it by a committee of its members. If the House of Lords were abolished that element of it which performs the work as the supreme court could continue with only formal change. The Courts Act, 1971, which made sweeping changes in the administration of justice, did not interfere with the judicial functions of the House of Lords, because there was no evidence that any change in this part of the system would be likely to produce any concrete advantages.

REFORM OF COMPOSITION, 1958 AND 1963

Two important statutes concerning the composition of the House of Lords have been passed in recent years, the Life Peerages Act of 1958 and the Peerage Act of 1963. Both made real innovations in the Constitution, supplanting practices not defined by statute, but authoritatively accepted as being so well entrenched that they could not be departed from except on the basis of new statutory definition.

The Act of 1958 allowed the Crown to grant peerages for life only. As the Crown had, year after year, granted new hereditary peerages, and as there was no statutory prohibition against the grant of life peerages, it might well be thought that the Crown was able to confer peerages for life only, if it should wish to do so, without any new authority. The matter was put to the test in 1856, when, on the Prime Minister's advice, the Crown did just that. (The Government wanted to add some senior judges to the House of Lords so as to strengthen it as the highest court, without adding to the House in perpetuity the heirs of ennobled judges.) But the House found that because all new peerages conferred in the past 300 years had been generally accepted as being hereditary, a peerage must by its nature be hereditary; there could be no such thing as a life peerage in the then existing Constitution, unless it were provided for by statute.

This particular problem was finally dealt with in 1876 when the Appellate Jurisdiction Act allowed life peerages to be given to two judges (Lords of Appeal in Ordinary). The number was increased to six in 1913, seven in 1929 and nine in 1947. It was not until 1958 that further legislation allowed life peerages to be given to people other than judges.

Since 1958 the new law has been filled out by undefined practices, which must be regarded as part of the effective Constitution in 1974.

From the earliest times the grant of a peerage had signified that the recipient had earned a great reward by his distinguished acts. The peerage recognised his illustriousness, and being hereditary perpetuated it. The political implication of this was that peerages were expected to be given only to people whom the Government wished to reward, such as retiring ministers. This doctrine had worn rather thin long before 1958, but it still meant that the Prime Minister did not recommend political opponents for peerages. The result was that, when the Labour Party became the alternative major party to the Conservatives but was out of office for a long time, the Opposition was grotesquely under-represented in what was, after all, still a House of Parliament in a political system based on interplay between Government and Opposition.

Ramsay MacDonald, as Prime Minister in the 1924 and 1929–31 Labour Governments, might well have redressed the balance by conferring numerous peerages on party supporters, but a lavish distribution of honours would have been too sharp an innovation for his taste, and anyway his party as a whole was hostile to all hereditary privilege. His recommendations were not exceptionally lavish. A few peerages were given to Labour supporters under the war-time coalition, when the Labour Party was in the Government, and between 1945 and 1951 Attlee was fairly liberal with his political awards. But by 1958 the Conservatives had been in power for seven years, and the work of opposition was languishing somewhat because it was shared among only a few people.

With the passing of the Life Peerages Act it became accepted that a life peerage was not necessarily, even in appearance, a great reward for great merit. In some cases the Prime Minister consulted the Leader of the Opposition before advising the Crown to confer peerages, and made it publicly known that he had done so, and this became a regular practice. The Life Peerages Act was not a necessary condition for such a development, but it facilitated it.

Under the Conservative Government of 1958–64 some hereditary peerages were conferred, in addition to the life peerages, and the distinction kept alive the old idea of reward. But in the six years of Labour

Government between 1964 and 1970 there were no hereditary honours at all. The position by 1970 well illustrates the nature of precedent in constitutional practice. Certainly quite a substantial body of precedent against the conferment of hereditary peerages had been built up, and there were sound and evident reasons for total discontinuance. It was still for the incoming Conservative Prime Minister to decide whether or not he would follow this precedent. He did follow it for his first three years in office, but made it known that he considered himself free to depart from it.

Meanwhile, the old idea of reward has been preserved, or suggested, in a rather subtle way. Some life peerages have been conferred in the Birthday and New Year Honours Lists, along with the numerous lesser orders by which the State rewards solid or brilliant services or achievements. Other life peerages have been given in separate lists at other convenient times. But this practice, if it is one, is not of much significance, and is certainly not binding.

The House of Lords even in 1974 still maintains a real continuity with its past; some of the principal notables in the land, having had peerages conferred on them, are included in its membership. The continuing presence of Members by right of succession is, however, not only in conflict with the fairly well-established rejection of hereditary privilege; it is also a source of dilution to the element of the 'notables'. The prestige derived from the mere fact of having succeeded to a peerage has greatly declined in recent years. Many peers by succession do in fact work hard to make a very useful and constructive contribution to the work of Parliament, so that it is wrong to judge their presence as though they were upholding class or personal interests. But much opinion sees them above all as a group whose claim to be part of Parliament is based on a false and rejected legitimacy.

As for the peers who have their places by personal appointment to life peerages, hereditary peerages or bishoprics, their collective legitimacy too is diluted – more so since the passing of the 1958 Life Peerages Act than before. Some indeed have their places through great merit (including solid work for their political parties). Their rewards for services to State or party are combined with a prospect that they may contribute usefully to the discussion of public policy. They both receive and give. Perhaps we may say that the greater their acknowledged achievements, the less their duty to work at routine parliamentary tasks. But peerages have also been conferred in order to give a voice in Parliament to particular groups of people, and the grounds of choice in these cases, already fuzzy thirty years ago, have become more indistinct since 1958. The ennobled doctors, academics and so on have been for the most part quite meritorious in their fields, but not invariably more meritorious than numerous colleagues who were not ennobled. They have been chosen, it seems, with a view to their potential useful contributions (probably after informal consultation with elite elements among their special groups). But they have neither election nor measurably recognised achievement to earn even a modest reflection of the deference which was paid in the past.

The confusion about the nature of a peerage was still further confused by the reform of 1963. After 1922, when Lord Curzon was passed over for the Prime Ministership, it looked as though that precedent had come near to establishing a convention that a peer could not be Prime Minister. Membership of the Upper House had become a clear disadvantage to a serious politician (particularly in the Labour Party whose values enjoin dislike of such an undemocratic body). However, it was not until 1960 that a peer attempted to renounce a peerage. That attempt produced a whole series of new constitutional definitions, beginning with the Peerage Act of 1963, under which a person who inherits a peerage may renounce it for his own lifetime, and thus become eligible to sit in the House of Commons. Before the Act was passed it was not clear what the constitutional position really was; but because no peerage had ever been renounced, the House of Commons decided, on the advice of its Committee of Privileges, that there was no right to renounce a peerage. The whole nature of peerage, and of membership of the House of Lords, was based on practice, so that positive and negative precedents must be regarded as authoritative. So long as no actual difficulty arose over people who inherited peerages, there was no cause for Parliament to look at the problem.

In 1895 the first Earl of Selborne died. His heir, then in the Commons, succeeded to the peerage and decided that he would prefer to remain in the Lower House. There was no law to prevent his doing so, so he tried the simple expedient of entering the Commons Chamber in the usual way as though nothing had happened. He was called up to withdraw on the ground that he had automatically lost his membership, and a committee was set up to decide just what his position was – and incidentally to produce a definition of a part of the Constitution that was uncertain.

The committee had before it two possibilities. Either it could say that peers were not eligible for the Commons merely because they were peers, and that a traditional practice had created an assumption that was part of the Constitution. Or it could say that the practice depended on a rational cause – that it was because they were already in Parliament, but in the Upper House, that peers were excluded from the Commons. If it took the second, more rational, line the consequence would be that any MP succeeding in future could continue to be eligible for the Com-

L

mons, because he would not have a seat in the Lords until he took the necessary steps to establish his claim.

The committee could have followed either line, and the advice of at least one high authority, the clerk of the House of Commons, was against automatic disqualification. But it did decide for disqualification, and in doing so it seemed to be upholding a general principle of much wider implications: that in case of uncertainty about a constitutional point, a practice when often repeated constituted a rule in its own right, without regard to the reason for the existence of the practice.

During the next sixty years several Members of Parliament succeeded to peerages and went uncomplaining to the House of Lords, though some of them had some regret, in particular Mr Quintin Hogg when he became Lord Hailsham. He seemed to have become ineligible for the premiership, but he was not shunted into obscurity. His standing in the Conservative Party did not suffer, as the events of 1963 were to show.

A front rank politician derives his standing not only from office as a minister or shadow minister, but from his standing in his party, and however much the Conservative Party may have been ready to accept its peers as serious politicians, a peer in the Labour Party was badly placed. In 1955 Mr Anthony Wedgwood Benn, a Labour MP but heir to his father's peerage, did not readily accept the prospect of being removed from the Commons. Any constitutional practice can be supplanted by legislation, so an attempt was made to have Parliament pass a personal bill to exempt Mr Benn from the consequences of the future succession to the peerage. The bill was rejected on government advice on the ground that no such bill had ever been passed before and that a general change in the law was required for a constitutional innovation of this kind. For a time no such change was made.

On 17 November 1960 Mr Benn succeeded to the peerage on his father's death. He wrote out a document purporting to be a renunciation of his peerage and deposited it at Buckingham Palace. Nobody had ever done such a thing before. The Palace knew nothing of any procedure for the renouncing of peerages, and Mr Benn's act of renunciation was disgorged on governmental advice, as though it was a non-document. So the question that had been asked in 1895 was reopened.

The 1895 decision may have been unreasonable, but it had created a precedent, and precedents are usually followed unless new arguments can be brought forward. The Commons Committee of Privileges, to which the matter was referred, followed the 1895 decision. Mr Benn's seat was therefore vacant. Arrangements were accordingly made for a by-election to be held. But although Benn was disqualified there was no constitutional provision to prevent him from offering himself as a candidate again. The local Labour Party adopted him, his candidature was accepted, the election took place and he won with an enormous majority – much bigger than at the previous general election. He was prevented from taking his seat by a ruling that he was disqualified. Mr Benn's defeated opponent brought the matter before the Election Court, consisting of two high court judges. They decided, after proceedings which cost £7,000 and lasted for more than a week, that Benn had not been properly elected because he was disqualified, and that therefore the candidate who had received the next largest number of votes (in other words the defeated Conservative candidate) was the duly elected member. He thereupon entered the House of Commons and sat for the constituency in the meantime. This outcome was obviously absurd and in a real sense unconstitutional.

In response to the pressure for legislation to set this wrong right, the Government introduced a bill to make it possible for a peer to renounce his peerage, and that bill was passed in 1963. Mr Benn renounced his peerage immediately, and was soon afterwards elected to the House of Commons again, the Conservative Member having resigned when Benn became eligible.

The Peerage Act of 1963 was passed in response to a new situation which arose not only from the changes in the relative positions of the two Houses of Parliament, but also in particular from the realities of power and influence within one of the two major political parties. Indirectly it implied recognition of the inferior standing of the House of Lords, and the sequel took the decline further. In October 1963, when Macmillan resigned as Prime Minister, two Conservative peers, Lords Hailsham and Home, were of sufficient standing in their party to be regarded as possible successors – and Lord Home was in fact appointed. Lord Hailsham had lost no time in announcing that he would give up his peerage, and Lord Home renounced his immediately after being appointed Prime Minister. There were grounds for believing that any peer who remained in the House of Lords, even in the Conservative Party, was opting out of the front rank of politics, and that the place of the House of Lords in the constitutional system could not fail to be affected by this development. In fact, however, this has not happened. Since 1970 the Upper House has included the Secretary of State for Defence; the Opposition's objections have seemed merely to follow a routine, and Lord Carrington's standing in Government and party has not been adversely affected. The Upper House's newfound vigour and effectiveness, derived from the Life Peerages Act, was not at all diminished.

The abortive Lords reform scheme of 1968–9 was ingenious, elegant and civilised. We need not now look at it in detail; having been once abandoned it is unlikely to be revived. Very briefly, it would have allowed all who were at that time members of the Upper House to continue to attend and speak. All those members who had themselves had peerages conferred on them would have been voting members for life too (so long as they maintained a reasonable record of attendance). And the scope for conferring life peerages, with a voting right, was so designed that most of those peers by succession who had already earned their passage by assiduity in attendance would also be able to keep their full membership. It was a solution marvellously in agreement with British constitutional traditions, respecting the interests which deserved to be respected and designed to enable the House of Lords to continue to perform its useful functions, a little more effectively than hitherto.

There were some apparent weaknesses, but they could all be reasonably defended. Democratic purists could complain at the preservation of some of the hereditary element, even for a term – but after all, those Members who owed their seats to heredity alone, being unable to vote, could take no part in the decisions of the reformed House. The opposite argument, that a House with two classes of Members, voting and non-voting, would be an embarrassingly artificial community, had caused objections to a two-writ scheme some years before, but the proposed regime was no longer attacked on this ground.

It was a little harder to counter the argument that the reform would leave too much scope for patronage, with too little control or restriction. Although the Prime Minister was to have appropriate consultations before making his new appointments, the voting membership of the reformed Upper House would still have been composed mainly of people who owed their seats and voting rights to the decisions of a few party leaders, currently in office or having recently been in office. However, Prime Ministers have already had this kind of patronage power for a long time, and have used it sensibly, and beneficiaries have not been expected to show gratitude by political subservience.

On balance, the scheme was quite a good one, so long as the intention was merely to retain an Upper House, continuing the same functions as the old House of Lords but on a more acceptable basis of membership. The House reformed in this way would have been well equipped to continue with the same role in the constitutional system as before – holding some well-informed debates, doing useful work in revising bills; useful but not absolutely necessary, because bills might well be considered more effectively as a result of quite different reforms. But it could not have equipped the second House of Parliament for performing any new functions – and there are some functions which are asking to be performed.

There are two potential and proper functions of Parliament which now go more or less by default: detailed examination of administrative policy, and representation of the nations and regions of the kingdom. The House of Commons has tried to fill the first gap to some extent, through the new committees which operated in the last four years of the Labour Government (1966–70). But by 1970 it had to be admitted that the new committees had only gone a short way towards filling this gap. The attempt to add a new role to the House of Commons ran into the difficulty that the House was already fully occupied with its existing tasks. The second gap, that of providing representation of regional interests in Parliament, could never be convincingly filled by the House of Commons.

The Second Chamber might well be the right body to fill these two gaps. But if it is to do this, it must be reconstructed much more thoroughly, in such a way that there is real representation of the public. This might be through direct or indirect election through region-wide constituencies, preferably each with several members chosen by proportional representation, which might provide a healthy counterweight to the majority-dominated Commons.

These two gaps are serious. For Scotland and Wales the big support for Nationalist candidates at by-elections reflects a need for national representation within the UK Parliament which is not now fulfilled. Within England regional consciousness is variable and fluctuating, but normally dormant mainly because it lacks means of expression. Membership of the EEC, within which geographical areas of 5 to 15 million people have some real political significance, gives new grounds for promoting a sense of identity in the English sub-divisions of this size. Distinct parliamentary representation is one device through which a meaningful regional sense could be promoted.

Politics operate on several dimensions of ideological commitment, of geography and of mere intelligent choice between options. The middle ranges, such as energy and transport policy, tend to be decided by professional administrators whose policies are not adequately examined.[1] Such examination is necessary, because it is at this level, a second level of politics, that bureaucratic incompetence and prejudice offer the most serious dangers.

The House of Commons takes care of the first and third levels of

---

[1] The Government's commitment to a third London airport, through the years 1969–73, was never adequately challenged. Its persistent failure to see the problem as a part of transport policy has been examined in the author's *Great White Elephant of Maplin Sands* (Paul Elek, 1973). As far as Parliament is concerned, the story suggests the importance of the gaps, both at regional level and at the level of the nuts and bolts of decision making.

politics reasonably well; its attempts to deal with the middle level, both geographical and ideological, have been unsuccessful. This level lacks political sex-appeal, but in reality it includes the most important fields of choice in the politics of the modern world.

So long as the Upper House remains unreformed, its formal powers are unlikely to be increased. A Labour Government may well be inclined to seek to reduce to six months its power to delay bills under the Parliament Act, and to remove or modify the power to reject statutory instruments. Such changes would have little significance, as the House has left its surviving formal powers almost unused. The background of the Parliament Act, together with a sense of political realism, has been more significant than the Act itself. That background showed that a significant conflict between the two Houses, being in effect a conflict between the Lords and a Government in power, could be resolved in a manner damaging to the Lords, either through creation of new peers or with the help of a general election in which the Lords and the Conservative Party would be represented in an unfavourable light. Such a conflict would be unlikely to arise even under a Labour Government unless the full Conservative leadership were to expect it to bring a real advantage to their party – and this would be unlikely.

Even a reformed Upper House might well have fewer powers than the Lords of 1974, but any rational reform would surely remove the Government's power to create unlimited numbers of peers so as to secure a majority for itself, and thus remove a major source of weakness. Even so, the new role of a Upper House might still involve more effective discussion, more effective probing, rather than a use of any formal powers.

Elections

THE FUNCTION OF ELECTIONS

Article III of the French Fifth Republic Constitution begins with these words: 'National Sovereignty belongs to the people, who exercise it through elected representatives and by process of referendum.' No British statute states or implies that the people are exercising a sovereign function when they choose representatives. However, as the Queen must rule through ministers who are responsible to the House of Commons, that House must presumably derive its authority from some source, and this can surely be none other than the people who have chosen it. So it would appear that a principle such as that of the French Constitution (and many others) is present; it is undefined because no need to define it has arisen.

To begin with, let us summarise the obvious characteristics of the electoral process:

1. Each local community chooses a person to represent it in Parliament. No matter how many candidates there may be, the one who gets most votes is elected.

2. The communities represented have ceased to have any necessary permanent identity; they are just geographical sub-divisions called by the neutral name 'constituencies'.

3. Each person elected is elected (a) because the leadership group of his local party chose him from several rivals as its candidate, and (b) because more people in the constituency voted for that party than for any other. So,

4. Each person elected holds his seat primarily as a party member.

5. Each seat is won by the candidate who receives most votes, and the effect of this is to encourage and maintain a two-party system.

6. The effective restriction of the choice of potential government to two parties tends to cause these two parties to cover most elements in the political spectrum.

7. Even between the two main parties the system can produce a 'wrong' result. In 1951 the Labour candidates collectively won 230,000 more votes than the Conservatives,[1] yet the Conservatives won more seats, and thus formed a Government. In 1974 the Conservatives won 300,000 more votes than Labour, but nine fewer seats.

There is no provision for a Member of Parliament to resign his seat. However, effective resignation is possible. A Member may ask to be given one of a number of sinecure 'offices of profit', and having been appointed to one of these he is automatically disqualified from membership. His seat is then vacant.

If a Member dies or resigns or becomes a peer a by-election is held to fill his seat. 'The Speaker issues his warrant to the clerk of the Crown for a new writ for the place represented by the Member whose seat is thus vacated.'[2] But the Speaker takes no action until some Member has moved a motion ordering him to do so, and by convention that motion is normally moved by the Chief Whip of the party to which the outgoing Member belonged. There is nothing to prevent excessive delay in the moving of the writ, and sometimes, if the party concerned calculates that delay will be advantageous to it, there is considerable delay. When Mr Dick Taverne resigned as Labour Member for Lincoln in 1972, with the intention of seeking re-election, but as an independent, there was such delay before the by-election that Lincoln was left unrepresented for half of the period of sitting of a parliamentary session.

A British general election is in modern times effectively a kind of plebiscite in which the whole nation chooses one of two parties to form the Government. Research into voting behaviour has shown that almost all British voters vote for a candidate because he is the party's candidate, and not because of his personal merits or policies. The form of a general election, still giving each seat in the House of Commons to the candidate who obtains the largest number of votes in his constituency,

---

[1] The actual percentages were: Labour 48·8 Conservative 48·0. Two Northern Ireland seats were uncontested, so no Unionist votes were counted in them. If they had been contested, Labour's overall lead in votes in the whole UK would have been about 0·6 per cent instead of 0·8 per cent. The number of seats won by the main parties would not have been affected. This unsatisfactory result was accepted with little complaint, and Herbert Morrison, deprived of office by the election result, used his spare time to write a book (*Government and Parliament*) in which he said that by and large the people get the government they want. The Conservative Government did not suffer in either authority or self-confidence from this essentially unsatisfactory basis for its power.

[2] Erskine May, op. cit., p. 176. A peerage does not disqualify if it is renounced under the 1963 Act.

was not devised in order to ensure that the voter's choice should be between only two parties, but the system does undoubtedly tend to prevent any other party from winning a number of seats commensurate with its nationwide electoral support.

The electors choose those whom they choose, rather than others, for some reason, which is presumably based on assumptions about what they will do during the period of office for which they have been elected. How far then are those who are elected bound to do the things which, when seeking election, they said they would do? How far ought they to abstain from doing other things, in particular things that are inconsistent with their election manifestoes?. Even if we could clearly find an answer to the question what they *ought* to do, by what means could they be obliged to do those things only? There is no clear answer.

Those who are elected have to act in response to circumstances which were unforeseeable at the time of the election. Edmund Burke's famous insistence on the MPs independence of his electors is often cited as though it had been a discovery of the true relationship. It involves a rejection of popular sovereignty exercised through elected persons. But Burke's theory can hardly be of much relevance to the behaviour of individual MPs elected for major parties, because (a) they are elected not as individuals but as party supporters, and (b) it is expected that they will vote with their parties in Parliament after they have been elected. Thus the relationship between the individual major party MP and his electors cannot be meaningfully discussed except in terms of the two-party system. Whether or not the British people's interests are adequately represented by an opportunity to choose between two parties, one of which forms the Government, the electoral system tends to ensure that one party wins a majority of seats in the House of Commons. In every general election from 1945 to 1970 the winning party obtained under half the votes cast, but was able to form a government with overall majority support in the House of Commons.

Accepting, then, that the people, through the electoral system, choose one of the parties to form the Government for up to five years, it is proper to ask what is the nature of the Government's commitment to the people? How far is it, and how far are its parliamentary supporters, bound by the terms of their election programme? How free are they to adopt new policies as they go along? Mandate theory, popular some fifty years ago, is useful only if it is accepted as a very general guide to action. It becomes unrealistic if it is applied rigidly. There are unsuperable practical difficulties in the way of a theory of the continuing dependence of elected representatives on popular sovereignty; such a theory, if expressed in a constitution, can be little more than a general statement of purpose, in a rather vague form: a Government ought not to do things which are clearly inconsistent with the approach to politics which it indicated when seeking election.

This basic question, with the tentative answer which is all that can be suggested, needs to be borne in mind in relation to the detailed study of constitutional rules and practices concerning elections, which can conveniently be divided into three main parts: the franchise, constituencies, and the timing of elections.

THE FRANCHISE

The right to vote is equal and universal for British resident citizens, and provided for by statute. Successive Acts of Parliament, passed with steadily-declining controversy over a period of 140 years, have defined new classes of people entitled to vote in parliamentary and local government elections. The last extensions of the suffrage, to women and, in 1969, to people aged between 18 and 21, seem to have brought the process of broadening to a point beyond which it can go no further.

The earlier British reforming statutes, up to that of 1918, were passed only after much argument and in some cases violence. The suffragettes' campaign before 1914 is still remembered, but the female victory in 1918 was probably due rather to the general recognition of women's new role in society rather than to the activities of the suffragettes. The later changes have come quietly. The last, the extension of the voting right to people aged under 21 but over 18, was not preceded by violent agitation, but followed as a reasonable consequence of the report of the Latey Committee which proposed that 18, instead of 21, should be the legal age of majority.

The Representation of the People Act, 1948, ended the inequality of plural voting. Until then, if a person lived in one constituency and occupied business premises he and his spouse could vote in both, and a university graduate could vote as an elector in a university constituency as well as that in which he lived. The university votes were ended by the abolition of the twelve university seats. The Conservative Opposition of that time objected strongly to the latter change, but a restoration of the university seats would now seem unthinkable.

The main class of persons excluded from voting (under the system in force up to 1974) is that of peers, on the ground that they are themselves already in Parliament as members of the House of Lords. Holders of peerages of Scotland (dating back before 1707) were put on the same footing as English or United Kingdom peers by the Peerage Act of 1963; previously they had been represented by sixteen of their number, elected by all the peers of Scotland at each general election to sit in the House of Lords for the duration of the Parliament. The reform, though it may at first sight seem trivial, illustrated some new movement in the spirit of the constitution, and also a delayed recognition of facts. On the one hand, we see the contemporary concern for eliminating all unfairness to individuals (here the forty or so Scottish peers who were not elected and before 1963 had no part in the normal process of representation through the House of Commons); on the other hand the complete disappearance of the reason for the rules of 1707. Then the Scottish peers were almost as numerous as the English, and would have affected the balance of a House of Parliament with real power; long before 1963 the automatic inclusion in the House of Lords of all the peers of Scotland had ceased to have any potential effect on politics.

Unlike the countries which make provision whereby citizens residing abroad may vote, Britain has remained content with a qualification based on actual residence in a place within the UK on a given date. This rule corresponds with the notion that each Member of Parliament represents the people of communities within the country.

LAWS ON THE CONDUCT OF ELECTIONS

As the constitutional assumptions have moved forward to the point of accepting the principle of one man one vote, together with secret ballot, so there has been a need for much detailed statutory provision aimed at ensuring that every person entitled to vote is in fact given an opportunity to do so, and that no person votes more than once. It is concerned also to prevent crude cheating, by introducing false ballot papers into the boxes, or by miscounting, and there must be confidence that the laws are obeyed. Some statutory provision has been introduced without controversy, so as to establish procedures whose object is to achieve agreed ends. Other provisions have been partisan, depending on arguable definitions of the objectives.

Nobody may vote unless registered as a voter. Local officers have the duty of compiling a new register of voters once each year. The head of each household is obliged to enter on a form the names of all the qualified persons residing in that house on 15 October, and on the basis of the information thus obtained the electoral register for each district is compiled. The qualification for inclusion is to be normally resident in a particular place at a certain date, and to be a British subject or Commonwealth citizen. The new register comes into force in February and remains in force for twelve months, during which time the right to vote is restricted to those persons whose names are on the register. Aothough voting is not compulsory, failure to register is punishable, and it is the duty of public officers to take all steps they can to see that everyone eligible is registered.

The register of electors is always somewhat out of date at the time when a general election takes place, and in the most popular month of November it is more than a year since the registration date. The 1969 Act provided for the advance registration of young people, so that any person aged 18 on election day should be registered and eligible to vote. Voting by proxy is allowed in the case of seamen resident in Britain.

If a person leaves the area in which he was living at the time of the registration he is still eligible to vote in the area in which he was registered, but not elsewhere. Until 1948 this meant that if he wanted to vote he had to travel to his old voting place, but the Representation of the People Act, 1948, provided that a person may apply for a postal vote if he has moved out of the constituency in which he was registered, or if he expects to be away for business reasons, or if he expects to be unable to go to the voting place through physical incapacity, and his vote is counted if he returns it before the day of the election.

Rather unreasonably, a person who intends to be away on holiday may not apply for a postal vote. It has been usual to avoid holiday periods for general elections. *The Observer* calculated that on 18 June 1970, 300,000 more Conservative than Labour supporters would be away. An electoral advisory conference argued that a change would be costly and open to abuse. The objections were cited by the Labour Government spokesman when a private member's bill proposed a change in May 1974.

THE FINANCING OF PERSUASION

Before the nineteenth-century reforms, corruption was common. Voters were bribed and treated, and in some cases threatened, and as the voting was not secret they could easily be rewarded or punished. So long as the franchise was restricted and irrational, bribery and similar practices were tolerated by the dominant opinion and by the law. The spirit that led to extensions of the franchise could not fail to deplore corrupt practices, but the main defence against corruption – secret voting – was not introduced until the passing of the Ballot Act of 1873.

With corrupt practices outlawed and condemned, there were still other matters connected with candidates' expenditure to be settled. Individual candidates, and parties on a wider scale, need to use resources to make their appeal effectively. Paper and printing, and the distribution of literature, are a minimum. These things [cost money. Modern democratic values would find it objectionable that a candidate should gain advantage from superior financial resources; to prevent this the law can either set a limit to what may be spent, or provide that the State shall supply each candidate (or each party) equally with means for propagating his ideas.

British electoral law uses a combination of these devices. The State-owned postal system delivers candidates' election communications to all electors free of charge. The maximum amount of money to be spent by any candidate during a campaign is fixed by a formula which takes into account the total number of electors and the density of population. In most constituencies the maximum permitted in 1970 was between £1,000 and £1,500. The law in this matter is rigidly applied, and is firmly supported both by a general respect for the rules, and by a requirement that accounts should be submitted. Average expenditure per candidate in 1970 is shown in the Table.[1]

Party	Average £ per candidate	% of permitted maximum
Conservative	949	79
Labour	828	68
Liberal	525	41
Other	424	36

The history of the law concerning the use of motor-cars in connection with the voting process on election-day gives us an instance of a difference between parties' attitudes, influenced by calculations of party advantage. When car-ownership was not widespread the Labour Party thought that the absence of regulation of cars was beneficial to the Conservatives. There was nothing inherently wrong in car-owners giving voters rides to the polling-place, but because it was thought that there were more Conservative-owned cars available the Labour Party, when it came into power, brought in legislation to restrict the number of cars helping each candidate to a figure supposed to be determined roughly by the number of cars available to the less car-owning party. The Conservatives considered this regulation to be a pettifogging interference with liberty, but they obeyed it until they were in a position to abolish it. They did abolish it, with the excuse that car-ownership had increased and spread so much that free use gave no significant advantage to either party. When the Labour Party returned to power in 1964 it did not restore the regulation. No doubt there were and still are more cars owned by Conservative supporters than by Labour supporters, but the difference has probably lost significance to such an extent that the business of restoring the regulation would not be worth while.

Access to television and radio channels is clearly important, and cannot well be determined by rules like those which limit individual candidates' expenditure during a campaign. In any case, the media are nation-wide or region-wide, and thus not very appropriate to individual

[1] D. Butler and M. Pinto-Duschinsky, *The British General Election of 1970* (Macmillan, 1971), p. 333.

general election candidates. It is the parties as such that can properly make use of them, and the rules must be made in recognition of this fact.

Both the BBC and commercial television operators are required by law to be impartial, and no advertiser or political party or candidate can buy time to make an election appeal. The broadcasting authorities have had little difficulty in deciding that the duty to be impartial obliges them to give equal treatment, equal time in equal conditions as far as practicable, to the two major parties, less to the Liberals, and very little indeed to any other parties. This applies most obviously to electioneering, but the rule is extended to all other matters, including coverage of party conferences. The assumption is that the Constitution works through Government and Opposition. The media recognise and fulfil an obligation to give almost equal time to the two major parties in their news coverage of an election campaign.

For party election broadcasts arrangements are made, within general rules (to which the Conference on Electoral Law devotes some care), by an *ad hoc* Committee on Political Broadcasting which meets as the campaign begins. In 1970 this committee met on 19 May, with representatives of the BBC, ITV and the three main parties. It decided that the Conservative and Labour Parties should have five ten-minute periods each on television, the Liberals three, all at 10 p.m. on weekdays. On sound the Liberals were less well treated. The committee did not include representatives of other parties, but decided to give Welsh and Scottish Nationalists five minutes each on their national transmitters on both sound and television. Any party putting up at least fifty candidates would have five minutes of a nationwide broadcast. The Communist Party qualified, but was given its five minutes at 6.30 p.m. – and at short notice, so that its broadcast was not scheduled in the programme weeklies.[1] Minor parties have complained at their treatment in the matter of election broadcasts, and on this occasion the short notice gave the Communists good cause to complain.

Expenditure by individual candidates during campaigns is strictly limited, but there is no restriction on advertising expenditure by parties between elections, either on posters or in newspapers. Uncommitted voters are more likely to respond to long-term than to short-term influences, so this is important. In 1958 the Conservatives, in power but faring badly in opinion polls and by-elections, ran an expensive advertising campaign, buying space in newspapers, while the Labour Party expressed disapproval. An improvement in Conservative

---

[1] D. Butler and M. Pinto-Duschinsky, *ibid.*, pp. 203 f.

opinion-poll showings followed, and the Conservatives went on to obtain an increased majority in the general election of 1959. It seems likely that the advertising helped their electoral recovery, and both parties have used this technique since then.

There is regulated equal access to television for the two major parties even outside the election periods. Here again the constitutional arrangements have been determined by an agreement based on common sense, and giving the major parties more time than the Liberals or the smaller groups. The provision of party-political broadcasts, together with ministerial statements followed by opportunities for the Opposition to make comments or counter-statements as it sees fit, can be regarded as a reasonable use of mass media with respect to the electoral process and the role of the parties in relation to it.

Although the law limits the money to be spent in support of any election candidature in a constituency during a campaign, it does not concern itself with the source of the money that is spent. As far as the law is concerned the whole cost may be met by the candidate himself, or by any other person or body. It is only in the past thirty years that heavy personal expenditure by a candidate has come to be considered objectionable, and the internal rules of the parties now provide effective authority for limitation.

As late as 1939 some local Conservative associations had a strong preference for a parliamentary candidate who would pay the whole of his election expenses and also a big subscription. An authoritative condemnation of such practices was made by a report of the Speaker's Conference on Electoral Reform in 1944, which

'. . . agreed to place on record the fact that they regarded with disapproval the direct or indirect payment or promise of payment of substantial contributions or annual subscriptions to party organisations (including local party organisations), designed to influence the action of such organisations in selecting any particular individual as a parliamentary candidate.'

The Conservative Party quickly responded by imposing limits on its candidates' personal contributions, and in 1948 introduced a rule that the constituency association should pay the whole election costs. The candidate should subscribe no more than £25 a year – or £50 after being elected.[1] The new (Maxwell Fyfe) rules of the Conservative Party reflected new egalitarian and anti-plutocratic values outside the party, and there is no evidence that they have affected political relations between Members and their local associations.

[1] Cf. M. Rush, *The Selection of Parliamentary Candidates* (Nelson, 1969), p. 30.

The Labour Party's rules, while imposing some restrictions (though less severe ones) on individual candidates' personal contributions, have never prevented a trade union from contributing so heavily that it effectively purchases a seat. The 'Hastings rules' (1933) allow a union to pay up to 80 per cent of the election costs, plus a large contribution to the funds of a constituency Labour Party. The practical effect of this is to ensure that at least a hundred Labour MPs are at any time beholden to unions. The six biggest trade unions dominate the local Labour parties in most of the constituencies which are safest for Labour.[1]

It could reasonably be argued that the sponsorship of Labour candidates by trade unions is in disagreement with the spirit of the Constitution – but what matters is that the Labour Party is one of the two major parties in the political system, and that the party's values can quite readily accommodate a relationship of this type. The Conservative Party 'does not approve the financing of its candidates by any trade union, trade association or organisation of employers'.[2] But the disapproval relates only to its own internal organisation. What is important from the constitutional angle is not whether or not the relationship between unions and their sponsored Members agrees with some theoretical standards of propriety – that is a merely academic question – but that that relationship is a necessary condition of the financing of the activities of one of the two major parties; that when Labour is in power action against the system is hardly to be expected; and that when the Conservatives have been in power they have not thought it useful to attempt to impose any restrictions on the system, because it would not be worth their while to face the accusations of discrimination, and the possible loss of votes, that such action would undoubtedly produce.

CONSTITUENCIES

The arrangement of the areas within which people vote is wholly provided for by statute, and new statutes revising the arrangements have been passed with some frequency – the last in 1958. Before 1832 each unit of representation, whether a county or a borough, returned two members. The Reform Act of 1832 established for the first time some districts returning one member each, and the Acts of 1867, 1884

[1] In 1970, trade unions sponsored 137 candidates of whom 112 were elected (or 85 per cent, as compared with 45 per cent of all Labour candidates and 35 per cent of non-sponsored candidates). In 1966 the union-sponsored candidates did better still; only 6 out of 138 were defeated.

[2] *Notes on Procedure for the Adoption of Conservative Candidates in England and Wales* (Conservative Central Office, 1960), p. 9. Quoted by Rush, *op. cit.*, p. 32.

and 1918 increased the number of one-member districts. Undivided two-member constituencies, in which the two candidates who obtained most votes were elected, survived the 1918 reforms in eleven towns, and were not abolished until 1948. Since then every constituency has returned one member.

'One man one vote' implies that all votes should be counted equally, in other words that each elected Member should represent approximately the same number of voters. Around 1800 some boroughs which returned two members each had less than fifty electors, while others had several thousands. This inequality of representation was a cause of even more indignation than the still-restricted franchise, especially because a small number of electors in a rotten borough could be controlled by an influential individual. The worst abuses were removed by the 1832 Reform Act, and there were further redistributions in 1867 and 1884. By 1918 the principle of equality of representation had been fully accepted, and the 1918 Act drew boundaries in such a way as to embody the principle that no parliamentary seat ought to represent very many more or fewer electors than the average. One exception was admitted: very sparsely populated areas might properly have generous representation because it was difficult for a Member of Parliament to perform his representative functions adequately if his constituency covered too great an area.

But the Act of 1918 made no provision for future redistributions, and twenty-five years later great inequalities had arisen because of population movement. Some newly-developed suburban areas round London, in particular, were grossly under-represented. Some constituencies had two or three times the average number of electors. Like most problems affecting the Constitution this was handled by an *ad hoc* procedure. A conference presided over by the Speaker of the House of Commons considered the matter, with all parties taking part, and it made proposals which provided the basis of legislation. The Redistribution Act of 1944 took account of this short-term inequity by creating twenty-five seats and dividing the most over-populated constituencies into two – and one of them into three. But this was just a temporary measure. The Act for the first time established permanent machinery for the periodic alteration of boundaries: four Boundary Commissions, one each for England, Wales, Scotland and Northern Ireland. Each commission had the Speaker of the House of Commons as its chairman, plus three other members also appointed in the expectation that they would be impartial: high court judges, the Director-General of the Ordnance Survey, and others whose offices set them apart from party politics. The 1944 Act provided that each commission should review the boundaries at intervals of between five and seven years. They were to ensure that no

M

constituency had many more or many fewer electors than the quota – that is the average number of electors per seat.

In providing for these impartial bodies, together with a review procedure, the 1944 Act made an honest attempt to ensure that a parliamentary majority in power should not be able to gain advantage either from maintaining existing constituency boundaries without change or by changing the boundaries in a particular way.

The 1944 Act not only set up the Boundary Commissions, but made elaborate provisions for the hearing of local objections to their proposals. However, it stopped short at the fundamental issue, by leaving the Government of the day to advise Parliament to bring new boundaries into operation. The Home Secretary must lay the Commissioners' reports before Parliament, together with a draft Order in Council giving effect to their recommendations, with or without modifications; but Parliament can then act as it sees fit.

One aspect of the 1944 Act was of significance for the theory of elections. By providing machinery by which the boundaries were to be changed at stipulated intervals it seemed to recognise that each constituency was just an artificial unit rather than a real community. This innovation in the interest of equal representation can be interpreted as a step towards recognition of a general election for what it really is – a plebiscite in which the electorate chooses a government.

Meanwhile, the concept of a constituency as a real community survives through the elected Member's role as its representative, and the parties have to build up and maintain their constituency organisations for choosing candidates, running election campaigns, and discussing national and local problems. An association which is supporting a Member in the House has to keep him in touch with local opinion and provide him with many services, and it has the power to refuse to readopt him.

Each boundary change involves some interference with the unity of the constituencies involved. When a couple of wards are added to a constituency their people are newcomers to that community, and it takes time to integrate them. The enforced transfer of leaders and other activists between party organisations produces some difficulties of adjustment.

A general revision of boundaries was made in 1948, and another, as required by the existing law, in 1954. But there was bitter complaint among activists of all parties against the damage that was done to their organisation and work. In response to the objections a new Act was passed in 1958. The Boundary Commissions were released from their obligation to keep electorates within 25 per cent of the quota, and the time limit between a revision and the completion of the next review was increased to fifteen years. The changes involved some sacrifice of the principle of maximum equality in electorates, in the interest of more continuity of representation and more meaningful communities.

The 1958 compromise was generally welcomed, but the initiative came from the Conservatives – in spite of the fact that, in the conditions of the mid-twentieth century, boundary changes in the interests of equalisation of population are likely to increase the number of seats won by the Conservative Party, while the absence of change is likely to help the Labour Party. The situation in 1969 illustrated this fact. With boundaries arranged in 1954 still in force, all the main urban areas had lost population, so that industrial Lancashire, central London and other Labour strongholds had more seats than their population warranted, while outer suburbs and the areas surrounding the towns (still formally classified as rural) were under-represented in terms of parliamentary seats because their population had grown enormously. In most of these growing regions the Conservatives could be sure of winning nearly all the seats no matter how the boundaries were drawn within them, because in most (but not all) of these growing regions a high proportion of new residents were relatively prosperous.

The Boundary Commissions reviewed the boundaries, as required by the 1958 Act, during 1965–8. Objections were properly heard, and led to some minor changes in their proposals. Early in 1969 everything was completed. It could easily be calculated that, in a general election taking place in the newly-proposed constituencies, the Conservative Party would win between five and twenty more seats, and Labour up to twenty fewer, than in the old, now out-of-date constituencies.

The 1958 Act did not specifically require the new boundaries to be put into effect by 1969. It only required the Home Secretary to lay the proposals before Parliament. The Government in power clearly had a duty to take the necessary steps to see that the new boundaries came into force by that year, but there was no means of forcing it to do its duty. Under the Parliament Act the next general election was due to take place not later than March 1971. The Labour Party, currently in power, could see that it was likely to benefit from a failure to redistribute, and was tempted to defer the next redistribution until after the next general election. Through the first half of 1969 it remained inactive, ignoring frequent demands from the Opposition that it should bring in the boundary proposals. Then, in July, the Home Secretary announced that he had succumbed to temptation. As a pretext for avoiding redistribution he was able to use the recent issue of the Redcliffe-Maud Report and the consequent probability that the boundaries between local government areas would be altered within five years. He introduced a bill whose effect would be to leave all constituency boundaries unchanged except in Greater London, where the recommended changes should be made forthwith (as local government reform was not impending there), and in a few grossly under-represented areas, where the Boundary Commissioners were to produce proposals for additional seats pending a new general review after local government had been reformed. The bill was rushed into the House of Commons and passed, but the House of Lords amended it so as to make the whole of the Boundary Commissioners' proposals effective right away – and thus destroy the bill's purpose.

This exceptional use by the House of Lords of its surviving powers reflected the preservation of its power to reject a bill to prolong the life of a Parliament. Spokesmen of the Conservative majority claimed that as the Commons majority was interfering with the electoral system there was a need for somebody to try to safeguard the people's rights, and the House of Lords was the only body available.

Faced with this action by the House of Lords the Government could not easily use the Parliament Act to pass the bill again, because the Home Secretary would probably have been in breach of the existing law until indemnified by the final passing of the Act. Instead, the Government abandoned its bill. When Parliament reassembled in November, the Home Secretary laid the Boundary Commissioners' proposals before Parliament, and thus fulfilled his legal duty. But he advised the House of Commons to reject all the proposals, on the ground that the expected implementation of the Redcliffe-Maud plan for local government had now made the new boundary proposals unsuitable. The Labour majority in the House of Commons voted in agreement with Mr Callaghan's advice, all of them to improve their party's chances of obtaining office at the next election, a few of them to maintain in existence their own individual constituencies which, being over-represented, would have disappeared as soon as the boundaries were brought up to date.

The 1970 general election was thus held in out-of-date constituencies. The number of electors per consituency varied between extremes of 18,884 (Birmingham, Ladywood) and 124,215 (Billericay). The bias of the inequities in favour of Labour was clear: Labour won three-quarters of the 77 seats with under 45,000 electors, Conservatives won 70 out of the 90 with over 80,000 electors. Such variations, and the procedures responsible for them, would be regarded as unconstitutional by the standards set by the United States Supreme Court, but its recent rulings were not brought into the argument. Conservative politicians and newspapers, and some commentators normally favour-able to Labour, agreed that the procedure followed was dishonest. Many called it 'unconstitutional', but there was no means of reversing the effect of a Commons majority vote.

When the Conservatives had after all won the 1970 election the new Home Secretary soon asked the new House of Commons to approve the Boundary Commissioners' recommendations, and it did so. This action, at this stage, was sure to be damaging both to equitable representation and to the interests of the Conservative Party. By February 1974, when the next election took place, 18 of the 24 English constituencies with below 45,000 electors, but none of the 29 with over 85,000, were in central parts of conurbations. Sixteen of the new rotten boroughs were won by Labour. Labour won more than two-thirds of the 53 English constituencies with under 50,000 electors, nearly all of which were compact and urban, but less than one-third of the 52 with over 80,000, and most of these covered large and unwieldy areas. In Scotland and Wales the same pattern was to be observed. The Government in 1970–71 would have served both the principle of equitable representation and its own interest by reintroducing the previous government's bill, so that new boundaries, based on the new local government areas, could have been operative by 1973, in time for any new election in 1974 or 1975. Instead, gross inequities of representation were installed and likely to distort election results increasingly in Labour's favour well into the 1980's.

One curious irregularity that has been allowed to survive is the over-generous representation of Scotland and Wales. The Representation of the People Act, 1918, gave Scotland seventy-one seats (plus three for the Scottish universities), and the figure of seventy-one has been kept by all subsequent legislation – though the university seats were abolished with the others in 1948. Wales had thirty-five seats in 1918, increased to thirty-six in 1948. Since 1918 the population-increase has been around 10 per cent in these countries while there has been a 25 per cent increase in England. The number of House of Commons seats for England is not precisely fixed by law, and has been varied from time to time. At the 1970 election the number of electors per seat was 64,000 in England, 54,500 in Wales and 51,500 in Scotland. In relation to a fair quota for the whole of Great Britain Scotland had eleven seats too many. The redistribution which followed did not change this situation, although it increased the English seats from 511 to 516 and thus went one-twentieth of the way to deal with it.

The over-representation of Scotland and Wales was originally justified by the fact that some areas of both of these countries are sparsely populated. It is not specifically provided in any statute that the Scottish and Welsh mountains and islands are to be generously treated, but scope for generous treatment was given by the statutory allocation of the national quotas – though the actual distribution of seats does not over-represent these areas alone. In 1966 300,000 voters in the sparsely-populated north and far west of Scotland had ten seats between them, but the rest of Scotland, including in particular the heavily-urbanised Glasgow area, was also over-represented, and so were the urban parts of south Wales. The Boundary Commissioners' revisions which were brought into effect after the 1970 election did not substantially change the situation.

In the current atmosphere, in which all parties are anxious to do everything that they can to give the greatest possible satisfaction to the Scots and Welsh, it is considered unwise to risk causing local annoyance (and possible gains of votes by the Nationalists) by reducing the unfair advantage which these countries have in their parliamentary representation.

The Government of Ireland Act, 1920, provided for Ireland to have fewer seats than its normal quota, to reflect the existence of a parliament and government for internal affairs. Northern Ireland has thus continued to have only twelve seats at Westminster; the replacement of Stormont by an assembly with less extensive powers in 1973 (following a period of suspension) might possibly be regarded as giving cause for increasing the number of Northern Irish seats, but this has not been done. If new national assemblies should be established for Wales and Scotland the number of seats at Westminster might be affected; however, any reduction would be likely to increase the Conservatives' chances of obtaining a majority in the UK Parliament, and any proposal for change would be likely to produce controversy which Conservatives would reasonably expect to be as damaging to them as the reduction of Welsh or Scottish seats would be beneficial.

THE TIMING OF ELECTIONS

Although there is nothing in any statute to define the relations between the electorate and those whom they elect, British constitutional theory and practice undoubtedly accept the principle of a maximum term of office. Locke's notion of the trusteeship of legislative bodies illustrates the position without defining it. It implies that the electors place a trust in those whom they elect, and that the trust expires at a known date. A written constitution may make this clear, but when a parliament already elected is itself 'sovereign', there cannot be a fully guaranteed limitation.

The Parliament Act provides for a maximum five-year interval between general elections, and gives the House of Lords exceptionally an absolute power to veto any bill increasing the period, and thus prolonging the life of the House of Commons then in session. There is in fact a high degree of confidence that no Parliament would overturn a principle so important as the limitation of its own mandate, except in circumstances which would, by general agreement, justify the irregularity. The qualification is necessary, because of both past and recent experience, and the qualification would seem to make nonsense of the principle. (Who is to decide what these exceptional justificatory circumstances would be?) The contradiction is tolerable just because politicians have hitherto observed the spirit of the rule – though the Labour majority's cheating over boundaries in 1969 gave cause for apprehension.

The Triennial Act of 1694 was one of the three major constitutional enactments arising out of the 1688 revolution, yet it lasted only twenty years. An election took place in 1714. In 1716 the King and his ministers were afraid that the new election, due to be held in 1717, might produce a House of Commons majority inconvenient to themselves (more specifically, a Jacobite majority, which might endanger the whole edifice that had recently been constructed). In order to prevent a general election in 1717 the ministers presented the Septennial Bill, providing that the maximum interval between general elections should in future be seven years instead of three. Both Houses of Parliament passed the bill, and this put off the date of the general election, then due by law in 1717, for four further years. In other words the Parliament, elected in 1714 for three years, by its own act extended its period of office for political motives.

Thirty-one peers protested against the bill:

'. . . it is agreed, that the House of Commons must be chosen by the people, and when so chosen, they are truly the representatives of the people, which they cannot be so properly said to be, when continued for a longer time than that for which they were chosen; for after that time they are chosen by the Parliament, and not the people, who are thereby deprived of the only remedy which they have against those, who either do not understand, or through corruption, do wilfully betray the trust reposed in them; which remedy is, to choose better men in their places.'[1]

There is no doubt that the passing of this Act 'violated the understandings of the Constitution', as Dicey puts it. Some commentators have suggested that it was not of much importance, that it was merely a normal exercise of power by Parliament. Dicey attacks that view, saying instead,

'That Act proves to demonstration that in a legal point of view Parliament is neither the agent of the electors nor in any sense a trustee for its constituents. It is legally the sovereign legislative power in the state, and

[1] Thorold Rogers, *Protests of the Lords* (1875), vol. 1, p. 218, quoted by A. V. Dicey, *Law of the Constitution* (Macmillan, 1885), p. 46.

the Septennial Act is at once the result and the standing proof of such Parliamentary sovereignty.'[1]

If Dicey's argument is correct, it provides strong grounds for introducing a written constitution. But we have to ask also what happened next. The Septennial Act of 1716 provided a precedent for an existing Parliament prolonging its own life beyond the period for which it had been elected, but for 200 years the rhythm of general elections was in fact left to be governed by the Act. In all this period no Parliament prolonged its own existence. By 1885, Dicey wrote, plausibly it seemed: 'No modern English Parliament would for the sake of keeping a government or party in office venture to pass say a Decennial Act and thus prolong its own duration.'

Indeed the 1716 Septennial Act was amended by the Parliament Act of 1911, which reduced the maximum life of a Parliament from seven years to five, and, by preserving the Lords' absolute power to reject any bill to amend the quinquennial provision, suggested an intention that there should be very special safeguards against any repetition of 1716. Even so, the safeguard has not been absolute. Within three years of the passing of the Parliament Act the First World War began. An election was due in 1915, but the parties agreed that it was unwise to hold an election as long as the war continued. Both Houses passed a bill to defer the election, and the King signed it. In 1940 the Parliament then sitting likewise put off the election for the duration of the war, with the agreement of all three major parties and the House of Lords. A coalition government was set up, but the Labour Party withdrew from the coalition when the war with Germany ended in 1945. The Conservatives formed a Government, and though they had a House of Commons majority they resentfully recognised that it was now their duty to dissolve Parliament and hold a new election without delay.

Thus there are recent precedents for Parliaments prolonging their own lives beyond the period for which they were elected, but only in wartime, and subject to the agreement of the major parties to suspend the normal political contest between them, and not to try to win seats from one another at by-elections. These arrangements, made in the interest of national unity, would have made any general election an artificial proceeding. The electorate was not wholly in agreement. In several by-elections the major party candidate was opposed by one or more independent candidates, or candidates of new or old parties or groupings which could normally have had no hope of success – and in a few cases such candidates (including one Scottish Nationalist and one Communist) were successful.

---

[1] Dicey, *op. cit.*, pp. 47–8.

We may say, then, that there is a constitutional convention that a Parliament should not defer a general election, except in war. But what exactly is war ? What potential crisis is serious enough for a government to claim that it creates conditions equivalent to war ? These questions are unanswerable, and agreement between the major parties could make use of the precedents.

Premature dissolution of parliament

Neither legislation nor convention prevents dissolution of Parliament before the expiry of the term for which the Parliament was elected. A Government which effectively can dissolve the elected assembly at any time derives an obvious advantage from such a power. Accepted usage, supported by many precedents, allows the Prime Minister to advise the Queen to dissolve Parliament at any time, and it is not clear whether there are any imaginable circumstances in which the Queen ought to refuse.

Dissolution in search of a mandate.   A Prime Minister might be expected to request a dissolution because his Government proposed to embark on policy so much at variance with the programme on which it won the last election that it considered that it must ask the people, through a new election, for approval.

In 1910 there were two general elections in search of a mandate, the first to prove that there was popular support for the budget which the Lords had rejected, the second to prove support for the plan to create enough new peers to give the Government a majority in the House of Lords if that House should reject a bill limiting its powers. In both these elections the Government was successful.

In November 1923 King George V was advised by Baldwin to dissolve Parliament. He demurred on the grounds that it was only a year since the previous general election, and that the party in power still enjoyed the support of a majority in the House of Commons. Baldwin insisted on the dissolution because his Government proposed to embark on a new line of policy (tariff protection) which had not been in his party's programme at the previous election. He considered himself bound by the pledge given by his predecessor, Bonar Law, that there would be no fundamental change in the fiscal arrangements; therefore he ought not to take a new step of this kind without referring the problem back to the people.

In retrospect Baldwin's insistence on dissolving Parliament for the sake of his 'mandate' seems to have been quixotic. If he had been returned with a majority, he would have gained some advantage and strengthened his position; the Opposition would have been able to attack the Government very strongly if it had introduced protection in contravention of Bonar Law's pledge. But in the event the Government lost office altogether. Something like a negative precedent against the mandate dissolution may have been set, and the artificiality of a general election over a single issue is now generally recognised; a Government must deal with many unforeseeable problems while in office, and research-findings show that few electors vote on issues. In the past forty years, governments have embarked on new lines of policy without thinking of referring their mandate back to the people, and it does not seem very likely that a Government will in the future ask for a dissolution for such a reason. The Labour Party's pressure for a 'mandate' general election in 1971 over the Common Market entry terms was part of the usual tactics of an opposition party, but not to be taken seriously to imply that it had been converted to the principle of mandate general elections as a guide to its own intended future policy.

Dissolution on defeat of a Government. There seems to be no doubt that a Government defeated on an important issue in the House of Commons might ask for a dissolution; the Queen would be bound to agree. It is not worth citing the Canadian precedent of 1926; the general principle is straightforward and clear.

Dissolution for the Government's advantage. Subject to uncertainties arising from states of emergency and the non-availability of the Monarch, a Prime Minister may ask for, and expect to be granted, a dissolution, at any time that he judges to be advantageous to him and his party. In general this means that a Prime Minister can choose any time, before the expiry of its five years, that he judges to be favourable. The activities of the opinion polling organisations are exceedingly helpful to him, though they are not infallible. Month by month several different organisations produce information about the likely result of an immediate election, and that information can be added to that produced by recent by-election results.

There is still an element of uncertainty. The election does not take place until nearly a month after the Prime Minister's decision to hold it. There is always the possibility that events during the campaign may lead some voters to change their intentions – and this surviving element of uncertainty gives us some comfort.

A request for a dissolution merely in the hope of increasing a Government's majority would almost certainly have to be granted, no matter how short the time since the last election. Two recent general elections have produced Governments with inconveniently small majorities in the House of Commons – those of 1950 and 1964. In each case speculation about a possible new general election began almost at once, and there was no question but that it was open to the Prime Minister to choose his time, as early as he wished. In the 1950 to 1951 Parliament Attlee carried on for a year and a half, and then dissolved it, although he had not been defeated in the Commons, at a time when his party's prospects of electoral victory were poor. The Government was discouraged by its own lack of policy (having already carried through the reforms it wanted during the previous Parliament) and by divisions within its own party. It apparently felt that it was just not worth continuing any longer in such uncomfortable conditions.

In October 1964 Mr Wilson had a new Labour Government, full of vigour, but it wanted more freedom of movement than it had with a majority of only six. The Prime Minister bided his time for a little, and in March 1966, encouraged by the findings of opinion polls and the results of by-elections, he asked for Parliament to be dissolved. His judgement was vindicated by the election result. This precedent seemed greatly to have strengthened the Executive. However, the elections of June 1970 and February 1974 were both held when the polls had suddenly swung in the ruling party's favour. The adverse results showed that opinion polls cannot be wholly relied upon to indicate the outcome of an election after the necessary month of campaigning and new happenings.

Governments have regularly timed elections to suit their own political advantage. They are now very well equipped for doing this, because they have highly reliable information about the likely result of an election at any time. By-election results have always been available as a guide, but in the past twenty years they have also had the benefit of the information provided at regular intervals by several opinion polls conducted by private organisations.[1] A Government has some freedom of manoeuvre

---

[1] It has been argued that the whole apparatus of opinion polls was discredited by the events of June 1970, when the actual result of the election on 18 June differed very significantly from the findings of six out of seven polling organisations published during the preceding few days. The triumphant shouts of those who are prejudiced against the polls were not wholly justified, however, for the following reasons: (a) trade figures damaging to the Labour Government were published just before the election, thus pricking the bubble of enthusiasm which had been growing during the preceding few months; (b) there was even more abstention from voting in 1970 than in 1966, and there is ample evidence that potential Labour supporters contributed the greatest part to the trend to more abstention in 1951–70; (c) in 1974 the polls' real error was very slight, with the result, affected by high turnout, support for minor parties and malrepresentation; (d) the overall reliability of the polls should be judged in relation to their performance on all occasions, not one.

In February 1974 the polls were not as wrong as is often supposed; the

in trying to time its policies so as to gain popularity, or reduce its unpopularity, as the time for an inevitable election approaches.

The power of a Government to dissolve Parliament because of difficulties caused by dissidents in its own side is not likely to be used, but the power is there, and its significance lies in the Prime Minister's power to threaten to use it. Such threats were heard in 1968 and 1972, though it is impossible to measure their effectiveness.

The election of February 1974 produced a House of Commons in which no party had a majority, and a minority Labour Government was formed in the expectation that it would call a new election if defeated on a major issue, or at any time which the Prime Minister judged to be advantageous. It was kept in office for its first few months partly by the desire of the Conservative Opposition, and of the minor parties who held the balance, to avoid a new election. As often happens during the first months of a new Government, opinion polls were favourable, suggesting that a new election would produce a solid Labour majority. Not until June did the Government suffer defeats on issues of any consequence, and these were not such as to constitute expressions of no confidence or censure. Considering that the Labour Party probably owed some of its House of Commons strength to a distribution of electoral boundaries favourable to itself, the strong position in which the Government found itself during this period was justifiable only on the basis of a somewhat cynical view of the need for a government to reflect the wishes of the electorate as expressed in an election.

Conservatives did indeed obtain more votes than Labour, though the Conservative lead had fallen during the campaign.

Cf. R. Hodder-Williams, *Public Opinion Polls and British Politics* (Routledge & Kegan Paul, 1970).

Regions and Local Government

In November 1973 the Constitutional Commission, set up by the Labour Government in 1966, made its report, with a variety of proposals for the establishment of new devices for the government of Scotland and Wales, and for the identification and presentation of interests peculiar to the main regions of England. The lack of agreement among the members of the commission suggested, in 1973, a probability that if any action were to follow before the end of the decade, it would not exactly follow any of the particular proposals put forward. Meanwhile, legislation had already provided for the reform of the system of local government in each of the nations of the kingdom, and the reforms came into effect in 1974. Although the reforms were less fundamental than those proposed by the Redcliffe-Maude Commission Report of 1969, they were never-theless very far-reaching. Thus in those aspects of the constitutional system which concern the relations between the central Government and the geographical sections of the UK the early 1970s saw on the one hand signs of impending change, and on the other hand a mass of changes already introduced.

We may look at the objects of this inquiry in two parts, first that concerned with the 'nations' united in the kingdom, and second the relation of the central Government with local bodies in general. Both aspects are fundamentally governed by the principle that the Crown is sovereign in relation to all the parts of the kingdom: if legislation were passed abrogating any existing powers, or abolishing existing sub-authorities or creating new ones, there would be little point in arguing that it was unconstitutional.

Wales, Scotland and Ireland were all in some degree under the

English Crown long before 1688. Wales had been incorporated in the kingdom of England by the *Statutum Walliae* of 1284, and the Laws in Wales Act, 1536, gave the Welsh all the privileges and rights of Englishmen. For government Wales was wholly assimilated. The Act of Union with Scotland was based on a treaty which commissioners negotiated on behalf of the two Parliaments; first the Scottish, then the English Parliament ratified the Articles of Union. The Act of Union, 1706, provided that the two kingdoms should 'for ever' be united in one kingdom called Great Britain. It included some religious guarantees. The Act of Union with Ireland, 1800, was not based on a treaty. It created the United Kingdom of Great Britain and Ireland, which was also to last 'for ever', though the absence of a treaty meant that the status of that intention was less impressive than in the Scottish case. However, the attempt of the Parliament of that time to bind its successors did not succeed, and in 1922 the Irish Free State (Constitution) Act separated Ireland (except for six northern counties) from the United Kingdom, and the Ireland Act of 1949 recognised the secession of the Republic of Ireland from the Commonwealth, though the northern part of Ireland remained, under a new regime, within what now became the United Kingdom of Great Britain and Northern Ireland.

From the nineteenth century onwards the new nationalism focussed long-standing discontents, and in recent decades devolutionary measures have been introduced; the Constitutional Commission of 1969 was concerned with the practicability of extending these without reducing the substantial benefits which all the parts of the kingdom are widely believed to derive from the union. For the future it was bound to consider the possibility of a federal structure for the kingdom, though the objections to this are almost insuperable. It could however propose further devolution through sub-parliaments, or it could suggest changes in the House of Lords which would give the Second Chamber a new role, similar to many other Second Chambers, as an assembly representing the parts of the kingdom as such.

Before 1969 various statutes, orders and executive measures had already created special devolutionary devices for each of the three countries other than England, and new changes were made in the 1960s. Taking Scotland first, the main device existing in 1974 was the office of Secretary of State for Scotland, created in 1927, though there had already been a Scottish Secretary since 1885. This office is the foundation of a substantial measure of administrative devolution, which in its turn flows from the distinctness of Scottish law. Local government in Scotland has always been a distinct system, and the operations of the central administration in Scotland are in the hands of the Scottish Office under the Secretary of State, assisted by a Minister of State and three Parliamentary Under-Secretaries of State, each of whom is in charge of one of the three departments into which the office is divided. They have been reorganised several times, by administrative procedures.

The existence of a separate administrative system implies separate legislation for Scotland, except in cases where English legislation is made to apply to Scotland too. For example, the Scottish educational system and National Health Service are provided for by Scottish legislation, though measures such as nationalisation statutes have included Scotland.

For parliamentary discussion of Scottish bills and of expenditure and administration in Scotland the procedure in force in 1974, after several modifications, represents rather a confused attempt to embody two principles: that Scottish affairs ought to be discussed by Members of Parliament representing Scottish constituencies, and thus that committees of the House composed only of Scottish Members are suitable devices for such discussion; while on the other hand Scottish susceptibilities would be offended if all matters concerning Scotland were relegated to committees and thus apparently neglected by Parliament itself.

The principles of bills relating to Scotland may be discussed on second reading in a committee consisting of Scottish Members, provided that no objection is raised in the House (and in fact a very important Scottish second reading would be taken on the floor); the committee stage is normally taken in a committee of Scottish Members. There is also a Scottish Grand Committee whose main function is to hold supply-type debates, about six times a year, on aspects of Scottish administration. All Members for constituencies in Scotland are automatically members of the Grand Committee, but that committee is held to be subject to the rule that members of all committees are to be appointed 'with regard to the composition of the House'. This means that the party composition of a committee must be in the same proportions as the whole House, so it is necessary for some non-Scottish Members to be added. The rule became important after the 1970 general election, which produced a Labour majority in Scotland, so that without the added non-Scottish Members the Government would have been in danger of defeat but for the addition of English Conservatives. The addition is generally rather artificial as normally the Grand Committee does not vote – though it would not be safe to say that there is a convention that there should be no votes. Usually it is clear in advance that the Opposition does not intend to divide the committee, so the non-Scottish added Members can safely stay away.

As the Grand Committee debates are analogous to what might be done by a Scottish Parliament in discussing administration, there would be advantages in holding these meetings in Scotland, but this had never been done up to 1974.

A further innovation was the establishment in 1969 of a Select Committee of the House of Commons on Scottish Affairs, a sessional committee composed of eleven Scottish Members, with the function of inquiring into any matter falling within the jurisdiction of the Scottish Office. Like other select committees this group receives memoranda, questions 'witnesses' (mainly officials), and makes reports which may be critical of current policies. It was part of the new system of select committees set up from 1966 onwards, and was set up anew (with some continuing members) in each session up to 1971–3.

The Secretary of State for Scotland and his juniors, together with the two Scottish Law officers, share the task of speaking for the Government on all these occasions, and they also answer parliamentary questions concerning internal Scottish administration. Until 1974 questions have always been taken on the floor of the House of Commons, though there are obvious arguments in favour of taking them in a specifically Scottish assembly, possibly meeting in Scotland – either the Commons Grand Committee or some new assembly which might emerge from the Constitutional Commission, or even an assembly of the Scottish Members of some second Chamber of Parliament. But changes on that scale are unlikely to be made in the near future.

The appointment of a Secretary of State for Wales in the Labour Government of 1964 was the last stage in a long series of arguments and responses with reference to this question. In the 1930s the more vocal elements in Wales began to press hard for the appointment of a minister in the Cabinet to be concerned entirely with Welsh affairs. The economic depression was affecting Wales particularly badly. Scotland had had its Secretary since 1885, so why not Wales too? The Welsh pressure was resisted by the Prime Ministers of the time, who were constantly under pressure both to appoint new ministers and to reduce the size of their Cabinets.

When Labour came to power in 1945, twenty-eight of the thirty-six Welsh seats were held by Labour. Welsh Labour Members pressed for the creation of a Welsh Office, but Attlee and his principal colleagues were unconvinced. They did not want to complicate the administrative machinery, and they argued that the quality of administration in Wales would suffer through the small scale of the operations. Specialisation in services could not be sufficiently developed.

When the Conservatives returned to power in 1951 the Home Secretary was given the additional function of Minister for Welsh Affairs. The innovation was not a fundamental one. The Home Secretary, Sir David Maxwell Fyfe, did not represent a Welsh constituency and was not a Welshman, though as a Liverpool barrister he had appeared 'in practically every court between the Dee and Caernarvon'.[1] As he had all the duties of Home Secretary to perform he could only devote some of his energies to the consideration of Welsh matters; he in fact managed to visit Wales about twenty-five times a year. In 1957 responsibility for Welsh affairs was transferred to the Minister of Housing and Local Government. A little later, in December 1957, Macmillan made the first appointment of a full-time Welsh minister. Under the Minister of Local Government he appointed a Minister of State for Welsh Affairs, giving the first holder of the office a peerage, with the idea that he should spend most of his time in Wales, reasonably free of parliamentary duties in London. This arrangement continued until 1964. For nearly seven years both Scotland and Wales had their Ministers of State, based largely in Edinburgh and Cardiff, speaking on their countries in the House of Lords and contributing in varying degrees to the general representation of the Government in the Upper House.

As a further device to meet Welsh demands the Conservative Government set up a Council for Wales, consisting of appointed members who were in fact prominent Welsh personalities. This body, which met at regular intervals, was empowered to make proposals about the administration of Welsh affairs. It quickly began to concern itself not only with current events in Wales, but also with questions of Welsh administrative reform. In its Third Memorandum, in January 1957, it recommended that there should be a Secretary of State for Wales, and that the powers exercised in Wales by the Ministers of Education, Agriculture, Fisheries and Food, and Housing and Local Government should be transferred to him. There should be a Welsh Office with a structure similar to the Scottish, with four Departments of State in Cardiff, a Secretary of State and two Parliamentary Under-Secretaries.

The establishment of the council was regarded in Wales not as a satisfaction of Welsh aspirations but as a new means of expressing those aspirations. The creation of a Welsh Office, with a Secretary of State having a seat in the Cabinet, in 1964, brought this plan to fruition, and the arrangement was continued under the Conservatives in 1970. At the parliamentary level there is now also a Welsh Grand Committee, and a parallel procedure for dealing with Welsh bills – though the devolution has not gone so far as to require separate Welsh bills except on the single case of the Welsh language.

The solution used for Northern Ireland under the legislation of 1920 and 1922 moved much further towards establishing a relationship of a federal character than anything that had yet been done in respect of Wales or Scotland. This was somewhat ironic in so far as the majority of

[1] Lord Kilmuir, *Political Adventure* (Weidenfeld, 1964), p. 203.

N

the Northern Irish population wanted nothing so much as to preserve their position within the United Kingdom, having little ambition for autonomy. But the minority had a deep resentment against the British, and an ambition to be united with the rest of Ireland. The degree of autonomy left to the province made it possible for the majority to maintain certain advantages for its community, but after disturbances which began in the 1960s the British Government exercised its influence to secure some reforms in the direction of removing minority grievances.

By the Government of Ireland Act, 1920 and the Irish Free State Act, 1922, the six northern counties remained within the United Kingdom, but were provided with a Parliament of two Houses (a popularly-elected House of Commons and a Senate mainly elected by it), and a Governor, representing the Queen, who acts on the advice of ministers responsible to the Northern Ireland House of Commons. The Northern Ireland Government and Parliament had jurisdiction over internal affairs; some matters clearly appropriate to a central authority were 'excepted' from the jurisdiction granted to it, and some others were 'reserved' to the UK Parliament, notably postal services and some taxation.

There is however nothing to prevent the UK Parliament from legislating in a field within the competence of the Northern Ireland Parliament, and any Act of the Northern Ireland Parliament would be void in so far as it was inconsistent with UK legislation.

The inclusion of Ireland within the United Kingdom has produced contradictions which have never been resolved. The attempt of the Parliament of 1801 to bind its successors, by incorporating all of Ireland 'for ever', failed fifty years ago. Northern Ireland still remains within the UK, but legislation of 1972, providing for a referendum in which its electors were asked to choose between continuing UK membership and union with the Republic of Ireland, clearly marked the end of the absolute claim that the union was 'for ever', even in the case of the North.

The Northern Irish devolutionary system, based on the Government of Ireland Act, 1920, which operated from 1921 to 1972, was suspended for a year in March 1972, but the suspension was renewed and it now seems unlikely that the 1920 scheme will ever come into effect again. By the Northern Ireland (Temporary Provisions) Act of 1972 the UK Government took over that responsibility for internal administration which had previously been devolved, but the system then established was intended to be replaced by another. The White Paper, *Northern Ireland Constitutional Proposals*, was published in March 1973, as a basis for new legislation which the Government proposed to present to Parliament after discussion, and after attempts to obtain the widest possible agreement.

The first question to be resolved was whether or not Northern

Ireland should continue to be within the United Kingdom. It was generally believed that a majority of the inhabitants did so wish, though a minority did not. In order to test opinion the Northern Ireland (Border Poll) Act of 1972 provided for the holding of periodical referenda on the question 'Do you want Northern Ireland to remain part of the United Kingdom ?' or 'Do you want Northern Ireland to be incorporated in the Irish Republic ?'.

On 8 March 1973 a referendum was held, with all registered electors in the province eligible to vote, and 57 per cent of the electorate voted in favour of continuing membership of the UK. This result obliged the Government to continue to make provision for the government of the province within the UK, under the temporary regime of 1972, until another could be instituted.

Under the devolutionary system of 1921–72 the number of Protestants supporting the Unionist Party was always great enough to give that party a parliamentary majority, which ruled the province in such a way as to maintain various advantages for the Protestant element. In the 1960s the UK Labour Government put pressure on the Northern Ireland Government to put an end to some practices which it considered repugnant to the spirit of the UK Constitution; in response to that pressure considerable movement towards change began.

Meanwhile there were civil disturbances, and the UK Government formed the opinion, in 1969, that the forces of law and order, as they had been operating under the Northern Ireland Government's responsibility and control, had been constituted and used in a manner which itself created grounds for grievance among the Catholic minority. There appeared to be some danger of a serious increase in violence, and though the Northern Ireland Government made changes in its police arrangements, the UK Government decided (with the Opposition's support) that British military forces should be sent in to calm the situation. The troops were at first widely accepted as impartial guarantors of civil peace.

It is not normal to use the army for such purposes, though there are precedents, and there is no doubt that a Government has power so to use it. However regrettable this reaction to the troubles, any other course then looked likely to produce more danger to persons and property. Whether or not this was correct cannot now be said. But it is true that the troops went in to deal with violence of the stone-throwing type, met up to that time with over-vigorous use of truncheons. The inception of a serious campaign of terrorism, with lethal weapons, followed the arrival of the troops, and it continued, gathering force, during the next four years.

In mid 1973 no end to the terrorist campaign was in sight. The experience strengthens doubts, already aroused by similar experiences elsewhere, whether national military forces, as distinct from forces under United Nations control, can ever be used, no matter how genuinely non-repressive the intention of their national controllers, for such purposes without their use being followed by an increase in the violence which they are intended to diminish. If military forces are used with a truly repressive purpose, and given unlimited means of action, they may well repress successfully. The constitutionally safeguarded compromise may be workable in some circumstances when the troops are servants of a world authority, if legitimated by a will to peace upon which no doubts can be plausibly cast; but it is only in rare circumstances that a national army can succeed in persuading all who need to be persuaded that its sole purpose is the protection of all innocent persons. The very source of its commands is bound to make it suspect; and even when its men, becoming themselves targets of terrorist attack, merely defend themselves, any death or injuries that they inflict on their attackers become the source of a mythology of martyrdom and revenge against them. That mythology thrives still more when the troops kill innocent people by mistake; and no precautions against such accidents can be wholly adequate. Outside Britain the troops were widely represented as agents of an oppressive regime, with serious damage to Britain's reputation.

Until early in 1972 the British troops in Northern Ireland were under the command of the Ministry of Defence, yet employed in support of the Northern Ireland Government, which remained responsible, under the devolution system, for the maintenance of law and order. The troops' position was made difficult in that the authority for which they worked was hated by part of the population. At the same time that authority was attempting, encouraged or prodded by the UK Government to remedy the wrongs (as they seemed even to the UK Government) which were part of the cause of the hatred in which they were held. 'Wrongs' like gerrymandered electoral boundaries and the employment of only a small proportion of members of the Catholic community in public posts of any substantial influence were capable of correction (though not in one day), and an intention to remove them as soon as practicable could not remove the resentment that they had caused. In the meantime some of that resentment was likely to affect people's views of the military forces – and hence to identify the UK Government with the very wrongs (not yet cured) that the UK Government was seeking to remedy.

The situation was complicated by the presence in the Catholic community of an element who could never be satisfied by any remedy short of the ending of Northern Ireland's place in the United Kingdom.

As terrorism developed the Northern Ireland Government used powers of internment, or arrest and deprivation of liberty without trial, under the Special Powers Act. The powers were used against persons suspected of being likely to be involved in the planning of terrorist activity. Soon it was being plausibly alleged that internees were being roughly treated. In 1971 a Committee of Privy Counsellors was set up to investigate the complaints. It reported that there had been some ill-treatment – mild by the standards of repressive regimes, but not normal according to the standards generally accepted in Britain. Some of the techniques employed for interrogation, though possibly justified in extreme circumstances, might constitute criminal assault under English law.[1] One member, the former Lord Chancellor, Lord Gardiner, gave it as his opinion that these techniques were unlawful. On the day on which the report was issued the UK Prime Minister announced that a directive had been sent to the General Officer Commanding in Chief in Northern Ireland, to the effect that the impugned techniques were not to be used any more. They had in fact not been used for several months.[2]

The difficulties involved in the relations between the British army and the Northern Ireland Government were shown early in 1972, when the normal procedures of Parliament had to be adapted to the passing of legislation in quite unusual haste.

On 23 February the Northern Ireland High Court upheld the appeals of five people (including members of the Northern Ireland Parliament) against conviction and sentence on charges of remaining in an assembly after being ordered to disperse by an army officer, in his role as a person qualified to give such an order under Regulation 38 of the Special Powers Act. The court upheld the appeal because the Government of Ireland Act, 1920, expressly denied the Northern Ireland Parliament the power of making laws respecting the armed forces; therefore, it appeared, the Northern Ireland Government had no authority to confer powers on the army under the Special Powers Act.

From 1969, when the army had been sent to Northern Ireland to support the civil power, until the Northern Ireland Court gave its ruling, it had been assumed that it would operate under powers conferred on it by the Special Powers Act. Now therefore the UK Government immediately introduced a bill to provide a legal basis for that former assumption.

After second reading (without a division), the bill went straight into a Committee of the Whole House, where an amendment was proposed,

---

[1] *Report of the Committee of Privy Counsellors Appointed to Consider Authorised Procedures for the Interrogation of Persons Suspected of Terrorism*, Cmnd. 4901 (1972). [2] H. C. Debs, 2 March 1972, col. 744.

to the effect that the legislation should be valid for one year only. However, the Attorney General replied that this would not be proper, as the bill's object was to declare the law rather than to innovate. The amendment was rejected. The remaining stages were dealt with quickly. Proceedings in the House of Lords began at 11.25 p.m., and the bill received the royal assent at 2 a.m. – less than twenty hours after the court's decision which had made the bill necessary. This was the first time since 1931 that a bill had passed all its stages up to royal assent without having been notified on the Order Paper.

The UK Parliament had undoubtedly power to transfer responsibility for law and order to itself, and it now seemed to the Government that, so long as the army was performing its role, the continuing responsibility of the Stormont Government must be unsatisfactory, However, the Northern Ireland Prime Minister informed the UK Government that he could not obtain support in the Stormont Parliament for such a transfer; it seemed that no such support could be forthcoming for any Government of the province which agreed to any such arrangement.

The UK Government considered that speedy action was needed, and on 24 March 1972 it was announced that the devolutionary powers of the Northern Ireland Government and Parliament were to be suspended. A Northern Ireland (Temporary Provisions) Act provided for the Stormont Parliament to be prorogued for one year; the prorogation would be renewable annually.

The bill was given a second reading in the Commons, with Opposition support, on 28 March, by a majority of 483 to 18. The committee and remaining stages were taken on the floor of the House next day, in a continuous sitting which lasted until 11.20 a.m. on 30 March, when the third reading was approved by 191 votes to 13.

In order to allow time for the Lords to debate the bill at adequate length without causing delay, a No. 2 bill was debated in the Lords on 29 March. Its second reading was passed without a division. At 11 a.m. on 29 March the No. 2 bill was withdrawn; the bill from the Commons passed through all its stages quickly, and the royal assent was given after adjournment of the Commons sitting.

The Act had to make new provisions for public expenditure on Northern Ireland's domestic services. As the Northern Ireland Parliament was not now available to pass the financial legislation, Orders in Council were needed to make the necessary provision.

The principle of parity of expenditure on services, as between Northern Ireland and Great Britain, was maintained, and along with it the need for a contribution from the national exchequer considerably in excess of the proceeds of taxes collected at the normal UK rates from the inhabitants of the province.

With no delay at all a Northern Ireland Department was set up, on lines similar to the Scottish Office, with a Secretary of State, assisted by two (later three) Ministers of State and a Parliamentary Under-Secretary. Unlike the Scottish and Welsh Offices the new Northern Ireland Office was staffed at the top by politicians and officials having no personal connection with the territory concerned, though some civil servants, the highest now being put at the level of Deputy-Secretary, were to work in Belfast.

Preparations for building new consultative machinery were quickly put in hand. On 25 May Mr Whitelaw announced the establishment of an Advisory Commission on Northern Ireland. The eleven members were residents of the province, chosen for their varied experience and knowledge of various aspects of Northern Ireland affairs. The commission's functions included the examination of any proposed Orders in Council, and a right to take the initiative in raising any matter that it might wish to discuss.

On 29 September Lord Diplock, a Lord of Appeal in Ordinary, was appointed chairman of a commission whose terms of reference were:

'to consider what arrangements for the administration of justice in Northern Ireland could be made in order to deal more effectively with terrorists' organisations by bringing to book, otherwise than by internment by the executive, individuals involved in terrorist activities, particularly those who plan and direct, but do not necessarily take part in, terrorist acts; and to make recommendations.'

This arrangement was made so as to establish the most effective available means for combining the preservation of individual rights with the attempt to protect a public against indiscriminate acts of terrorism.

The Detention of Terrorists (Northern Ireland) Order was laid before Parliament on 6 November and came into force the next day. It ended detention and internment by the Executive, but empowered the Secretary of State to order a person suspected of being concerned with terrorism to be detained for up to twenty-eight days. Within that period the Chief Constable of the Royal Ulster Constabulary may either release the person detained or bring him before a commissioner. Three commissioners were appointed; at least three days before being brought before a commissioner a detainee must be served with a written statement about the nature of the terrorist activities which are to be the subject of inquiry. Appeal from a commissioners' decision could be made to a Detention Appeals Tribunal.

Before the suspension of its functions the Northern Ireland Government had already introduced substantial reforms of local administration, transferring many powers from local authorities to itself. This was not remarkable; after all, the population of the province is less than that of some English counties. At the provincial level there were moves towards a committee system, through which elected members of minority parties would be taken into the process of discussion in relation to policy making, instead of being merely members of a permanent opposition with no hope of any voice. But the provincial reforms being introduced under Stormont were suspended with Stormont itself.

In 1972 the new Secretary of State began to prepare a new plan for the government of the province. *The Future of Northern Ireland: a Paper of Discussion* was published in October 1972, followed, after debates in both Houses of the UK Parliament, and extensive consultations in Northern Ireland, by a White Paper, *Northern Ireland Constitutional Proposals*, on 20 March 1973.

The discussions had shown that there was no prospect of agreement among all sections of Northern Ireland opinion on any possible set of proposals; however, there was much support, not restricted to any one element in the community, for certain principles as elements of a new arrangement. On the basis of these principles, a bill was brought in, during the following month to provide for the restoration of some devolution, with a single-chamber elected Assembly of seventy-eight members elected for the same twelve constituencies as the Westminster MPs, but with five to eight members for each, elected by single transferable vote. Associated with each new department there would be a committee of members of the Assembly, whose members would reflect the balance of parties. The chairmen of these committees would be political heads of departments and collectively form the Executive of the province. The Assembly would legislate 'in respect of most matters affecting Northern Ireland', subject to the overriding legislation power of the UK Parliament.

However, the devolution would be more restricted than under the regime suspended in March 1972. Several matters previously the responsibility of the Northern Ireland Government would be permanently the responsibility of the UK Government: the appointment of certain judges and magistrates; the conduct of public prosecutions; elections and the franchise, and exceptional measures in the law and order field.

The special situation created by the persistence of terrorist activity would be dealt with by new measures. The UK Government would retain full responsibility for law and order; the Special Powers Act would be repealed and replaced by UK legislation.

There would be safeguards against any action by the Northern Ireland authorities which might discriminate against any section of the community; a continuation of the 'ombudsman' system, set up in 1971;

and devices to provide the individual with the safeguards and protections of a charter of human rights.

The system for Northern Ireland, proposed in the White Paper, would involve a greater degree of autonomy for Northern Ireland than had been devolved to any other part of the UK in the past, though the fact that the (Crowther-Kilbrandon) Constitutional Commission's report was then still awaited raised the question whether a similar arrangement might ultimately be proposed for Wales and Scotland.

Meanwhile, the Northern Irish situation was fundamentally different from that of Wales and Scotland in one sense. The Union of Wales and Scotland with some other nation state could not be realistically contemplated; in the case of Northern Ireland room was now left for possible union with the Irish Republic, provided that the majority should wish it.

Though the White Paper accepted the present status of Northern Ireland as part of the United Kingdom, it also explicitly accepted 'the possibility – which would have to be compatible with the principle of consent – of subsequent change in that status.' Meanwhile there should be 'effective consultation and co-operation in Ireland for the benefit of North and South alike'.

Thus the possibility of change was left open. Presumably the scheme assumed that if at any time a majority should be found to favour union with the Irish Republic such arrangements might be made; and that principle would reasonably imply that if either a majority in either Scotland or Wales should ever wish to withdraw from the United Kingdom, arrangements for such withdrawal should be made.

These assumptions, immediate and speculative, would seem to imply that the precedent of the Northern Irish referendum over UK membership might be repeated, certainly in Northern Ireland, possibly in Wales and Scotland too. But the Northern Irish referendum of March 1973, the first such exercise ever undertaken in the United Kingdom, had been a depressing start, with under 1 per cent of the electorate voting in favour of union with Ireland, and 42 per cent abstaining.

In 1974 the previous year's attempt at a solution was in doubt. The provincial assembly contained a majority of members opposed to its structure and to each other. At the UK general election of February 1974 ten of the Northern Irish seats were won by Unionists opposed to the Assembly (and to all UK parties). Their number alone exceeded the difference between Conservative and Labour seats in the House of Commons, Meanwhile, for the first time, seats held by Welsh and Scottish Nationalists alone also exceeded that difference. It seemed that, with the Kilbrandon Report's various devolutionary proposals newly in the background, some new reforms were to be expected, even from a Parliament once again dominated by a single party.

21

Local Government

The greater part of civil administration, if we take the number of people employed as the criterion, is carried on by local authorities – 'authorities' because the central sovereign power has conferred on them by law many powers and duties within the territorial limits of the areas to which their jurisdiction extends. If there were a legal concept of 'the Administration' in Britain they and their activities could well be part of it. In the absence of any legally-defined administration they must be regarded as agencies subject to the Crown and to the jurisdiction of the ordinary courts yet with functions outside the responsibility of ministers. The commission under Lord Redcliffe-Maud, which reported in 1969, with recommendations for sweeping changes in the whole structure of local government, was not asked to raise fundamental questions about their relations with the central government.

Within England, as in Wales, Scotland and Northern Ireland, the UK central authority is the origin of the existence, and of the powers and functions, of agencies which perform functions of particular interest to the inhabitants of particular localities. There is no doubt that the Sovereign's powers in relation to local government are unlimited. The Act of 1972 completely rearranged the local areas, abolished most of those which had existed for nearly 100 years and set up new ones to come into force in 1974. The Queen in Parliament can take away power and functions, or redistribute them, or create new ones. An Act could even abolish all local councils and bring the whole of local government into a single undifferentiated system of central administration. Alternatively it could go in the opposite direction and hand over to local agencies a large part of the powers now held by the centre.

British practice provides for no general purpose central government supervisors over local administration scattered through the country; there is no functionary equivalent to the Prefect in the French system. The Queen appoints a Lord Lieutenant for each county, but his functions are ceremonial. Each of the local authorities has an independent existence and within the powers granted to it by Parliament it can legally decide how it will do the things which it is required or allowed to do. If there is ground for complaint against a local authority because it appears to be exceeding its powers or misusing them, or to be failing to do something which it is obliged to do, recourse may be had to the courts of law, but not to any body analogous to the French Council of State – though the reforms of 1974 instituted a system of local government ombudsmen.

Education is the biggest of local activities. Many Acts of Parliament define the duties of local authorities in this sphere. They have some autonomy, but the breadth of their discretion may be varied from time to time, and there is room for disagreement about the extent to which the central government 'ought' to control them. The Education Act of 1944 obliges every parent to ensure that his children receive education appropriate to their age and ability; this and other Acts oblige local authorities to ensure that there are sufficient schools to provide primary and secondary education for children up to the age of sixteen, and beyond that age for those who may be able to benefit from it. But local authorities make their own arrangements about selecting children for particular types of schools. Some authorities began on their own account to introduce a comprehensive secondary system in the 1950s, and others followed. In 1965 the Minister requested all local authorities to prepare schemes for comprehensive secondary schools, but a few refused, and others had not produced schemes by 1969. A bill to reduce the local authorities' autonomy in this matter had not been passed when Parliament was dissolved, and the new Government would not thus encroach on local discretion; then in 1974 its successor withheld funds for non-comprehensive developments.

Local authorities are empowered to raise revenue by imposing taxes on property within their areas. They themselves determine the rate of tax, but the central government concerns itself with the valuation of the property. Local authorities also derive revenue from some of the services which they provide, and they may borrow. As there are big variations in the value of property per inhabitant, and many poorer authorities have to meet heavy demands for services, financial independence for each authority would produce obvious difficulties. The central government claims an interest in preventing great disparity of ability to provide services, and indeed recognises a duty to create conditions favourable to the reduction of disparity. Hence the system of grants from the central government, some earmarked to particular functions, some to be spent at the local bodies' discretion. The system of grants necessarily implies a degree of control.

The central sovereign power has not been the creator of all local units. At two levels we see local agencies still surviving from the time when they spontaneously developed an existence of their own. The smallest subdivision, that of the parish, was a community within reach of a church, before it was a political unit, and outside towns the parish is still a unit with a few surviving powers, slightly extended by the Act of 1972, though far smaller than those of its French equivalent, the *commune*. The counties, or shires, already existed as recognised units before the Norman conquest. Their origins go back into antiquity so far that we know little about them, and until 1974 they survived with the boundaries between them unchanged except in so far as they had lost jurisdiction over designated urban enclaves or encroachments – and a few had lost their separate identity be being wholly incorporated in neighbouring counties.

Within the county boundaries the map of local government, apart from the parishes, is wholly the Sovereign's creation. At various dates, beginning before 1066 but mostly after 1200 and in some cases very much later, towns have been granted charters of incorporation by which they received a status partially independent of the counties in which they were situated. The incorporated towns, whether boroughs or cities, thus derived their existence as authorities as well as their functions from specific actions of the central authority. The Municipal Corporations Act of 1835 made new definitions of local government within 178 towns in England and Wales; each was to have a council elected by the ratepayers (except that a quarter of each council was to consist of aldermen elected by the elected councillors). The councils were given responsibility for law and order, and were empowered to make by-laws for the good rule and government of their areas. But this Act, interestingly, did not change the existing boundaries; Parliament accepted ancient creations which it could well have altered. Then, as industrialisation created new needs for governmental action, Parliament created a network of *ad hoc* authorities for different purposes.

A few decades of experience of administration by different *ad hoc* bodies with geographically overlapping jurisdictions produced a movement for new reforms, replacing the patchwork by a series of all-purpose authorities. The reforms were brought about be a series of statutes. Their overall effect was to create, by 1894, a pattern of local government which had survived, with a few minor changes, or special provisions for a few areas, until 1971. In 1888 each large town's council became as a 'county borough' the sole all-purpose authority for the town.[1] Outside the large towns there were two tiers. The county

---

[1] At this time the County of London was created. Until 1963, when it was enlarged, with a new structure of boroughs within it. The ancient City survived both reforms.

councils were responsible for major services, and each county was divided into subdivisions of three types: non-county boroughs, urban districts and rural districts. These lower-level authorities were not subordinate to their counties, but each was responsible for services which Parliament considered likely to be best run by authorities closer to their public than the county councils. Room was left for some flexibility. In general, municipal borough councils had the most functions, rural districts the least. Later legislation made changes in the provisions for distribution between the tiers, and gave scope for variations from the standard pattern.

Thus Parliament, giving effect to policies worked out by the central government, made provision by legislation for the whole pattern of local government and administration. It left room for changes. The Local Government Act of 1888 gave county borough status to towns with at least 50,000 inhabitants. Later other towns, which grew beyond 50,000 people, promoted Acts of Parliament which gave them county borough status. Parliament made its decision in each case after a small committee of its members had heard arguments submitted by counsel, hired at the cost of the inhabitants of the would-be county borough, and by counsel engaged by the county and district authorities which stood to lose powers and therefore tended to oppose change.

The system created in the late nineteenth century was based on two main assumptions: first that some functions were best performed by authorities close to the people, while others needed to be run on a fairly large scale, so that closeness had to be sacrificed; and secondly that the needs of people living in towns were different in character from the needs of people living outside towns, because the conditions of urban life created needs essentially different from the needs of the countryside. To these assumptions we might add the acceptance of the historic boundaries between counties. Although the Sovereign could have interfered with them she chose not to.

By the mid-twentieth century new conditions had arisen. Neighbouring towns had grown outwards and became physically joined; suburbs had spread far into once-rural areas. Mechanised agriculture required an ever-dwindling farm labour force, and the motor-car made town and country more accessible to one another and less distinct. Many local services were felt to be working on too small a scale for efficiency. It was recognised that Parliament might usefully make some new and more fundamental changes in the system; but it was reluctant to impose changes brutally. From 1947 onwards a series of commissions inquired and produced recommendations, but every proposal for change was resisted by those existing authorities which would lose territory or powers. By the 1960s little in the way of real change had been accomplished. A few changes were made, notably the creation of a new greater London county in 1963, of five enlarged county boroughs to comprehend the area around Birmingham, and of a merged county borough of Teesside.

In 1966 a commission under Lord Redcliffe-Maud was set up with wide terms of reference, and its report in 1969 recommended a completely new structure, dividing England into sixty-one areas based partly on central towns. The plan recognised that some of the boundaries between historic counties made little administrative sense because of the great changes in population and urban development since the counties came into being. The nineteenth-century distinction between the needs of town and countryside was thought to be no more of primary importance; and it was assumed that a big enough scale for all services was more important than closeness to their clients. The old system was in part to be turned upside down. A new two-tier pattern was to be created in conurbations, mainly affecting people hitherto living in single-tier county boroughs. In all the rest of the country, most of which had hitherto lived under a two-tier pattern, single-tier all-purpose authorities were to be set up.

The Labour Government quickly accepted the Redcliffe-Maud proposals, and announced an intention of bringing in legislation embodying their principles, with some minor modifications. After the general election of 1970 the new Conservative Government announced that it would indeed bring in a bill for comprehensive local government reform, using for the most part the areas drawn on the Redcliffe-Maud (though with substantial changes in some parts of the country), but that its bill would provide for second-tier authorities throughout the country. Thus the scheme which had been produced by an independent body with so much labour and after so much discussion was to be replaced by another, described in a White Paper which the new Government produced only eight months in office.

The 1972 Local Government Act preserved the ancient counties as the basis for its new scheme, though it modified them, for administrative purposes, in two main ways, firstly by creating six new metropolitan counties, secondly by various boundary adjustments and amalgamations. The new metropolitan counties were all on border areas between two or more ancient counties, and mainly composed of areas which had previously been 'county boroughs', or independently governed urban enclaves, so the reform of 1972, becoming effective in 1974, was not fundamentally revolutionary. In fact the legislation involved a considerable watering-down of the reforms proposed in 1969 after three years of concentrated work by the commission under Lord Redcliffe-Maud.

Each of the thirty-eight non-metropolitan counties is divided into 'districts', fewer in number and with larger population than the urban and rural districts which the reform replaces. Some of the new districts are former county boroughs, which after more than eighty years of wholly independent local government now lose the largest-scale functions to the counties.

Under the terms of the Act the new system of local government was duly brought into effect, in the whole of England outside Greater London, in 1974. New county and district councils were elected in the spring of 1973, to prepare themselves to take over their new functions a year later.

The Act of 1972 may have produced reforms less fundamental than those proposed by the Redcliffe-Maud Commission, but the commission's report assumed, and the Act confirmed, Parliament's complete power to alter the structure of local government, free from any constraint. The complete dependence of local units on Parliament for their very existence was emphasised even more strongly than at the time of the reforms of the late nineteenth century. Under the Redcliffe-Maud scheme some boroughs (created by Parliament several centuries ago) would have wholly lost their identity, though some would perhaps have been allowed a shadowy existence for the purpose of a machinery of consultation which was never defined in detail. The legislation of 1972 was passed on the assumption that there was no obligation to preserve ancient units as such; however, early in 1973 a circular from the Department of the Environment indicated that cities and boroughs which became districts would keep the trappings associated with their ancient incorporation, including the titles of Lord Mayor and Mayor.

The British system leaves to the local units rather greater independence than that enjoyed by local units in France or some other countries, but the extent of Parliament's actual interferences with the very substance of local government within the past hundred years, without the express consent of the units concerned and in at least one case against the wishes of a majority, as ascertained by an unofficial referendum, suggest that even conventional constraints on the central power are peculiarly slight in the English constitutional systems. The extreme nature of Parliament's power has the great advantage that it enables the local government system to be altered in response to the great changes in the social structure to which it relates.

Population increase, migration, new means of transport and the increase in social services within these hundred years have altered the nature and the scale of local government functions so profoundly that structural changes must be desirable to cope with changed conditions. Given the propensity of sections of the public to reject changes likely to damage their short-term local and sectional interests, a strong parliamentary power to reorganise, even against local wishes, is a necessary condition of an effective local government system.

REGIONS

Whatever emerges from the Kilbrandon Commission, it will be concerned not only with the nations of the United Kingdom, but with the regions of England too. Until 1974 there had been little recognition in any part of the constitutional system of regions (as distinct from local government areas) within England. Various measures of administrative devolution to regional offices of central government departments had been made, then modified, during the previous thirty years, and in 1940 Regional Commissioners were appointed, ready to assume powers in case a breakdown of communications should lead the central government to call upon them to act. Their offices were not continued, and the scale of administrative devolution was reduced for a period after the war, then increased again. None of this really affected the Constitution, nor did the regional Economic Planning Councils which were set up in 1964, mainly to give advice to the Secretary of State for Economic Affairs – though they continued to function and to advise the Government after that office was abolished.

The new regionalist ideas recognise that there are meaningful and identifiable geographical parts of England which could usefully, in the late twentieth century, have institutions with defined functions, corresponding in some degree with governmental structures in Germany, Italy and, more recently, France. There is also the fact that the UK already includes, in Wales, Scotland and Northern Ireland, three ready-made 'regions'. If the devolution of powers to these national regions is justified on pragmatic grounds, as distinct from merely sentimental grounds, it is presumably desirable to establish regional institutions within England, which has more than five times as many inhabitants as the three together. But regional sentiment remains rather weak, except in the regions most remote from London, and constitutional change has generally responded only to needs which are expressed with real urgency.

The members of the Kilbrandon Commission were confronted with evidence to suggest that there was not enough identifiable difference between English regions, nor enough momentum behind regionalist aspirations, to provide spontaneous support for substantial innovations in this direction. At the same time they also found that there was widespread disillusion with the system of communication on which central decisions were based, whether or not such decisions required parliamentary endorsement. Means of communication through regional machinery of some kind is an obvious device, but the commission's members had good reason for doubting the potential efficacy of any machinery that might be imposed from the centre.

The minority report by Lord Crowther-Hunt and Professor Peacock proposed the establishment of regional bodies, mainly elected by local authorities, for the identification, measurement and expression of regional needs, together with some formal provision for regional representation in the second House of Parliament. The latter point could be important for the development of a region's sense of sharing in its special way in the broader national interest (and ultimately in the interests of Europe), because if each regional body saw itself merely as a claimant for benefits, the existence of such bodies could merely produce a series of newly-articulated demands between which the central Government would need ultimately to adjudicate.

22

Britain and the EEC

In 1972 the British Constitution was modified by adherence to the EEC. Other treaties too, by which Britain's freedom of action has been restrained, have involved the voluntary relinquishment of an element of national sovereignty and a consequent restriction of the action of future Parliaments; but the EEC membership involves in addition both the subjection of British citizens to Community regulations, and the duty of British courts to enforce those regulations, subject to appeal to the European Court.

Adherence to the treaty, confirmed by British legislation, involves acceptance of the principle that the provisions of the treaty, and of regulations made under it, prevail in any case of conflict between those provisions and British domestic law.

The words of a ruling of the European Court, given on 13 July 1972, describe the situation as it applies to every member state. For all member states, adherence to the treaty 'implies in fact a definitive limitation of their sovereign powers, over which no appeal to provisions of internal law of any kind can prevail'.

Britain is, through adherence to the treaty, subject to the regulations already in force, having been made without Britain's participation. Many of these were temporary in their effect, but the permanent ones are substantial, and a steady flow of new regulations will continue to affect British citizens. Although formally they all deal with commercial practices they have far-reaching effects on the conditions of life of the Community as a whole.

The authority now having final power to make regulations affecting British law is the Council of Ministers, and British political processes are involved in a remote and complex way with the exercise of this power.

Draft regulations are produced by the EEC Commission and its staff, who, like the Commission members, are outside the control of national governments. The draft regulations may be discussed in national parliaments, and in the Community Parliament, before going to the Council of Ministers, which consists of national government spokesmen, assisted by a permanent staff who work for their national governments. The essential problem is to provide a means of democratic control over the vast mass of activity by national and community officials, much of which is influenced by pressure groups.

The members of the Commission are appointed by their national governments for four-year terms (which may be renewed). From 1970 until the accession of Britain, Ireland and Denmark, the EEC Commission had consisted of nine members, two from each of the three larger countries and one from each of the others. Now Britain was allocated two offices, Ireland and Denmark one each, bringing the total to thirteen. The two British offices were given to Sir Christopher Soames and Mr George Thomson, one a former member of a Conservative Cabinet, the other of a Labour Cabinet. They took the portfolios of external relations and regional policy respectively. Primary responsibility for Britain's relations with the Community was given to a minister with a seat in the Cabinet; the ancient sinecure office of Chancellor of the Duchy of Lancaster was used for this purpose, though the title may be rather mystifying to non-British members of the Community.

Like the other larger countries Britain was allocated thirty-six seats in the enlarged European Parliament, the assumption being that, as with other national parliamentary delegations, the seats would be distributed on a proportional basis among the parties according to their strength in the Lower House of the legislature. However, because of its opposition to the whole process, the Parliamentary Labour Party decided (on the recommendation of the Shadow Cabinet) not to take up its allocation, so the British delegation, when its members took their place in the Parliament, consisted of only twenty members: eighteen Conservatives, chosen by the Government, twelve from the Commons and six from the Lords, together with one Liberal from each of the two Houses. The absence of the Labour Party distorted the whole EEC Parliament, by reducing the voice both of British members collectively and of the political element generally described as Social Democratic. The allocation of one-third of the places to peers is arbitrary, and cannot well be justified except on the ground that the House of Lords is part of Parliament and ought to be given a share in the European delegation; once this is accepted one-third of the seats seems a fair proportion. Also, whatever theoretical arguments there may be for or against the arrangement, the inclusion of the Lords element is sensible, useful and appropriate in relation to parliamentary procedure.

Among the Community institutions the Parliament balances the

Commission, and neither has either final power or answerability to any public or to any elected body.

The EEC Parliament has little effective power; it cannot itself reject draft regulations, though it may give its opinion on them, after debate and vote. Much of its work is done in committees. Members of it are not subject to effective checks by their national Parliaments. When the British Members took their places there was already a movement within the EEC Parliament for extending its powers in relation to the Commission. Mr Kirk, the leader of the British Conservative group, proposed that a form of procedure analogous to the British question-hour should be introduced (to supplement the already-existing provision for written questions) and the reform was made. But the British MPs, like members of other national parliamentary delegations, could presumably best be controlled through their own party committees or subject-groups.

Within the EEC Parliament members group themselves on party rather than national lines. Such grouping is easy for Communists and Social Democrats, and for Christian Democrats from most sections of the Community. The British Conservatives might well have grouped themselves along with the fairly large Christian Democrat Group, but (up to early 1973 at least) remained aloof. As few avowed 'Conservatives' have been elected to EEC parliaments in recent years the British Conservatives constituted a separate group, like the French Gaullists.

The life of the House of Commons is much affected by the absence of even twelve of its Members in the European Parliament for a considerable part of the parliamentary year. Given the informal manner of their choice, the role of these MPs is not altogether satisfactory or capable of adequate definition; their absences are not helpful to their work as representatives of their constituencies.

The enlargement of the Community in 1972 gave new force to the movement for greater integration, which could lead to direct election of members of its Parliament. Such election might well be by proportional representation, and British politics themselves would be much affected – and brought out of their present rigid two-party mould – by a need to elect members on a proportional representation basis.

The European Commission and Parliament in themselves do not directly affect the British Constitution. The Constitution is directly affected however at two points: through the ability of the British Parliament itself to discuss draft regulations and to express opinions about them, and through the participation of a British minister, responsible to Parliament in the normal way, in the decision-making work of the EEC's Council of Ministers.

Proposals from the Commission are considered by the Community's

Council of Ministers, which has sovereign power to amend or reject them. Each member-country is represented by a minister, normally the minister in charge of foreign affairs, together, if necessary, with a department minister. For a meeting at which, for example, agricultural policy is involved, the national ministers concerned with agriculture may be present too. For the actions they take in relation to community policy British ministers are responsible to Parliament just as they are for their normal activities at home. Normal parliamentary procedures, such as questions, adjournments and supply days can be used within the House of Commons to make their responsibility effective; though the usefulness of the procedures depends on the British MPs' energy and patience in informing themselves of the issues which they might wish to discuss.

In order to make the Parliament's involvement more effective, a special committee was set up to examine draft regulations and directives from the Commission before they go to the EEC Council of Ministers for decision. The committee is somewhat analogous to the Select Committee on Statutory Instruments, except that it is not prevented from discussing the merits of the draft EEC regulations; it may make reports to the House, which may be made the subject of debate. But the task of parliamentary scrutiny of draft regulations cannot easily be performed except through a complete system of parliamentary committees, and the need for such scrutiny creates new arguments in favour of a committee system of this kind – if not in the House of Commons, then in a reformed Second Chamber with an elected element: elected preferably on a basis different from the House of Commons.

THE PROCESS OF JOINING THE EEC

Britain's accession to the European Communities was analogous to a constitutional amendment of an unprecedented kind, and the process followed for the decision to join was in itself a constitutional exercise. Wholly new processes might have been used, but instead the ordinary parliamentary legislative procedure was made to serve this unusual purpose. But Parliament's contribution was on a different scale from what is normal with even the most important legislation. More time was spent, first at several preliminary stages and then over the legislation itself, than on any other single item of policy for many decades past; and the freedom of voting, allowed at least to government supporters, meant that Parliament as such was participating in the decisions at a level more intense than on any other major proposal of recent times.

Serious negotiations for accession were begun, after an earlier failure, by the Labour Government and taken over by the Conservative Government in 1970. Both parties included promises to seek entry in their manifestos in June 1970. As the negotiations proceeded the Government took pains both to give information to Parliament about the progress that was being made and to give Parliament an opportunity to discuss the various stages and to vote. The process illustrated a difficult part of the interpretation of the constitution. Negotiations are undoubtedly for the Executive, the making of treaties falls within the Crown's prerogative powers, broadly interpreted so as to include 'acts of state'; but there is also the convention that treaties should be made only if there is good reason to believe that the majority in the House of Commons is in agreement.[1] However, there is a procedure whereby a treaty may be expressly made subject to confirmation by Parliament,[2] and treaties which affect the rights of British subjects need to be confirmed by the legislature. The treaty of accession to the EEC needed to be treated under the last of these procedures, but the steps taken in 1971 recognised a role for Parliament at all stages.

Consent of Parliament, expressed by majority vote, usually means an automatic endorsement of the Government's policy by its party. In relation to a treaty, agreement by the Opposition is desirable if it can be achieved. Here the Government was carrying forward a policy initiated by the previous (Labour) Government. Not all Conservative MPs supported the policy, and some Labour MPs had been hostile to it in 1968–70, but it seemed reasonable to expect bi-partisan support. However, early in 1971, the Labour Party leadership was at first uncertain of its position, and its MPs were split, some for, some against and some uncertain.

The House of Commons held a two-day debate on the EEC application on 21 and 22 January 1971. There was no vote, and the negotiations proceeded. On 21 and 22 June important agreements were reached, and on 7 July a White Paper, *The United Kingdom and the European Communities* (Cmnd 4715) was published. The White Paper was debated in the Commons on 21, 22, 23 and 26 July, and in the Lords on 26, 27, 28 and 29 July. There was no division in either House, and the White Paper was attacked and supported from both sides. Mr Wilson, speaking as Leader of the Opposition, opposed entry on the present terms, and on 28 July the Labour Party's National Executive voted against entry. The Labour Party thereupon held a special conference, which met for one day and approved a resolution allowing the parliamentary leaders to take a position unfavourable to entry on the terms negotiated; the

---

[1] Cf. O. Hood Phillips, *Constitutional and Administrative Law* (Sweet & Maxwell, 4th edn, 1967), p. 88.
[2] *ibid.*, p. 265.

regular annual conference in October passed a resolution more force-fully hostile.

Both Houses held debates at the end of October, before prorogation, on the motion to approve the Government's 'decision of principle to join the European Communities on the basis of the arrangements which have been negotiated'. The debates in the two Houses were remarkable for their length, extending over six sittings, and for the free vote that the Government allowed to its supporters, although asking the Parliamentary Party for its support.

The official Opposition now claimed that the Government had no electoral mandate for entry, though both parties had looked forward to entry in their election programme; Mr Wilson based his attack on the terms negotiated.

In the event, thirty-nine Conservatives voted with the Opposition against the motion in the Commons, and if the Opposition had voted solidly the motion would have been defeated. The Parliamentary Labour Party voted to ask its members to oppose the motion, but sixty-nine Labour Members, including Mr Roy Jenkins, the Deputy-Leader, six other members of the Shadow Cabinet and twenty-four lesser party spokesmen voted with the Government. Twenty Members abstained. The overall voting was 356 in favour, 244 against. The breach of solidarity among the front-benchers went against the current trend towards a kind of collective shadow responsibility, but Mr Jenkins was re-elected as Deputy-Leader of the P L P shortly afterwards. It was indicated that less freedom would be allowed or taken during the debates on the ensuing legislation in 1972.

The Opposition argued at this time that a general election should be held on the question, thus reviving the notion of mandate and single-issue general elections. However exceptional this particular issue may have been, its nature made it even more unsuitable than most other single issues as a basis for a general election, and, with the terms of entry certainly no more unfavourable than could reasonably have been expected in 1970, the Government could quite properly claim to have a mandate from the electorate. When the mandate argument was used the Opposition could well be said to have no mandate for its changed attitude.

Granted that a new general election at this stage would have been contrary to constitutional expectations, another solution was available. A referendum might have been appropriate. The lack of precedent for such a device in Britain cannot reasonably be taken to present a consti-tutional obstruction incapable of being overcome. An argument against a referendum on constitutional grounds was in any case severely weakened by the fact that already early in 1972 the Government was considering legislation to provide for the holding of a referendum in Northern Ireland; that legislation was in fact brought in and passed in 1972, and the referendum held in March 1973.

A further argument in favour of a referendum was created by the fact that the three other countries confronted by the need to make similar decisions, did hold referenda on the EEC question in 1972.

On 22 January 1972, together with Denmark, the Irish Republic and Norway, and the six countries already members of the European Communities, Britain signed the treaty of accession. In one of the six original member states, France, a referendum was held on the expansion of the EEC, and a majority voted in favour. However, the turnout was rather low, and it appeared that, as in an earlier French referendum of 1969, many of the electorate used the referendum as a means of expressing their feelings about the government of France as a whole, as distinct from their views on the issue before them.

In Denmark and the Irish Republic referenda were held on the question, with a positive result. In Norway a consultative referendum was held, with a negative result, and the Norwegian Government decided to abide by the result of the popular decision. Accordingly, Norway dropped out.

For Britain the story of the changes in the official Opposition's attitude on the referendum issue has important long-term significance, as it ended with the acceptance by one of the two major parties of the principle that such a device was an appropriate means of deciding a major issue. The Labour Party's own constitution and decision-making process were also involved.

23

Conclusion

In every one of the ten years between 1964 and 1973, the House of Commons appointed a select committee of its members to examine some aspect of parliamentary procedure and to recommend changes. The last procedural review before 1964 was in 1958, and previous intervals had run at about fifteen years. This simple fact gives us some indication of the characteristics of the period, in which this Constitution's quality of flexibility has been predominant. Never before has there been so much talk about change or so much actual change, always within a framework which has been kept intact.

The point may seem irrelevant. Under written constitutions parliamentary procedure is not treated as part of the constitution. Where a written constitution assigns a specific limited role to an assembly, the assembly's internal process is not of so much concern. In Britain, where some of the main constitutional principles are found in parliamentary standing orders or practices, parliamentary change is more significant, and the search for change in these ten years illustrates the vigour of a new quest for adaptation to changing circumstances.

At no time since 1688 has the constitutional system been reformed according to a single coherent plan devised by like-minded people. Each increment of change has been brought in to deal with a particular situation according to the ideas of a dominant element currently capable of obtaining a House of Commons majority, either with or without the opposition of a minority. Almost every change has been made by a similar process. The first push towards each change has come from some small group, possibly concerned with rationality rather than with fundamental change. After discussion, in Parliament and outside, the Government has set up a committee, either of MPs or of persons it judges to be suitably qualified, to gather facts and hear opinions. The committee's report has been debated in Parliament and discussed in the Press; the Government has presented a White Paper, summarising the position and putting forward its own proposals for action. After an interval, with further discussion of the Government's plan, the Government has taken action, which may or may not have involved legislation; and when legislation has been involved, the bill has been discussed in principle and in detail through the successive parliamentary stages in both Houses of Parliament. Not every reform needs every one of these stages; reforms of parliamentary procedure do not need legislation, even though the Constitution may be affected.

The process still leaves ultimate decision, on action and its form, in the hands of the Government currently in power, subject to the support of a majority of the House of Commons. But the form of proceeding is devised to ensure a basis of impartial fact-finding. The device of the Green Paper, introduced in the 1960s, is designed to allow public discussion of government plans while they are still at a tentative stage, so that the ensuing White Paper, involving more commitment by the Government, can take into account the Government's reactions to criticisms of its first Green Paper proposals.

This machinery for change has worked energetically since 1965, with some preliminary movement before then. The House of Lords in its capacity as the highest court of appeal began to sit outside the House, but at first only in order to facilitate rebuilding operations, in 1948. This reform was both simple and trivial, but we do well to remember that as recently as 1949 there was virtually no support for the notion that even this minor reform should be permanent. The Life Peerages Act of 1958 seemed at the time a daring step – particularly in allowing women to receive peerages – and it has led to a new invigoration of the House of Lords which has not been damped by the 1963 provision for renunciation of peerages. Indeed the upper House of Parliament is entering the last quarter of the century ripe for another bout of reforms. The Lords may have led the way to the new constitutional flexibility of the 1960s, and the political activity of the House in that period has not been concerned with attempts to impose restraint, but the changes of this recent period have left unchanged its formal functions and slightly modified the basis of its composition.

In Parliament these years of change have seen a rationalisation of financial procedure: the abandonment of the inconvenient practice of the old Committee of Supply showed a readiness to sweep away time-honoured practices which no longer served the purposes for which they were originally intended. More important, the introduction of rolling five-year estimates of future expenditure, separated from and additional to the annual vote, together with the setting up of the new Select Committee on Public Expenditure Votes, created new forms which gave scope for a new effectiveness in traditional parliamentary functions.

The transfer of part of the annual debates on taxation, through the committee stage of the Finance Bill, represents another departure from constitutional purism for the sake of effectiveness.

These reforms are one aspect of a recognition that parliamentary control of ministers through traditional methods and assumptions has become hazy and uncertain. The creation of the office of Parliamentary Commissioner was another such recognition, creating a practical piece of machinery, devised to protect citizens against maladministration less haphazardly than they were protected before. Constitutional purity was upheld by the rule that all complaints must be forwarded by MPs, not directly by the complainants themselves.

During this same period the whole structure of local government was completely changed, for the first time for nearly a century. The system of courts was completely reformed by legislation, in a manner without precedent. The National Health Service was reconstructed. These three major changes were all first approached with real determination under the Labour Government of 1964–70, and carried through by the succeeding Conservative Government in its own way.

The franchise was extended to the 18 to 21 age group in 1969, and a complete reform of the House of Lords was abandoned only because opposition of two minority groups in the House of Commons would have caused the legislative proceedings to take more time in that House than the Government was prepared to sacrifice.

Although the initiative for these changes came from a Labour Government, they did not reflect socialist ideology or the main long-term objectives of the Labour Party. They were informed rather by a radical purpose, in the old sense of that term, in the spirit of old-fashioned Liberalism. They have left the constitution more open than it was before, more likely to be receptive to further changes in the future.

The prelude to these changes was the conversion of the old colonial empire into a commonwealth of equal, independent states, first with the Queen as nominal sovereign, then, in most cases, as republics within the Commonwealth. With Britain no longer the centre of government for a third of the world's population, Britain itself had scope for interpreting its own structure less rigidly than before. The surrender of an element of national sovereignty in the European Economic Community has been one major ensuing change; changes in the relation between the central power and the constituent parts of the United Kingdom may come later.

Administrative devolution to Wales has proceeded piecemeal, moving by small steps towards the position already established for Scotland, and minor devices for extending devolution have affected Scotland too. The possibility of further change in this direction must await action on the report of the Crowther-Kilbrandon Constitutional Commission produced in 1973 after four years of study. The obstacle to a federal solution is not so much objection to its principle but rather the unequal size and population of the nations of the kingdom, combined with a homogeneity of England (as indicated by voting behaviour) so great that regionalism has no spontaneous foundation.

But the terms of reference given to Lord Crowther's Commission did point to two constitutional problems waiting to be solved: how to secure wider participation in decision making and less centralisation of power. The two problems are interconnected, because the larger the unit of decision the less the scope for wider 'participation'. (This word, widely used in the late 1960s, faded out of use soon after. Its meaning is too varied and uncertain though it expresses aspirations which are widely approved).

At one level, participation exists already through the relations between interest-group spokesmen and ministers and civil servants, and links between these groups and MPs supplement the consultations in Whitehall. But well-organised producer-groups in the economy are better placed than other groups: each group pursues its selfish interests; and the Government may in the long run merely hold the ring between the various producer-interests. Members of Parliament themselves have some part to play in the participatory process: and today's procedures do not much favour such activity.

The extension of parliamentary committee work is the first require-ment for a fulfilment of the movement of the past ten years. Such committee work cannot all take place at Westminster; some can well be moved down to the people.

But the House of Commons is fully occupied with its current roles in relation to constituencies and the national struggle for power, and hence electoral support.

It may well be that within the next ten years Britain's membership of Europe will show the way to a modification of the second House of Parliament in two directions: first as a device for representing the nations and regions of the kingdom, and second as a new link in the participatory process. For this, the second House would need an elected element, and the representation of the main zones of the kingdom would be a natural basis. With the House still lacking formal power to remove a Government, and its members seeking election on a special basis, there would be scope for them to make a new and effective parliamentary contribution to the decision-making process in its many aspects.

It could be argued that the new readiness of members of the House of Commons to disobey their whips has brought enough new flexibility into the system. But, except on joining Europe, no Government has been in danger of defeat over a serious issue; the rebellious have always been contained within a scope acceptable to the Government and have not seriously threatened its power. Governments may have been forced to make concessions here and there; but there is still room for more effective machinery to ensure that ministers have really and publicly identified the options through which agreed objectives may be attained.

SELECT BIBLIOGRAPHY

This bibliography cites only a selection of the books and articles in easily-accessible quarterly journals directly relevant to the study of the political aspects of the Constitution which have been discussed in this book. It does not include references to the daily and weekly press, or to the innumerable official reports, of the Select Committees on Procedure, Privileges, Estimates, Public Expenditure, Public Accounts, Nationalised Industries, the Parliamentary Commissioner, European Community Secondary Legislation, etc., or to statutes, statutory instruments or parliamentary debates. Nor does it include any of the numerous one-volume books on the British political system, many of them recent and good, such as those by Birch, Moodie, Punnett, Stacey and others.

A number of recurrent publications may be mentioned as relevant to constitutional studies: the surveys of general elections which have been published one by one by Macmillan for each general election since the war; the annual surveys of constitutional developments and (in recent years) of public legislation published in *Parliamentary Affairs*, and the annual surveys of administrative developments in *Public Administration*.

BOOKS

Acton Society Trust, *Regionalism in England*, 3 vols (Acton Society, 1966).
W. Bagehot, *The English Constitution* with Introduction by R. H. S. Crossman (Fontana, 1963).
A. P. Barker and M. Rush, *The Member of Parliament and his Information* (P.E.P. and Allen and Unwin, 1970).
R. Bassett, *1931 Political Crisis* (Macmillan, 1958).
Humphrey Berkeley, *The Power of the Prime Minister* (Allen & Unwin, 1968).
L. Blom-Cooper and G. Drewry, *Final Appeal: A Study of the House of Lords in its Judicial Capacity* (O.U.P., 1972).
F. Boyd, *British Politics in Transition, 1945–63* (Pall Mall Press, 1964).
Jeremy Bray, *Decision in Government* (Gollancz, 1969).
P. Bromhead, *Private Members' Bills in the British Parliament* (Routledge, 1956).
Lord George-Brown, *In My Way* (Gollancz, 1971).
R. G. S. Brown, *The Administrative Process in Britain* (Methuen, 1970).
David Butler and Jennie Freeman, *British Political Facts, 1900–67* (Macmillan, 1968).
David Butler and M. Pinto-Duschinsky, *The British General Election of 1970* (Macmillan, 1971).
Ronald Butt, *The Power of Parliament* (Constable, 1967).
Richard A. Chapman (ed.), *The Role of Commissions in Policy-Making* (Allen & Unwin, 1973).

Richard A. Chapman and A. Dunsire (eds), *Style in Administration* (Allen & Unwin, 1971).

D. N. Chester and Nora Bowring, *Questions in Parliament* (O.U.P., 1960).

W. S. Churchill, *The Second World War* (Cassell, 1948).

Sir Richard Clarke, *New Trends in Government* (Civil Service College, 1972).

David Coombes, *The Member of Parliament and the Administration: The Case of the Select Committee on Nationalised Industries* (Allen & Unwin, 1966).

B. R. Crick, *The Reform of Parliament* (Weidenfeld, 2nd edn, 1968).

B. R. Crick (ed), *Essays on Reform* (OUP, 1967).

J. A. Cross, *British Public Administration* (University Tutorial Press, 1970).

Richard Crossman, *Inside View* (Cape, 1972).

A. V. Dicey, *Law of the Constitution* (Macmillan, 1965).

P. Gordon Walker, *The Cabinet* (Cape, 1970).

J. A. G. Griffith, *Central Departments and Local Administration* (Allen & Unwin, 1966).

Lord Halifax, *Fullness of Days* (1957).

A. H. Hanson and B. Crick, *The Commons in Transition* (Fontana, 1970).

A. Hauriou, *Droit constitutionnel et institutions politiques* (Montchrestien, 1966).

Patrick Howarth, *Questions in the House* (The Bodley Head, 1956).

Robert Rhodes James, *Ambitions and Realities: British Politics 1964–70* (Weidenfeld, 1972).

W. I. Jennings, *Parliament* (CUP, 1939, 1957).

Nevil Johnson, *Parliament and Administration: The Estimates Committee, 1945–65* (Allen & Unwin, 1966).

J. G. Kellas, *The Scottish Political System* (CUP, 1973).

Lord Kilmuir, *Political Adventure* (Weidenfeld, 1964).

D. Leonard and V. Herman, *The Backwater and Parliament* (Macmillan, 1972).

N. MacCormick, *The Scottish Debate* (OUP, 1970).

J. P. Mackintosh, *The Devolution of Power* (Chatto, 1968).

J. P. Mackintosh, *The British Cabinet* (Stevens, 1962).

Harold Macmillan: *Memoirs*, 3 vols (Macmillan, 1971–3).

G. Marshall and G. C. Moodie, *Some Problems of the Constitution* (Hutchinson, 1967).

G. Marshall, *Constitutional Theory* (OUP, 1971).

T. Erskine May, *Parliamentary Practice* (Butterworth, 1971).

R. Mosley, *The Story of the Cabinet Office* (Routledge, 1969).

J. Murray-Brown (ed.), *The Monarchy and its Future* (Allen & Unwin, 1969).

Harold Nicolson, *George V* (Constable, 1952).

Sir C. Petrie, *The Modern British Monarchy* (Eyre & Spottiswoode, 1961).

O. Hood Phillips; *Constitutional and Administrative Law* (Sweet & Maxwell, 4th ed. 1967).

Peter Pulzer, *Political Representation and Election in Britain* (Allen & Unwin, 2nd ed, 1972).

P. G. Richards, *Patronage in British Government* (Allen & Unwin, 1962).

P. G. Richards, *The Backbenchers* (Faber, 1972).

P. G. Richards, *Parliament and Conscience* (Allen & Unwin, 1970).

M. Rush, *The Selection of Parliamentary Candidates* (Nelson, 1970).

B. C. Smith, *Advising Ministers* (Routledge, 1969).

S. A. De Smith, *Constitutional and Administrative Law* (Penguin, 1971).

Frank Stacey, *The British Ombudsman* (OUP, 1971).

E. S. Taylor, *The House of Commons at Work* (Penguin, 1971).

D. R. Turner, *The Shadow Cabinet in British Politics* (Routledge, 1969).

E. C. S. Wade and G. Godfrey Phillips, *Constitutional Law* 8th revised edn, A. W. Bradley (Longman, 1970).

S. A. Walkland, *The Legislative Process in Great Britain* (Allen & Unwin, 1968).

J. Wheeler-Bennett, *King George VI* (Macmillan, 1958).

Corinne Comstock Westow, *English Constitutional Theory and the House of Lords* (Routledge, 1965).

Harold Wilson, *The Labour Government 1964–70* (Michael Joseph, 1971).

R. E. Wraith and G. B. Lamb, *Public Inquiries as an Instrument of Government* (Allen & Unwin, 1971).

ARTICLES

A. Alexander, 'British Politics and the Royal Prerogative of Appointment since 1945', *Parliamentary Affairs* (1970), pp. 248–57.

D. E. Apter, 'The Premise of Parliamentary Planning', *Government and Opposition* (1973), pp. 3–23.

A. Barker, 'Party and Supply', *Parliamentary Affairs* (1963–4), pp. 287–317.

A. Barker, 'The Most Important and Venerable Function: A Study of Commons Supply Procedure', *Political Studies* (1965), pp. 45–64.

M. J. Barnett, 'Back Bench Behaviour in the House of Commons', *Parliamentary Affairs* (1968–9), pp. 38–61.

E. H. Beet, 'Parliament and Delegated Legislation', *Public Administration* (1955), pp. 325–32.

G. Borrie, 'The Wedgwood Benn Case', *Public Law* (1961), pp. 349–61.

R. L. Borthwick, 'The Welsh Grand Committee', *Parliamentary Affairs* (1968), pp. 264–76.

C. J. Boulton, 'Result Developments in House of Commons Procedure', *Parliamentary Affairs* (1969–70), pp. 61–71.

Sir H. Brittain, 'The Treasury's Responsibilities', *Public Administration* (1961), pp. 1–15.

P. Bromhead, 'The Commons and Supply', *Parliamentary Affairs* (1958–9), pp. 337–48.

P. Bromhead, 'Mr Wedgwood Benn, the Peerage and the Constitution', *Parliamentary Affairs* (1960–1), pp. 493–506.

D. E. Butler, 'The Redistribution of Seats', *Public Administration* (1955), pp. 125–47.

Sir Richard Clarke, 'Parliament and Public Expenditure', *The Political Quarterly* (1973), pp. 137–53.

Sir Richard Clarke, 'The Machinery for Economic Planning: The Public Sector', *Public Administration* (1966), pp. 61–72

L. H. Cohen, 'Local Government Complaints', *Public Administration* (1973), pp. 175–84.

D. Coombes, 'The Scrutiny of Ministers' Powers by the Select Committee on Nationalised Industries', *Public Law* (1965), pp. 9–29.

B. Crick, 'The Life Peerages Act', *Parliamentary Affairs* (1957–8), pp. 455–65.

G. H. Daniel, 'Public Accountability of the Nationalised Industries', *Public Administration* (1960), pp. 27–34.

Myfyr Evans and John Reynolds, 'A New Constitutional Structure for Wales', *The Political Quarterly* (1971), pp. 191–202.

G. K. Fry, 'Thoughts on the Present State of Ministerial Responsibility', *Parliamentary Affairs* (1969–70), pp. 10–20.

E. N. Gladden, 'The Estimates Committee looks at the Civil Service', *Parliamentary Affairs* (1965–6), pp. 233–40.

Sir Samuel Goldman, 'The Presentation of Public Expenditure Proposals to Parliament', *Public Administration* (1970), pp. 247–62.

J. A. G. Griffith, 'The Council and the Chalkpit', *Public Administration* (1961), pp. 369–74.

H. Grisewood, 'The BBC and Political Broadcasting in Britain', *Parliamentary Affairs* (1962–3), pp. 42–5.

Lewis A. Gunn, 'Politicians and Officials: Who is Answerable?', *The Political Quarterly* (1972), pp. 253–60.

W. Hampton, 'Parliament and the Civil Service', *Parliamentary Affairs* (1963–4), pp. 430–8.

A. H. Hanson, 'Parliamentary Control of the Nationalised Industries', *Parliamentary Affairs* (1957–8), pp. 328–40.

A. H. Hanson, 'Ministers and Boards', *Public Administration* (1969), pp. 65–74.

D. J. Heasman, 'The Monarch, the Prime Minister and the Dissolution of Parliament', *Parliamentary Affairs* (1960–1), pp. 94–107.

N. Johnson, 'Servicemen and Parliamentary Elections', *Parliamentary Affairs* (1962–3), pp. 201–12 and 440–4.

G. Jones, B. Smith and H. V. Wiseman, 'Regionalism and Parliament', *The Political Quarterly* (1967), pp. 403–10.

G. W. Jones, 'The Local Government Act 1972 and the Redcliffe-Maud Commission', *The Political Quarterly* (1973), pp. 154–66.

G. W. Jones, 'The Prime Minister and the Cabinet . . . and his Advisers', *Political Studies* (1972), pp. 213–25, (1973), pp. 363–75.

B. Keith Lucas, 'Three Questions on Electoral Procedure', *Parliamentary Affairs* (1963–4), pp. 195–9.

P

R. Kimber and J. J. Richardson, 'Specialisation and Standing Committees', *Political Studies* (1968), pp. 97–101.

R. Klein, 'The Politics of PPB', *The Political Quarterly* (1972), pp. 270–81.

J. M. Lee, 'Select Committees and the Constitution', *The Political Quarterly* (1970), pp. 182–94.

Sir T. Low, 'The Select Committee on Nationalised Industries', *Public Administration* (1962), pp. 1–16.

J. P. Mackintosh, 'The Prime Minister and the Cabinet', *Parliamentary Affairs* (1967–8), pp. 53–68.

J. P. Mackintosh, 'Devolution, Regionalism and the Reform of Local Government: the Scottish Case', *Public Law* (1964), pp. 19–32.

G. Marshall, 'The Franks Report on Administrative Tribunals and Inquiries', *Public Administration* (1957), pp. 347–58.

G. Marshall, 'Tribunals and Inquiries: Developments since the Franks Report', *Public Administration* (1958), pp. 261–70.

G. C. Moodie, 'The Crown and Parliament', *Parliamentary Affairs* (1956–7), pp. 256–64.

G. C. Moodie, 'The Monarch and the Selection of the Prime Minister', *Political Studies* (1957), pp. 1–20.

E. Leslie Normanton, 'In Search of Value for Public Money', *The Political Quarterly* (1968), pp. 156–68.

C. O'Leary, 'The Wedgwood Benn Case and the Doctrine of Wilful Perversity', *Political Studies* (1965), pp. 65–79.

E. P. Pritchard, 'The Responsibility of the Nationalised Industries to Parliament', *Parliamentary Affairs* (1963–4), pp. 439–49.

R. M. Punnett, 'Ministerial Representation in the House of Lords', *The Table* (1961), pp. 67–71; (1964), pp. 69–80.

A. Ranney, 'Inter-Constituency Movement of British Parliamentary Candidates, 1951–9', *American Political Science Quarterly* (1964), pp. 36–45.

J. Rasmussen, 'The Implications of Safe Seats for British Democracy', *Western Political Quarterly* (1966), pp. 517–29.

W. A. Robson, 'The Missing Dimension of Government', *The Political Quarterly* (1971), pp. 233–46.

M. Ryle, 'Parliamentary Control of Expenditure and Taxation', *The Political Quarterly* (1967), pp. 435–46.

M. Tyle, 'Private Members' Bills', *The Political Quarterly* (1966), pp. 385–93.

L. J. Sharpe, 'Theories and Values of Local Government', *Political Studies* (1970), pp. 153–74.

S. A. De Smith, 'The Council on Tribunals', *Parliamentary Affairs* (1958–9), pp. 320–8.

Study of Parliament Group, 'Parliament and Legislation', *Parliamentary Affairs* (1969), pp. 210–5.

A. H. Taylor, 'The Effects of Party Organisation: Correlation between Campaign Expenditure and Voting in the 1970 Election', *Political Studies* (1972), pp. 329–31.

K. C. Wheare, 'The Redress of Grievances', *Public Administration* (1962), pp. 125–8.

M. Wheeler-Booth, 'The Stansgate Case', *The Table* (1961), pp. 23–56.

P. M. Williams, 'The Politics of Redistribution', *The Political Quarterly* (1968), pp. 239–54.

H. V. Wiseman, 'Supply and Ways and Means: Procedural Changes in 1966', *Parliamentary Affairs* (1967–8), pp. 10–15.

M. Wright, 'The Professional Conduct of Civil Servants', *Public Administration* (1973), pp. 1–16.

INDEX